GNU Gnulib 2/2

A catalogue record for this book is available from the Hong Kong Public Libraries.

Published in Hong Kong by Samurai Media Limited.

Email: info@samuraimedia.org

ISBN 978-988-8381-76-0

Table of Contents

9   ISO C and POSIX Function Substitutes 68

10 Past POSIX Function Substitutes 417

10 Past POSIX Function Substitutes

This chapter describes which functions and function-like macros specified by older versions of POSIX are substituted by Gnulib, which portability pitfalls are fixed by Gnulib, and which (known) portability problems are not worked around by Gnulib.

The notation "Gnulib module: —" means that Gnulib does not provide a module providing a substitute for the function. When the list "Portability problems not fixed by Gnulib" is empty, such a module is not needed: No portability problems are known. Otherwise, it indicates that such a module would be useful but is not available: No one so far found this function important enough to contribute a substitute for it. If you need this particular function, you may write to <bug-gnulib at gnu dot org>.

10.1 bcmp

POSIX specification: http://www.opengroup.org/susv3xsh/bcmp.html

Gnulib module: —

Portability problems fixed by Gnulib:

Portability problems not fixed by Gnulib:

- This function is missing on some platforms: Solaris 2.4, mingw, MSVC 9.
- This function is marked as "legacy" in POSIX. Better use memcmp instead.

10.2 bcopy

POSIX specification: http://www.opengroup.org/susv3xsh/bcopy.html

Gnulib module: bcopy

Portability problems fixed by Gnulib:

- This function is missing on some platforms: Solaris 2.4, mingw, MSVC 9.

Portability problems not fixed by Gnulib:

- This function is marked as "legacy" in POSIX. Better use memcpy or memmove instead.

10.3 bsd_signal

POSIX specification: http://www.opengroup.org/susv3xsh/bsd_signal.html

Gnulib module: —

Portability problems fixed by Gnulib:

Portability problems not fixed by Gnulib:

- This function is missing on some platforms: Mac OS X 10.5, FreeBSD 6.0, NetBSD 5.0, IRIX 5.3, Solaris 2.5.1, Cygwin, mingw, MSVC 9, Interix 3.5.

10.4 `bzero`

POSIX specification: `http://www.opengroup.org/susv3xsh/bzero.html`

Gnulib module: —

Portability problems fixed by Gnulib:

Portability problems not fixed by Gnulib:

- This function is missing on some platforms: Solaris 2.4, mingw, MSVC 9.
- This function is marked as "legacy" in POSIX. Better use `memset` instead.

10.5 `ecvt`

POSIX specification: `http://www.opengroup.org/susv3xsh/ecvt.html`

Gnulib module: —

Portability problems fixed by Gnulib:

Portability problems not fixed by Gnulib:

- This function is missing on some platforms: FreeBSD 6.0, NetBSD 5.0.
- This function is marked as "legacy" in POSIX. Better use `sprintf` instead.

10.6 `fcvt`

POSIX specification: `http://www.opengroup.org/susv3xsh/fcvt.html`

Gnulib module: —

Portability problems fixed by Gnulib:

Portability problems not fixed by Gnulib:

- This function is missing on some platforms: FreeBSD 6.0, NetBSD 5.0.
- This function is marked as "legacy" in POSIX. Better use `sprintf` instead.

10.7 `ftime`

POSIX specification: `http://www.opengroup.org/susv3xsh/ftime.html`

Gnulib module: —

Portability problems fixed by Gnulib:

Portability problems not fixed by Gnulib:

- This function is missing on some platforms: Mac OS X 10.5, FreeBSD 6.0, NetBSD 5.0, OpenBSD 3.8, IRIX 5.3, Solaris 2.4.
- This function is marked as "legacy" in POSIX. Better use `gettimeofday` or `clock_gettime` instead, and use `ftime` only as a fallback for portability to Windows platforms.

10.8 gcvt

POSIX specification: `http://www.opengroup.org/susv3xsh/gcvt.html`

Gnulib module: —

Portability problems fixed by Gnulib:

Portability problems not fixed by Gnulib:

- This function is missing on some platforms: Mac OS X 10.5, FreeBSD 6.0, NetBSD 5.0.
- This function is marked as "legacy" in POSIX. Better use `sprintf` instead.

10.9 getcontext

POSIX specification: `http://www.opengroup.org/susv3xsh/getcontext.html`

Gnulib module: —

Portability problems fixed by Gnulib:

Portability problems not fixed by Gnulib:

- This function is missing on some platforms: Mac OS X 10.4, OpenBSD 3.8, Cygwin, mingw, MSVC 9, Interix 3.5, BeOS.

10.10 gethostbyaddr

POSIX specification: `http://www.opengroup.org/susv3xsh/gethostbyaddr.html`

Gnulib module: —

Portability problems fixed by Gnulib:

Portability problems not fixed by Gnulib:

- This function is missing on some platforms: mingw, MSVC 9.

10.11 gethostbyname

POSIX specification: `http://www.opengroup.org/susv3xsh/gethostbyname.html`

Gnulib module: —

Portability problems fixed by Gnulib:

Portability problems not fixed by Gnulib:

- This function is missing on some platforms: mingw, MSVC 9.

10.12 getwd

POSIX specification: `http://www.opengroup.org/susv3xsh/getwd.html`

Gnulib module: —

Portability problems fixed by Gnulib:

Portability problems not fixed by Gnulib:

- This function is missing on some platforms: Solaris 2.4, mingw, MSVC 9, BeOS.

- The size of the buffer required for this function is not a compile-time constant. Also, the function truncates a result that would be larger than the minimum buffer size. For these reasons, this function is marked as "legacy" in POSIX. Better use the `getcwd` function instead.

10.13 h_errno

POSIX specification: http://www.opengroup.org/susv3xsh/h_errno.html

Gnulib module: —

Portability problems fixed by Gnulib:

Portability problems not fixed by Gnulib:

- This function is missing on some platforms: IRIX 6.5, OSF/1 5.1, Cygwin, mingw, MSVC 9, Interix 3.5.

10.14 index

POSIX specification: http://www.opengroup.org/susv3xsh/index.html

Gnulib module: —

Portability problems fixed by Gnulib:

Portability problems not fixed by Gnulib:

- This function is missing on some platforms: Solaris 2.4, mingw, MSVC 9.
- This function is marked as "legacy" in POSIX. Better use `strchr` instead.

10.15 makecontext

POSIX specification: http://www.opengroup.org/susv3xsh/makecontext.html

Gnulib module: —

Portability problems fixed by Gnulib:

Portability problems not fixed by Gnulib:

- This function is missing on some platforms: Mac OS X 10.4, OpenBSD 3.8, Cygwin, mingw, MSVC 9, Interix 3.5, BeOS.

10.16 mktemp

POSIX specification: http://www.opengroup.org/susv3xsh/mktemp.html

Gnulib module: —

Portability problems fixed by Gnulib:

Portability problems not fixed by Gnulib:

- This function is not appropriate for creating temporary files. (It has security risks.) Therefore it is marked as "legacy" in POSIX. Better use `mkstemp` instead.

10.17 pthread_attr_getstackaddr

POSIX specification: http://www.opengroup.org/susv3xsh/pthread_attr_getstackaddr.html

Gnulib module: —

Portability problems fixed by Gnulib:

Portability problems not fixed by Gnulib:

- This function is missing on some platforms: HP-UX 11, Solaris 2.4, Cygwin 1.7.9, mingw, MSVC 9, BeOS.

10.18 pthread_attr_setstackaddr

POSIX specification: http://www.opengroup.org/susv3xsh/pthread_attr_setstackaddr.html

Gnulib module: —

Portability problems fixed by Gnulib:

Portability problems not fixed by Gnulib:

- This function is missing on some platforms: HP-UX 11, IRIX 5.3, Solaris 2.4, Cygwin 1.7.9, mingw, MSVC 9, BeOS.

10.19 rindex

POSIX specification: http://www.opengroup.org/susv3xsh/rindex.html

Gnulib module: —

Portability problems fixed by Gnulib:

Portability problems not fixed by Gnulib:

- This function is missing on some platforms: Solaris 2.4, mingw, MSVC 9.
- This function is marked as "legacy" in POSIX. Better use strrchr instead.

10.20 scalb

POSIX specification: http://www.opengroup.org/susv3xsh/scalb.html

Gnulib module: —

Portability problems fixed by Gnulib:

Portability problems not fixed by Gnulib:

10.21 setcontext

POSIX specification: http://www.opengroup.org/susv3xsh/setcontext.html

Gnulib module: —

Portability problems fixed by Gnulib:

Portability problems not fixed by Gnulib:

- This function is missing on some platforms: Mac OS X 10.4, OpenBSD 3.8, Cygwin, mingw, MSVC 9, Interix 3.5, BeOS.

- The effects of this call are system and compiler optimization dependent, since it restores the contents of register-allocated variables but not the contents of stack-allocated variables.

10.22 `swapcontext`

POSIX specification: `http://www.opengroup.org/susv3xsh/swapcontext.html`

Gnulib module: —

Portability problems fixed by Gnulib:

Portability problems not fixed by Gnulib:

- This function is missing on some platforms: Mac OS X 10.4, OpenBSD 3.8, Cygwin, mingw, MSVC 9, Interix 3.5, BeOS.

10.23 `ualarm`

POSIX specification: `http://www.opengroup.org/susv3xsh/ualarm.html`

Gnulib module: —

Portability problems fixed by Gnulib:

Portability problems not fixed by Gnulib:

- This function is missing on some platforms: Solaris 2.4, mingw, MSVC 9, BeOS.

10.24 `usleep`

POSIX specification: `http://www.opengroup.org/susv3xsh/usleep.html`

Gnulib module: usleep

Portability problems fixed by Gnulib:

- On some systems, `usleep` rejects attempts to sleep longer than 1 second, as allowed by POSIX: mingw.
- This function is missing on some platforms. However, the replacement is designed to be lightweight, and may round to the nearest second; use `select` or `nanosleep` if better resolution is needed: IRIX 5.3, Solaris 2.4, older mingw, MSVC 9, BeOS.

Portability problems not fixed by Gnulib:

- According to POSIX, the `usleep` function may interfere with the program's use of the `SIGALRM` signal. On Linux, it doesn't; on other platforms, it may.

10.25 `vfork`

POSIX specification: `http://www.opengroup.org/susv3xsh/vfork.html`

Gnulib module: —

Portability problems fixed by Gnulib:

Portability problems not fixed by Gnulib:

- This function is missing on some platforms: IRIX 6.5, mingw, MSVC 9, BeOS.

10.26 `wcswcs`

POSIX specification: `http://www.opengroup.org/susv3xsh/wcswcs.html`

Gnulib module: —

Portability problems fixed by Gnulib:

Portability problems not fixed by Gnulib:

- This function is missing on some platforms: Mac OS X 10.5, FreeBSD 6.0, IRIX 5.3, Solaris 2.5.1, Cygwin, mingw, MSVC 9, BeOS.
- On AIX and Windows platforms, `wchar_t` is a 16-bit type and therefore cannot accommodate all Unicode characters.
- This function is marked as "legacy" in POSIX. Better use `wcsstr` instead.

11 Glibc Header File Substitutes

This chapter describes which header files contained in GNU libc but not specified by ISO C or POSIX are substituted by Gnulib, which portability pitfalls are fixed by Gnulib, and which (known) portability problems are not worked around by Gnulib.

The notation "Gnulib module: —" means that Gnulib does not provide a module providing a substitute for the header file. When the list "Portability problems not fixed by Gnulib" is empty, such a module is not needed: No portability problems are known. Otherwise, it indicates that such a module would be useful but is not available: No one so far found this header file important enough to contribute a substitute for it. If you need this particular header file, you may write to <bug-gnulib at gnu dot org>.

11.1 a.out.h

Describes the structure of executables (and object files?) in the old a.out format.

Gnulib module: —

Portability problems fixed by Gnulib:

Portability problems not fixed by Gnulib:

- This header file is missing on some platforms: Mac OS X 10.5, Solaris 11 2011-11, mingw, MSVC 9, Interix 3.5, BeOS.
- This header file is useless because most executables and object files are in ELF format on some platforms: glibc 2.3.6, FreeBSD 6.0, NetBSD 5.0, OpenBSD 3.8.

11.2 aliases.h

Defines the type struct aliasent and declares the functions setaliasent, endaliasent, getaliasent, getaliasent_r, getaliasbyname, getaliasbyname_r.

Documentation:

- man setaliasent.

Gnulib module: —

Portability problems fixed by Gnulib:

Portability problems not fixed by Gnulib:

- This header file is missing on all non-glibc platforms: Mac OS X 10.5, FreeBSD 6.0, NetBSD 5.0, OpenBSD 3.8, Minix 3.1.8, AIX 5.1, HP-UX 11, IRIX 6.5, OSF/1 5.1, Solaris 11 2011-11, Cygwin, mingw, MSVC 9, Interix 3.5, BeOS.

11.3 alloca.h

Declares the alloca function of function-like macro.

Documentation:

- http://www.gnu.org/software/libc/manual/html_node/Variable-Size-Automatic. html,
- man alloca.

Gnulib module: alloca

Portability problems fixed by Gnulib:

- This header file is missing on some platforms: FreeBSD 6.0, NetBSD 5.0, OpenBSD 3.8, AIX 4.3.2, mingw, MSVC 9.

Portability problems not fixed by Gnulib:

11.4 ar.h

Describes the structure of files produced by the 'ar' program. Defines the type struct ar_hdr and the macros ARMAG, SARMAG, ARFMAG.

Gnulib module: —

Portability problems fixed by Gnulib:

Portability problems not fixed by Gnulib:

- This header file is missing on some platforms: mingw, MSVC 9, BeOS.

11.5 argp.h

Documentation:

- http://www.gnu.org/software/libc/manual/html_node/Argp.html.

Gnulib module: argp

Portability problems fixed by Gnulib:

- This header file is missing on all non-glibc platforms: Mac OS X 10.5, FreeBSD 6.0, NetBSD 5.0, OpenBSD 3.8, Minix 3.1.8, AIX 5.1, HP-UX 11, IRIX 6.5, OSF/1 5.1, Solaris 11 2011-11, Cygwin, mingw, MSVC 9, Interix 3.5, BeOS.

Portability problems not fixed by Gnulib:

11.6 argz.h

Documentation:

- http://www.gnu.org/software/libc/manual/html_node/Argz-Functions.html,
- man argz.

Gnulib module: argz

Portability problems fixed by Gnulib:

- This header file is missing on some platforms: Mac OS X 10.5, FreeBSD 6.0, NetBSD 5.0, OpenBSD 3.8, Minix 3.1.8, AIX 5.1, HP-UX 11, IRIX 6.5, OSF/1 5.1, Solaris 11 2011-11, mingw, MSVC 9, Interix 3.5, BeOS.
- The argz functions do not work on some platforms: Cygwin.

Portability problems not fixed by Gnulib:

11.7 `byteswap.h`

Defines the functions or function-like macros `bswap_16`, `bswap_32`, `bswap_64`.

Gnulib module: byteswap

Portability problems fixed by Gnulib:

- This header file is missing on some platforms: Mac OS X 10.5, FreeBSD 6.0, NetBSD 5.0, OpenBSD 3.8, Minix 3.1.8, AIX 5.1, HP-UX 11, IRIX 6.5, OSF/1 5.1, Solaris 11 2011-11, mingw, MSVC 9, Interix 3.5, BeOS.

Portability problems not fixed by Gnulib:

11.8 `crypt.h`

Defines the type `struct crypt_data` and declares the functions `crypt`, `crypt_r`, `setkey`, `setkey_r`, `encrypt`, `encrypt_r`.

Documentation:

- http://www.gnu.org/software/libc/manual/html_node/crypt.html, http://www.gnu.org/software/libc/manual/html_node/DES-Encryption.html,
- man crypt, man encrypt.

Gnulib module: —

Portability problems fixed by Gnulib:

Portability problems not fixed by Gnulib:

- This header file is missing on some platforms: Mac OS X 10.5, FreeBSD 6.0, NetBSD 5.0, OpenBSD 3.8, Minix 3.1.8, mingw, MSVC 9, Interix 3.5, BeOS.
- The functions `crypt`, `setkey`, `encrypt` are missing on some platforms: HP-UX 11, OSF/1 5.1.
- The type `struct crypt_data` and the functions `crypt_r`, `setkey_r`, `encrypt_r` are missing on some platforms: IRIX 6.5, Solaris 11 2011-11, Cygwin.

11.9 `endian.h`

Describe's the platform's endianness (byte ordering of words stored in memory). Defines the macros `BYTE_ORDER`, `LITTLE_ENDIAN`, `BIG_ENDIAN`, `PDP_ENDIAN`.

Gnulib module: —

Portability problems fixed by Gnulib:

Portability problems not fixed by Gnulib:

- This header file is missing on some platforms: Mac OS X 10.5, FreeBSD 6.0, NetBSD 5.0, OpenBSD 3.8, Minix 3.1.8, AIX 5.1, HP-UX 11, IRIX 6.5, OSF/1 5.1, Solaris 11 2011-11, mingw, MSVC 9, Interix 3.5.

11.10 envz.h

Documentation:

- http://www.gnu.org/software/libc/manual/html_node/Envz-Functions.html,
- man envz.

Gnulib module: —

Portability problems fixed by Gnulib:

Portability problems not fixed by Gnulib:

- This header file is missing on some platforms: Mac OS X 10.5, FreeBSD 6.0, NetBSD 5.0, OpenBSD 3.8, Minix 3.1.8, AIX 5.1, HP-UX 11, IRIX 6.5, OSF/1 5.1, Solaris 11 2011-11, mingw, MSVC 9, Interix 3.5, BeOS.

11.11 err.h

Declares the functions `warn`, `vwarn`, `warnx`, `vwarnx`, `err`, `verr`, `errx`, `verrx`.

Documentation:

- http://www.gnu.org/software/libc/manual/html_node/Error-Messages.html,
- man err.

Gnulib module: —

Portability problems fixed by Gnulib:

Portability problems not fixed by Gnulib:

- This header file is missing on some platforms: AIX 5.1, HP-UX 11, IRIX 6.5, OSF/1 5.1, Solaris 10, mingw, MSVC 9, BeOS.

11.12 error.h

Declares the functions `error`, `error_at_line` and the variables `error_print_progname`, `error_message_count`, `error_one_per_line`.

Documentation:

- http://www.gnu.org/software/libc/manual/html_node/Error-Messages.html,
- man error.

Gnulib module: error

Portability problems fixed by Gnulib:

- This header file is missing on many platforms: Mac OS X 10.5, FreeBSD 6.0, NetBSD 5.0, OpenBSD 3.8, Minix 3.1.8, AIX 5.1, HP-UX 11, IRIX 6.5, OSF/1 5.1, Solaris 11 2011-11, Cygwin, mingw, Interix 3.5, BeOS.
- This header file contains unrelated definitions on some platforms: MSVC 9.

Portability problems not fixed by Gnulib:

11.13 `execinfo.h`

Declares the functions `backtrace`, `backtrace_symbols`, `backtrace_symbols_fd`.

Documentation:

*   http://www.gnu.org/software/libc/manual/html_node/Backtraces.html,
*   man backtrace.

Gnulib module: —

Portability problems fixed by Gnulib:

*   This header file is missing on some platforms: Mac OS X 10.3, FreeBSD 6.0, NetBSD 5.0, OpenBSD 3.8, Minix 3.1.8, AIX 5.1, HP-UX 11, IRIX 6.5, OSF/1 5.1, Solaris 10, Cygwin, mingw, MSVC 9, Interix 3.5, BeOS.

Portability problems not fixed by Gnulib:

*   On platforms where the header file is missing, the Gnulib substitute implementation is just a stub, and does nothing.

11.14 `fpu_control.h`

Handling of the FPU control word. Defines the `fpu_control_t` type, declares the `__fpu_control` variable, and defines the `_FPU_GETCW`, `_FPU_SETCW` macros.

Gnulib module: —

Portability problems fixed by Gnulib:

Portability problems not fixed by Gnulib:

*   This header file is missing on all non-glibc platforms: Mac OS X 10.5, FreeBSD 6.0, NetBSD 5.0, OpenBSD 3.8, Minix 3.1.8, AIX 5.1, HP-UX 11, IRIX 6.5, OSF/1 5.1, Solaris 11 2011-11, Cygwin, mingw, MSVC 9, Interix 3.5, BeOS.

11.15 `fstab.h`

Defines the type `struct fstab`, the macros `FSTAB_*`, `_PATH_FSTAB`, and declares the functions `setfsent`, `endfsent`, `getfsent`, `getfsspec`, `getfsfile`.

Documentation:

*   http://www.gnu.org/software/libc/manual/html_node/fstab.html,
*   man setfsent.

Gnulib module: —

Portability problems fixed by Gnulib:

Portability problems not fixed by Gnulib:

*   This header file is missing on some platforms: Minix 3.1.8, IRIX 6.5, Solaris 11 2011-11, Cygwin, mingw, MSVC 9, Interix 3.5, BeOS.
*   The macro `_PATH_FSTAB` is missing on some platforms: AIX 5.1, HP-UX 11.

11.16 `fts.h`

Defines the types `FTS`, `FTSENT` and the macros `FTS_*`, and declares the functions `fts_open`, `fts_read`, `fts_children`, `fts_set`, `fts_close`.

Documentation:

- man fts.

Gnulib module: —

Portability problems fixed by Gnulib:

Portability problems not fixed by Gnulib:

- This header file is missing on some platforms: AIX 5.1, HP-UX 11, IRIX 6.5, OSF/1 5.1, Solaris 11 2011-11, mingw, MSVC 9, BeOS.

11.17 `getopt.h`

Defines the type `struct option` and declares the variables `optarg`, `optind`, `opterr`, `optopt` and the functions `getopt`, `getopt_long`, `getopt_long_only`.

Documentation:

- http://www.gnu.org/software/libc/manual/html_node/Getopt.html,
- man getopt.

Gnulib module: getopt-gnu

Portability problems fixed by Gnulib:

- This header file is missing on some platforms: AIX 5.1, HP-UX 11, MSVC 9, Interix 3.5.
- The function `getopt_long` is missing on some platforms: IRIX 6.5, OSF/1 5.1, Solaris 9.
- The function `getopt_long_only` is missing on some platforms: Mac OS X 10.3, FreeBSD 5.2.1, NetBSD 5.0, IRIX 6.5, OSF/1 5.1, Solaris 9, mingw.
- The method to reset options is incompatible on some platforms: FreeBSD 6.0, NetBSD 5.0(?), OpenBSD 3.8, Cygwin 1.5.x, mingw.
- The function `getopt` does not handle a leading '+' character in the options string on some platforms: Solaris 11 2010-11.

Portability problems not fixed by Gnulib:

11.18 `gshadow.h`

Defines the type `struct sgrp` and declares the functions `setsgent`, `endsgent`, `getsgent`, `getsgnam`, `sgetsgent`, `fgetsgent`, `putsgent`, `getsgent_r`, `getsgnam_r`, `sgetsgent_r`, `fgetsgent_r`.

Gnulib module: —

Portability problems fixed by Gnulib:

Portability problems not fixed by Gnulib:

- This header file is missing on all non-glibc platforms: Mac OS X 10.5, FreeBSD 6.4, NetBSD 5.0, OpenBSD 3.8, Minix 3.1.8, AIX 7.1, HP-UX 11.31, IRIX 6.5, OSF/1 5.1, Solaris 11 2011-11, Cygwin, mingw, MSVC 9, Interix 3.5, BeOS.

11.19 `ieee754.h`

Defines the types `union ieee754_float`, `union ieee754_double`, `union ieee854_long_double`.

Gnulib module: —

Portability problems fixed by Gnulib:

Portability problems not fixed by Gnulib:

- This header file is missing on all non-glibc platforms: Mac OS X 10.5, FreeBSD 6.0, NetBSD 5.0, OpenBSD 3.8, Minix 3.1.8, AIX 5.1, HP-UX 11, IRIX 6.5, OSF/1 5.1, Solaris 11 2011-11, Cygwin, mingw, MSVC 9, Interix 3.5, BeOS.

11.20 `ifaddrs.h`

Defines the type `struct ifaddrs` and declares the functions `getifaddrs`, `freeifaddrs`.

Documentation:

- `http://ecos.sourceware.org/docs-latest/ref/net-common-tcpip-manpages-getifaddrs.html`.

Gnulib module: —

Portability problems fixed by Gnulib:

Portability problems not fixed by Gnulib:

- This header file is missing on some platforms: AIX 5.1, HP-UX 11, IRIX 6.5, OSF/1 5.1, Solaris 10, Cygwin, mingw, MSVC 9, Interix 3.5, BeOS.

11.21 `libintl.h`

Defines the macros `__USE_GNU_GETTEXT`, `__GNU_GETTEXT_SUPPORTED_REVISION`, and declares the functions `gettext`, `dgettext`, `dcgettext`, `ngettext`, `dngettext`, `dcngettext`, `textdomain`, `bindtextdomain`, `bind_textdomain_codeset`.

Documentation:

- `http://www.gnu.org/software/libc/manual/html_node/Message-catalogs-with-gettext.html`,

- `http://www.gnu.org/software/gettext/manual/html_node/gettext.html`.

Gnulib module: gettext

Portability problems fixed by Gnulib, if GNU gettext is installed:

- This header file is missing on some platforms: Mac OS X 10.5, FreeBSD 6.0, OpenBSD 3.8, Minix 3.1.8, AIX 5.1, HP-UX 11, IRIX 6.5, OSF/1 5.1, mingw, MSVC 9, Interix 3.5, BeOS.

- The functions cannot deal with GNU .mo files with system-dependent strings (of major version 1 or of minor version 1) on some non-glibc platforms: NetBSD 3.0, Solaris 10.

Portability problems not fixed by Gnulib:

11.22 `mcheck.h`

Defines the type `enum mcheck_status` and declares the functions `mcheck`, `mcheck_pedantic`, `mcheck_check_all`, `mprobe`, `mtrace`, `muntrace`.

Documentation:

- `http://www.gnu.org/software/libc/manual/html_node/Heap-Consistency-Checking.html`.

Gnulib module: —

Portability problems fixed by Gnulib:

Portability problems not fixed by Gnulib:

- This header file is missing on all non-glibc platforms: Mac OS X 10.5, FreeBSD 6.0, NetBSD 5.0, OpenBSD 3.8, Minix 3.1.8, AIX 5.1, HP-UX 11, IRIX 6.5, OSF/1 5.1, Solaris 11 2011-11, Cygwin, mingw, MSVC 9, Interix 3.5, BeOS.

11.23 `mntent.h`

Defines the type `struct mntent` and the macros `MNTTAB`, `MOUNTED`, `MNTTYPE_*`, `MNTOPT_*`, and declares the functions `setmntent`, `getmntent`, `getmntent_r`, `addmntent`, `endmntent`, `hasmntopt`.

Documentation:

- `http://www.gnu.org/software/libc/manual/html_node/mtab.html`,
- man setmntent.

Gnulib module: —

Portability problems fixed by Gnulib:

Portability problems not fixed by Gnulib:

- This header file is missing on some platforms: Mac OS X 10.5, FreeBSD 6.0, NetBSD 5.0, OpenBSD 3.8, Minix 3.1.8, AIX 4.3.2, OSF/1 5.1, Solaris 11 2011-11, mingw, MSVC 9, Interix 3.5, BeOS.
- The function `getmntent_r` is missing on all non-glibc platforms: AIX 5.1, HP-UX 11, IRIX 6.5, Cygwin.

Gnulib module `mountlist` provides a higher-level abstraction.

11.24 `obstack.h`

Documentation:

- `http://www.gnu.org/software/libc/manual/html_node/Obstacks.html`.

Gnulib module: obstack

Portability problems fixed by Gnulib:

- This header file is missing on some platforms: Mac OS X 10.5, FreeBSD 6.0, NetBSD 5.0, OpenBSD 3.8, Minix 3.1.8, AIX 5.1, HP-UX 11, IRIX 6.5, OSF/1 5.1, Solaris 11 2011-11, Cygwin, mingw, MSVC 9, Interix 3.5.

Portability problems not fixed by Gnulib:

11.25 `paths.h`

Defines the macros `_PATH_*`.

Gnulib module: —

Portability problems fixed by Gnulib:

Portability problems not fixed by Gnulib:

- This header file is missing on some platforms: Minix 3.1.8, HP-UX 11, Solaris 11 2010-11, mingw, MSVC 9, BeOS.
- The set of `_PATH_*` macros is platform dependent.

11.26 `printf.h`

Defines the type `struct printf_info` and the macros and enum values `PA_*`, and declares the functions `printf_function`, `printf_arginfo_function`, `register_printf_function`, `parse_printf_format`, `printf_size`, `printf_size_info`.

Documentation:

- `http://www.gnu.org/software/libc/manual/html_node/Parsing-a-Template-String.html`.

Gnulib module: —

Portability problems fixed by Gnulib:

Portability problems not fixed by Gnulib:

- This header file is missing on some platforms: Mac OS X 10.5, FreeBSD 6.0, NetBSD 5.0, OpenBSD 3.8, Minix 3.1.8, AIX 5.1, HP-UX 11, IRIX 6.5, OSF/1 5.1, Solaris 11 2011-11, Cygwin, mingw, MSVC 9, Interix 3.5.

11.27 `pty.h`

Declares the functions `openpty` and `forkpty`.

Documentation:

- `http://www.gnu.org/software/libc/manual/html_node/Pseudo_002dTerminal-Pairs.html`,
- man openpty.

Gnulib module: pty

Portability problems fixed by Gnulib:

- This header file is missing on some platforms that declare the `forkpty` and `openpty` functions in `util.h` or `libutil.h` instead: Mac OS X 10.5, FreeBSD 6.0, NetBSD 5.0, OpenBSD 3.8.
- This header file is missing on some platforms: Minix 3.1.8, AIX 5.1, HP-UX 11, IRIX 6.5, Solaris 11 2011-11, BeOS.

Portability problems not fixed by Gnulib:

- This header file is missing on some platforms: mingw, MSVC 9.

11.28 `resolv.h`

Defines the types `res_sendhookact`, `res_send_qhook`, `res_send_rhook`, `res_state`, struct `res_sym` and the macros `_PATH_RESCONF`, `RES_*`, and declares the functions `fp_nquery`, `fp_query`, `hostalias`, `p_query`, `res_close`, `res_init`, `res_isourserver`, `res_mkquery`, `res_query`, `res_querydomain`, `res_search`, `res_send`.

Documentation:

- man res_init.

Gnulib module: —

Portability problems fixed by Gnulib:

Portability problems not fixed by Gnulib:

- This header file is missing on some platforms: Cygwin, mingw, MSVC 9, Interix 3.5, BeOS.
- The functions are missing on some platforms: HP-UX 11.

11.29 `shadow.h`

Defines the type struct `spwd` and declares the functions `setspent`, `endspent`, `getspent`, `getspent_r`, `getspnam`, `getspnam_r`, `sgetspent`, `sgetspent_r`, `fgetspent`, `fgetspent_r`, `putspent`, `lckpwdf`, `ulckpwdf`.

Documentation:

- man setspent.

Gnulib module: —

Portability problems fixed by Gnulib:

Portability problems not fixed by Gnulib:

- This header file is missing on some platforms: Mac OS X 10.5, FreeBSD 6.0, NetBSD 5.0, OpenBSD 3.8, Minix 3.1.8, AIX 5.1, OSF/1 5.1, Cygwin, mingw, MSVC 9, Interix 3.5, BeOS.
- The functions `getspent_r`, `getspnam_r`, `sgetspent_r`, `fgetspent`, `fgetspent_r`, `putspent` are missing on some platforms: HP-UX 11.
- The functions `sgetspent`, `sgetspent_r` are missing on some platforms: HP-UX 11, IRIX 6.5, Solaris 11 2011-11.

11.30 `sys/ioctl.h`

Declares the function `ioctl`.

Documentation:

- http://www.gnu.org/software/libc/manual/html_node/IOCTLs.html,
- man ioctl.

Gnulib module: sys_ioctl

Portability problems fixed by Gnulib:

- This header file is missing on some platforms: mingw, MSVC 9.

- This header file does not declare the `ioctl` function on some platforms: AIX 5.1, Solaris 11 2011-11.

Portability problems not fixed by Gnulib:

11.31 sysexits.h

Defines the `EX_*` macros, including `EX_OK`.

Gnulib module: sysexits

Portability problems fixed by Gnulib:

- This header file is missing on some platforms: mingw, MSVC 9, Interix 3.5, BeOS.
- The macro `EX_CONFIG` is missing on some platforms: HP-UX 11.

Portability problems not fixed by Gnulib:

11.32 ttyent.h

Defines the type `struct ttyent` and declares the functions `setttyent`, `endttyent`, `getttyent`, `getttynam`.

Documentation:

- man setttyent.

Gnulib module: —

Portability problems fixed by Gnulib:

Portability problems not fixed by Gnulib:

- This header file is missing on some platforms: HP-UX 11, IRIX 6.5, Solaris 11 2011-11, Cygwin, mingw, MSVC 9, Interix 3.5, BeOS.

12 Glibc Function Substitutes

This chapter describes which functions and function-like macros provided as extensions by at least GNU libc are also supported by Gnulib, which portability pitfalls are fixed by Gnulib, and which (known) portability problems are not worked around by Gnulib.

The notation "Gnulib module: —" means that Gnulib does not provide a module providing a substitute for the function. When the list "Portability problems not fixed by Gnulib" is empty, such a module is not needed: No portability problems are known. Otherwise, it indicates that such a module would be useful but is not available: No one so far found this function important enough to contribute a substitute for it. If you need this particular function, you may write to `<bug-gnulib at gnu dot org>`.

This list of functions is sorted according to the header that declares them.

12.1 Glibc Extensions to `<aio.h>`

12.1.1 `aio_init`

Gnulib module: —

Portability problems fixed by Gnulib:

Portability problems not fixed by Gnulib:

- This function is missing on some platforms: Mac OS X 10.5, FreeBSD 6.0, NetBSD 5.0, OpenBSD 3.8, Minix 3.1.8, AIX 5.1, HP-UX 11, OSF/1 5.1, Solaris 11 2011-11, Cygwin, mingw, MSVC 9, Interix 3.5, BeOS.

12.2 Glibc `<aliases.h>`

12.2.1 `endaliasent`

Gnulib module: —

Portability problems fixed by Gnulib:

Portability problems not fixed by Gnulib:

- This function is missing on all non-glibc platforms: Mac OS X 10.5, FreeBSD 6.0, NetBSD 5.0, OpenBSD 3.8, Minix 3.1.8, AIX 5.1, HP-UX 11, IRIX 6.5, OSF/1 5.1, Solaris 11 2011-11, Cygwin, mingw, MSVC 9, Interix 3.5, BeOS.

12.2.2 `getaliasbyname`

Gnulib module: —

Portability problems fixed by Gnulib:

Portability problems not fixed by Gnulib:

- This function is missing on all non-glibc platforms: Mac OS X 10.5, FreeBSD 6.0, NetBSD 5.0, OpenBSD 3.8, Minix 3.1.8, AIX 5.1, HP-UX 11, IRIX 6.5, OSF/1 5.1, Solaris 11 2011-11, Cygwin, mingw, MSVC 9, Interix 3.5, BeOS.

12.2.3 `getaliasbyname_r`

Gnulib module: —

Portability problems fixed by Gnulib:

Portability problems not fixed by Gnulib:

- This function is missing on all non-glibc platforms: Mac OS X 10.5, FreeBSD 6.0, NetBSD 5.0, OpenBSD 3.8, Minix 3.1.8, AIX 5.1, HP-UX 11, IRIX 6.5, OSF/1 5.1, Solaris 11 2011-11, Cygwin, mingw, MSVC 9, Interix 3.5, BeOS.

12.2.4 `getaliasent`

Gnulib module: —

Portability problems fixed by Gnulib:

Portability problems not fixed by Gnulib:

- This function is missing on all non-glibc platforms: Mac OS X 10.5, FreeBSD 6.0, NetBSD 5.0, OpenBSD 3.8, Minix 3.1.8, AIX 5.1, HP-UX 11, IRIX 6.5, OSF/1 5.1, Solaris 11 2011-11, Cygwin, mingw, MSVC 9, Interix 3.5, BeOS.

12.2.5 `getaliasent_r`

Gnulib module: —

Portability problems fixed by Gnulib:

Portability problems not fixed by Gnulib:

- This function is missing on all non-glibc platforms: Mac OS X 10.5, FreeBSD 6.0, NetBSD 5.0, OpenBSD 3.8, Minix 3.1.8, AIX 5.1, HP-UX 11, IRIX 6.5, OSF/1 5.1, Solaris 11 2011-11, Cygwin, mingw, MSVC 9, Interix 3.5, BeOS.

12.2.6 `setaliasent`

Gnulib module: —

Portability problems fixed by Gnulib:

Portability problems not fixed by Gnulib:

- This function is missing on all non-glibc platforms: Mac OS X 10.5, FreeBSD 6.0, NetBSD 5.0, OpenBSD 3.8, Minix 3.1.8, AIX 5.1, HP-UX 11, IRIX 6.5, OSF/1 5.1, Solaris 11 2011-11, Cygwin, mingw, MSVC 9, Interix 3.5, BeOS.

12.3 Glibc `<argp.h>`

12.3.1 `argp_err_exit_status`

Gnulib module: —

Portability problems fixed by Gnulib:

Portability problems not fixed by Gnulib:

- This variable is missing on all non-glibc platforms: Mac OS X 10.5, FreeBSD 6.0, NetBSD 5.0, OpenBSD 3.8, Minix 3.1.8, AIX 5.1, HP-UX 11, IRIX 6.5, OSF/1 5.1, Solaris 11 2011-11, Cygwin, mingw, MSVC 9, Interix 3.5, BeOS.

12.3.2 `argp_error`

Gnulib module: —

Portability problems fixed by Gnulib:

Portability problems not fixed by Gnulib:

- This function is missing on all non-glibc platforms: Mac OS X 10.5, FreeBSD 6.0, NetBSD 5.0, OpenBSD 3.8, Minix 3.1.8, AIX 5.1, HP-UX 11, IRIX 6.5, OSF/1 5.1, Solaris 11 2011-11, Cygwin, mingw, MSVC 9, Interix 3.5, BeOS.

12.3.3 `argp_failure`

Gnulib module: —

Portability problems fixed by Gnulib:

Portability problems not fixed by Gnulib:

- This function is missing on all non-glibc platforms: Mac OS X 10.5, FreeBSD 6.0, NetBSD 5.0, OpenBSD 3.8, Minix 3.1.8, AIX 5.1, HP-UX 11, IRIX 6.5, OSF/1 5.1, Solaris 11 2011-11, Cygwin, mingw, MSVC 9, Interix 3.5, BeOS.

12.3.4 `argp_help`

Gnulib module: —

Portability problems fixed by Gnulib:

Portability problems not fixed by Gnulib:

- This function is missing on all non-glibc platforms: Mac OS X 10.5, FreeBSD 6.0, NetBSD 5.0, OpenBSD 3.8, Minix 3.1.8, AIX 5.1, HP-UX 11, IRIX 6.5, OSF/1 5.1, Solaris 11 2011-11, Cygwin, mingw, MSVC 9, Interix 3.5, BeOS.

12.3.5 `argp_parse`

Gnulib module: —

Portability problems fixed by Gnulib:

Portability problems not fixed by Gnulib:

- This function is missing on all non-glibc platforms: Mac OS X 10.5, FreeBSD 6.0, NetBSD 5.0, OpenBSD 3.8, Minix 3.1.8, AIX 5.1, HP-UX 11, IRIX 6.5, OSF/1 5.1, Solaris 11 2011-11, Cygwin, mingw, MSVC 9, Interix 3.5, BeOS.

12.3.6 `argp_program_bug_address`

Gnulib module: —

Portability problems fixed by Gnulib:

Portability problems not fixed by Gnulib:

- This variable is missing on all non-glibc platforms: Mac OS X 10.5, FreeBSD 6.0, NetBSD 5.0, OpenBSD 3.8, Minix 3.1.8, AIX 5.1, HP-UX 11, IRIX 6.5, OSF/1 5.1, Solaris 11 2011-11, Cygwin, mingw, MSVC 9, Interix 3.5, BeOS.

12.3.7 `argp_program_version`

Gnulib module: —

Portability problems fixed by Gnulib:

Portability problems not fixed by Gnulib:

- This variable is missing on all non-glibc platforms: Mac OS X 10.5, FreeBSD 6.0, NetBSD 5.0, OpenBSD 3.8, Minix 3.1.8, AIX 5.1, HP-UX 11, IRIX 6.5, OSF/1 5.1, Solaris 11 2011-11, Cygwin, mingw, MSVC 9, Interix 3.5, BeOS.

12.3.8 `argp_program_version_hook`

Gnulib module: —

Portability problems fixed by Gnulib:

Portability problems not fixed by Gnulib:

- This variable is missing on all non-glibc platforms: Mac OS X 10.5, FreeBSD 6.0, NetBSD 5.0, OpenBSD 3.8, Minix 3.1.8, AIX 5.1, HP-UX 11, IRIX 6.5, OSF/1 5.1, Solaris 11 2011-11, Cygwin, mingw, MSVC 9, Interix 3.5, BeOS.

12.3.9 `argp_state_help`

Gnulib module: —

Portability problems fixed by Gnulib:

Portability problems not fixed by Gnulib:

- This function is missing on all non-glibc platforms: Mac OS X 10.5, FreeBSD 6.0, NetBSD 5.0, OpenBSD 3.8, Minix 3.1.8, AIX 5.1, HP-UX 11, IRIX 6.5, OSF/1 5.1, Solaris 11 2011-11, Cygwin, mingw, MSVC 9, Interix 3.5, BeOS.

12.3.10 `argp_usage`

Gnulib module: —

Portability problems fixed by Gnulib:

Portability problems not fixed by Gnulib:

- This function is missing on all non-glibc platforms: Mac OS X 10.5, FreeBSD 6.0, NetBSD 5.0, OpenBSD 3.8, Minix 3.1.8, AIX 5.1, HP-UX 11, IRIX 6.5, OSF/1 5.1, Solaris 11 2011-11, Cygwin, mingw, MSVC 9, Interix 3.5, BeOS.

12.4 Glibc `<argz.h>`

12.4.1 `argz_add`

Gnulib module: argz

Portability problems fixed by Gnulib:

- This function is missing on some platforms: Mac OS X 10.5, FreeBSD 6.0, NetBSD 5.0, OpenBSD 3.8, Minix 3.1.8, AIX 5.1, HP-UX 11, IRIX 6.5, OSF/1 5.1, Solaris 11 2011-11, mingw, MSVC 9, Interix 3.5, BeOS.
- This function is broken on some platforms: Cygwin 1.5.24.

Portability problems not fixed by Gnulib:

12.4.2 `argz_add_sep`

Gnulib module: argz

Portability problems fixed by Gnulib:

- This function is missing on some platforms: Mac OS X 10.5, FreeBSD 6.0, NetBSD 5.0, OpenBSD 3.8, Minix 3.1.8, AIX 5.1, HP-UX 11, IRIX 6.5, OSF/1 5.1, Solaris 11 2011-11, mingw, MSVC 9, Interix 3.5, BeOS.
- This function is broken on some platforms: Cygwin 1.5.24.

Portability problems not fixed by Gnulib:

12.4.3 `argz_append`

Gnulib module: argz

Portability problems fixed by Gnulib:

- This function is missing on some platforms: Mac OS X 10.5, FreeBSD 6.0, NetBSD 5.0, OpenBSD 3.8, Minix 3.1.8, AIX 5.1, HP-UX 11, IRIX 6.5, OSF/1 5.1, Solaris 11 2011-11, mingw, MSVC 9, Interix 3.5, BeOS.
- This function is broken on some platforms: Cygwin 1.5.24.

Portability problems not fixed by Gnulib:

12.4.4 `argz_count`

Gnulib module: argz

Portability problems fixed by Gnulib:

- This function is missing on some platforms: Mac OS X 10.5, FreeBSD 6.0, NetBSD 5.0, OpenBSD 3.8, Minix 3.1.8, AIX 5.1, HP-UX 11, IRIX 6.5, OSF/1 5.1, Solaris 11 2011-11, mingw, MSVC 9, Interix 3.5, BeOS.
- This function is broken on some platforms: Cygwin 1.5.24.

Portability problems not fixed by Gnulib:

12.4.5 `argz_create`

Gnulib module: argz

Portability problems fixed by Gnulib:

- This function is missing on some platforms: Mac OS X 10.5, FreeBSD 6.0, NetBSD 5.0, OpenBSD 3.8, Minix 3.1.8, AIX 5.1, HP-UX 11, IRIX 6.5, OSF/1 5.1, Solaris 11 2011-11, mingw, MSVC 9, Interix 3.5, BeOS.
- This function is broken on some platforms: Cygwin 1.5.24.

Portability problems not fixed by Gnulib:

12.4.6 `argz_create_sep`

Gnulib module: argz

Portability problems fixed by Gnulib:

- This function is missing on some platforms: Mac OS X 10.5, FreeBSD 6.0, NetBSD 5.0, OpenBSD 3.8, Minix 3.1.8, AIX 5.1, HP-UX 11, IRIX 6.5, OSF/1 5.1, Solaris 11 2011-11, mingw, MSVC 9, Interix 3.5, BeOS.

- This function is broken on some platforms: Cygwin 1.5.24.

Portability problems not fixed by Gnulib:

12.4.7 `argz_delete`

Gnulib module: argz

Portability problems fixed by Gnulib:

- This function is missing on some platforms: Mac OS X 10.5, FreeBSD 6.0, NetBSD 5.0, OpenBSD 3.8, Minix 3.1.8, AIX 5.1, HP-UX 11, IRIX 6.5, OSF/1 5.1, Solaris 11 2011-11, mingw, MSVC 9, Interix 3.5, BeOS.
- This function is broken on some platforms: Cygwin 1.5.24.

Portability problems not fixed by Gnulib:

12.4.8 `argz_extract`

Gnulib module: argz

Portability problems fixed by Gnulib:

- This function is missing on some platforms: Mac OS X 10.5, FreeBSD 6.0, NetBSD 5.0, OpenBSD 3.8, Minix 3.1.8, AIX 5.1, HP-UX 11, IRIX 6.5, OSF/1 5.1, Solaris 11 2011-11, mingw, MSVC 9, Interix 3.5, BeOS.
- This function is broken on some platforms: Cygwin 1.5.24.

Portability problems not fixed by Gnulib:

12.4.9 `argz_insert`

Gnulib module: argz

Portability problems fixed by Gnulib:

- This function is missing on some platforms: Mac OS X 10.5, FreeBSD 6.0, NetBSD 5.0, OpenBSD 3.8, Minix 3.1.8, AIX 5.1, HP-UX 11, IRIX 6.5, OSF/1 5.1, Solaris 11 2011-11, mingw, MSVC 9, Interix 3.5, BeOS.
- This function is broken on some platforms: Cygwin 1.5.24.

Portability problems not fixed by Gnulib:

12.4.10 `argz_next`

Gnulib module: argz

Portability problems fixed by Gnulib:

- This function is missing on some platforms: Mac OS X 10.5, FreeBSD 6.0, NetBSD 5.0, OpenBSD 3.8, Minix 3.1.8, AIX 5.1, HP-UX 11, IRIX 6.5, OSF/1 5.1, Solaris 11 2011-11, mingw, MSVC 9, Interix 3.5, BeOS.
- This function is broken on some platforms: Cygwin 1.5.24.

Portability problems not fixed by Gnulib:

12.4.11 `argz_replace`

Gnulib module: argz

Portability problems fixed by Gnulib:

- This function is missing on some platforms: Mac OS X 10.5, FreeBSD 6.0, NetBSD 5.0, OpenBSD 3.8, Minix 3.1.8, AIX 5.1, HP-UX 11, IRIX 6.5, OSF/1 5.1, Solaris 11 2011-11, mingw, MSVC 9, Interix 3.5, BeOS.
- This function is broken on some platforms: Cygwin 1.5.24.

Portability problems not fixed by Gnulib:

12.4.12 `argz_stringify`

Gnulib module: argz

Portability problems fixed by Gnulib:

- This function is missing on some platforms: Mac OS X 10.5, FreeBSD 6.0, NetBSD 5.0, OpenBSD 3.8, Minix 3.1.8, AIX 5.1, HP-UX 11, IRIX 6.5, OSF/1 5.1, Solaris 11 2011-11, mingw, MSVC 9, Interix 3.5, BeOS.
- This function is broken on some platforms: Cygwin 1.5.24.

Portability problems not fixed by Gnulib:

12.5 Glibc Extensions to `<arpa/inet.h>`

12.5.1 `inet_aton`

Gnulib module: —

Portability problems fixed by Gnulib:

Portability problems not fixed by Gnulib:

- This function is missing on some platforms: mingw, MSVC 9, BeOS.

12.5.2 `inet_lnaof`

Gnulib module: —

Portability problems fixed by Gnulib:

Portability problems not fixed by Gnulib:

- This function is missing on some platforms: Minix 3.1.8, Cygwin, mingw, MSVC 9, BeOS.

12.5.3 `inet_makeaddr`

Gnulib module: —

Portability problems fixed by Gnulib:

Portability problems not fixed by Gnulib:

- This function is missing on some platforms: Minix 3.1.8, mingw, MSVC 9, BeOS.

12.5.4 `inet_net_ntop`

Gnulib module: —

Portability problems fixed by Gnulib:

Portability problems not fixed by Gnulib:

- This function is missing on some platforms: Minix 3.1.8, HP-UX 11.00, IRIX 6.5, OSF/1 4.0, Cygwin, mingw, MSVC 9, Interix 3.5, BeOS.

12.5.5 `inet_net_pton`

Gnulib module: —

Portability problems fixed by Gnulib:

Portability problems not fixed by Gnulib:

- This function is missing on some platforms: Minix 3.1.8, HP-UX 11.00, IRIX 6.5, OSF/1 4.0, Cygwin, mingw, MSVC 9, Interix 3.5, BeOS.

12.5.6 `inet_neta`

Gnulib module: —

Portability problems fixed by Gnulib:

Portability problems not fixed by Gnulib:

- This function is missing on some platforms: Minix 3.1.8, HP-UX 11.00, IRIX 6.5, OSF/1 4.0, Solaris 10, Cygwin, mingw, MSVC 9, Interix 3.5, BeOS.

12.5.7 `inet_netof`

Gnulib module: —

Portability problems fixed by Gnulib:

Portability problems not fixed by Gnulib:

- This function is missing on some platforms: Minix 3.1.8, mingw, MSVC 9, BeOS.

12.5.8 `inet_network`

Gnulib module: —

Portability problems fixed by Gnulib:

Portability problems not fixed by Gnulib:

- This function is missing on some platforms: mingw, MSVC 9, BeOS.

12.5.9 `inet_nsap_addr`

Gnulib module: —

Portability problems fixed by Gnulib:

Portability problems not fixed by Gnulib:

- This function is missing on some platforms: Minix 3.1.8, HP-UX 11.00, IRIX 5.3, Cygwin, mingw, MSVC 9, Interix 3.5, BeOS.

12.5.10 `inet_nsap_ntoa`

Gnulib module: —

Portability problems fixed by Gnulib:

Portability problems not fixed by Gnulib:

- This function is missing on some platforms: Minix 3.1.8, HP-UX 11.00, IRIX 5.3, Cygwin, mingw, MSVC 9, Interix 3.5, BeOS.

12.6 Glibc `<byteswap.h>`

12.6.1 `bswap_16`

Gnulib module: —

Portability problems fixed by Gnulib:

Portability problems not fixed by Gnulib:

- This function is missing on some platforms: Mac OS X 10.5, FreeBSD 6.0, NetBSD 5.0, OpenBSD 3.8, Minix 3.1.8, AIX 5.1, HP-UX 11, IRIX 6.5, OSF/1 5.1, Solaris 11 2011-11, Cygwin, mingw, MSVC 9, Interix 3.5, BeOS.

12.6.2 `bswap_32`

Gnulib module: —

Portability problems fixed by Gnulib:

Portability problems not fixed by Gnulib:

- This function is missing on some platforms: Mac OS X 10.5, FreeBSD 6.0, NetBSD 5.0, OpenBSD 3.8, Minix 3.1.8, AIX 5.1, HP-UX 11, IRIX 6.5, OSF/1 5.1, Solaris 11 2011-11, Cygwin, mingw, MSVC 9, Interix 3.5, BeOS.

12.6.3 `bswap_64`

Gnulib module: —

Portability problems fixed by Gnulib:

Portability problems not fixed by Gnulib:

- This function is missing on some platforms: Mac OS X 10.5, FreeBSD 6.0, NetBSD 5.0, OpenBSD 3.8, Minix 3.1.8, AIX 5.1, HP-UX 11, IRIX 6.5, OSF/1 5.1, Solaris 11 2011-11, Cygwin, mingw, MSVC 9, Interix 3.5, BeOS.

12.7 Glibc Extensions to `<complex.h>`

12.7.1 `clog10`

Gnulib module: —

Portability problems fixed by Gnulib:

Portability problems not fixed by Gnulib:

- This function is missing on some platforms: Mac OS X 10.5, FreeBSD 6.0, NetBSD 5.0, OpenBSD 3.8, Minix 3.1.8, AIX 5.1, HP-UX 11, IRIX 6.5, OSF/1 5.1, Solaris 11 2011-11, Cygwin, mingw, MSVC 9, Interix 3.5.

12.7.2 `clog10f`

Gnulib module: —

Portability problems fixed by Gnulib:

Portability problems not fixed by Gnulib:

- This function is missing on some platforms: Mac OS X 10.5, FreeBSD 6.0, NetBSD 5.0, OpenBSD 3.8, Minix 3.1.8, AIX 5.1, HP-UX 11, IRIX 6.5, OSF/1 5.1, Solaris 11 2011-11, Cygwin, mingw, MSVC 9, Interix 3.5.

12.7.3 `clog10l`

Gnulib module: —

Portability problems fixed by Gnulib:

Portability problems not fixed by Gnulib:

- This function is missing on all non-glibc platforms: Mac OS X 10.5, FreeBSD 6.0, NetBSD 5.0, OpenBSD 3.8, Minix 3.1.8, AIX 5.1, HP-UX 11, IRIX 6.5, OSF/1 5.1, Solaris 11 2011-11, Cygwin, mingw, MSVC 9, Interix 3.5, BeOS.

12.8 Glibc `<crypt.h>`

12.8.1 `crypt_r`

Gnulib module: —

Portability problems fixed by Gnulib:

Portability problems not fixed by Gnulib:

- This function is missing on all non-glibc platforms: Mac OS X 10.5, FreeBSD 6.0, NetBSD 5.0, OpenBSD 3.8, Minix 3.1.8, AIX 5.1, HP-UX 11, IRIX 6.5, OSF/1 5.1, Solaris 11 2011-11, Cygwin, mingw, MSVC 9, Interix 3.5, BeOS.

12.8.2 `encrypt_r`

Gnulib module: —

Portability problems fixed by Gnulib:

Portability problems not fixed by Gnulib:

- This function is missing on some platforms: Mac OS X 10.5, FreeBSD 6.0, NetBSD 5.0, OpenBSD 3.8, Minix 3.1.8, HP-UX 11, IRIX 6.5, OSF/1 5.1, Solaris 11 2011-11, Cygwin, mingw, MSVC 9, Interix 3.5, BeOS.

12.8.3 `setkey_r`

Gnulib module: —

Portability problems fixed by Gnulib:

Portability problems not fixed by Gnulib:

- This function is missing on some platforms: Mac OS X 10.5, FreeBSD 6.0, NetBSD 5.0, OpenBSD 3.8, Minix 3.1.8, HP-UX 11, IRIX 6.5, OSF/1 5.1, Solaris 11 2011-11, Cygwin, mingw, MSVC 9, Interix 3.5, BeOS.

12.9 Glibc Extensions to `<ctype.h>`

12.9.1 `isctype`

Gnulib module: —

Portability problems fixed by Gnulib:

Portability problems not fixed by Gnulib:

- This function is missing on some platforms: Mac OS X 10.5, FreeBSD 6.0, NetBSD 5.0, OpenBSD 3.8, Minix 3.1.8, AIX 5.1, IRIX 6.5, OSF/1 5.1, Solaris 11 2011-11, Cygwin, mingw, MSVC 9, Interix 3.5, BeOS.

12.10 Glibc Extensions to `<dirent.h>`

12.10.1 `getdirentries`

Gnulib module: —

Portability problems fixed by Gnulib:

Portability problems not fixed by Gnulib:

- This function is missing on some platforms: Minix 3.1.8, AIX 4.3.2, IRIX 6.5, Solaris 11 2011-11, Cygwin, mingw, MSVC 9, Interix 3.5, BeOS.
- On platforms where `off_t` is a 32-bit type, this function may not work correctly on huge directories larger than 2 GB. The fix is to use the `AC_SYS_LARGEFILE` macro.

12.10.2 `scandirat`

Gnulib module: —

Portability problems fixed by Gnulib:

Portability problems not fixed by Gnulib:

- This function is missing on many non-glibc platforms: glibc 2.14, Mac OS X 10.5, FreeBSD 6.4, NetBSD 5.0, OpenBSD 3.8, Minix 3.1.8, AIX 7.1, HP-UX 11.31, IRIX 6.5, OSF/1 5.1, Solaris 11 2011-11, Cygwin 1.7.10, mingw, MSVC 9, Interix 3.5, BeOS.

12.10.3 `versionsort`

Gnulib module: —

Portability problems fixed by Gnulib:

Portability problems not fixed by Gnulib:

- This function is missing on all non-glibc platforms: Mac OS X 10.5, FreeBSD 6.0, NetBSD 5.0, OpenBSD 3.8, Minix 3.1.8, AIX 5.1, HP-UX 11, IRIX 6.5, OSF/1 5.1, Solaris 11 2011-11, Cygwin, mingw, MSVC 9, Interix 3.5, BeOS.

12.11 Glibc Extensions to `<dlfcn.h>`

12.11.1 `dladdr`

Gnulib module: —

Portability problems fixed by Gnulib:

Portability problems not fixed by Gnulib:

- This function is missing on some platforms: Minix 3.1.8, AIX 5.1, IRIX 6.5, OSF/1 5.1, Cygwin, mingw, MSVC 9, Interix 3.5, BeOS.

12.11.2 `dladdr1`

Gnulib module: —

Portability problems fixed by Gnulib:

Portability problems not fixed by Gnulib:

- This function is missing on some platforms: Mac OS X 10.5, FreeBSD 6.0, NetBSD 5.0, OpenBSD 3.8, Minix 3.1.8, AIX 5.1, HP-UX 11, IRIX 6.5, OSF/1 5.1, Cygwin, mingw, MSVC 9, Interix 3.5, BeOS.

12.11.3 `dlinfo`

Gnulib module: —

Portability problems fixed by Gnulib:

Portability problems not fixed by Gnulib:

- This function is missing on some platforms: Mac OS X 10.5, NetBSD 5.0, OpenBSD 3.8, Minix 3.1.8, AIX 5.1, HP-UX 11, IRIX 6.5, OSF/1 5.1, Cygwin, mingw, MSVC 9, Interix 3.5, BeOS.

12.11.4 `dlmopen`

Gnulib module: —

Portability problems fixed by Gnulib:

Portability problems not fixed by Gnulib:

- This function is missing on some platforms: Mac OS X 10.5, FreeBSD 6.0, NetBSD 5.0, OpenBSD 3.8, Minix 3.1.8, AIX 5.1, HP-UX 11, IRIX 6.5, OSF/1 5.1, Cygwin, mingw, MSVC 9, Interix 3.5, BeOS.

12.11.5 `dlvsym`

Gnulib module: —

Portability problems fixed by Gnulib:

Portability problems not fixed by Gnulib:

- This function is missing on all non-glibc platforms: Mac OS X 10.5, FreeBSD 6.0, NetBSD 5.0, OpenBSD 3.8, Minix 3.1.8, AIX 5.1, HP-UX 11, IRIX 6.5, OSF/1 5.1, Solaris 11 2011-11, Cygwin, mingw, MSVC 9, Interix 3.5, BeOS.

12.12 Glibc <envz.h>

12.12.1 envz_add

Gnulib module: —

Portability problems fixed by Gnulib:

Portability problems not fixed by Gnulib:

- This function is missing on some platforms: Mac OS X 10.5, FreeBSD 6.0, NetBSD 5.0, OpenBSD 3.8, Minix 3.1.8, AIX 5.1, HP-UX 11, IRIX 6.5, OSF/1 5.1, Solaris 11 2011-11, mingw, MSVC 9, Interix 3.5, BeOS.

12.12.2 envz_entry

Gnulib module: —

Portability problems fixed by Gnulib:

Portability problems not fixed by Gnulib:

- This function is missing on some platforms: Mac OS X 10.5, FreeBSD 6.0, NetBSD 5.0, OpenBSD 3.8, Minix 3.1.8, AIX 5.1, HP-UX 11, IRIX 6.5, OSF/1 5.1, Solaris 11 2011-11, mingw, MSVC 9, Interix 3.5, BeOS.

12.12.3 envz_get

Gnulib module: —

Portability problems fixed by Gnulib:

Portability problems not fixed by Gnulib:

- This function is missing on some platforms: Mac OS X 10.5, FreeBSD 6.0, NetBSD 5.0, OpenBSD 3.8, Minix 3.1.8, AIX 5.1, HP-UX 11, IRIX 6.5, OSF/1 5.1, Solaris 11 2011-11, mingw, MSVC 9, Interix 3.5, BeOS.

12.12.4 envz_merge

Gnulib module: —

Portability problems fixed by Gnulib:

Portability problems not fixed by Gnulib:

- This function is missing on some platforms: Mac OS X 10.5, FreeBSD 6.0, NetBSD 5.0, OpenBSD 3.8, Minix 3.1.8, AIX 5.1, HP-UX 11, IRIX 6.5, OSF/1 5.1, Solaris 11 2011-11, mingw, MSVC 9, Interix 3.5, BeOS.

12.12.5 envz_remove

Gnulib module: —

Portability problems fixed by Gnulib:

Portability problems not fixed by Gnulib:

- This function is missing on some platforms: Mac OS X 10.5, FreeBSD 6.0, NetBSD 5.0, OpenBSD 3.8, Minix 3.1.8, AIX 5.1, HP-UX 11, IRIX 6.5, OSF/1 5.1, Solaris 11 2011-11, mingw, MSVC 9, Interix 3.5, BeOS.

12.12.6 `envz_strip`

Gnulib module: —

Portability problems fixed by Gnulib:

Portability problems not fixed by Gnulib:

- This function is missing on some platforms: Mac OS X 10.5, FreeBSD 6.0, NetBSD 5.0, OpenBSD 3.8, Minix 3.1.8, AIX 5.1, HP-UX 11, IRIX 6.5, OSF/1 5.1, Solaris 11 2011-11, mingw, MSVC 9, Interix 3.5, BeOS.

12.13 Glibc `<err.h>`

12.13.1 `err`

Gnulib module: —

Portability problems fixed by Gnulib:

Portability problems not fixed by Gnulib:

- This function is missing on some platforms: AIX 5.1, HP-UX 11, IRIX 6.5, OSF/1 5.1, Solaris 10, mingw, MSVC 9, BeOS.

12.13.2 `errx`

Gnulib module: —

Portability problems fixed by Gnulib:

Portability problems not fixed by Gnulib:

- This function is missing on some platforms: AIX 5.1, HP-UX 11, IRIX 6.5, OSF/1 5.1, Solaris 10, mingw, MSVC 9, BeOS.

12.13.3 `verr`

Gnulib module: —

Portability problems fixed by Gnulib:

Portability problems not fixed by Gnulib:

- This function is missing on some platforms: AIX 5.1, HP-UX 11, IRIX 6.5, OSF/1 5.1, Solaris 10, mingw, MSVC 9, BeOS.

12.13.4 `verrx`

Gnulib module: —

Portability problems fixed by Gnulib:

Portability problems not fixed by Gnulib:

- This function is missing on some platforms: AIX 5.1, HP-UX 11, IRIX 6.5, OSF/1 5.1, Solaris 10, mingw, MSVC 9, BeOS.

12.13.5 `vwarn`

Gnulib module: —

Portability problems fixed by Gnulib:

Portability problems not fixed by Gnulib:

- This function is missing on some platforms: AIX 5.1, HP-UX 11, IRIX 6.5, OSF/1 5.1, Solaris 10, mingw, MSVC 9, BeOS.

12.13.6 `vwarnx`

Gnulib module: —

Portability problems fixed by Gnulib:

Portability problems not fixed by Gnulib:

- This function is missing on some platforms: AIX 5.1, HP-UX 11, IRIX 6.5, OSF/1 5.1, Solaris 10, mingw, MSVC 9, BeOS.

12.13.7 `warn`

Gnulib module: —

Portability problems fixed by Gnulib:

Portability problems not fixed by Gnulib:

- This function is missing on some platforms: AIX 5.1, HP-UX 11, IRIX 6.5, OSF/1 5.1, Solaris 10, mingw, MSVC 9, BeOS.

12.13.8 `warnx`

Gnulib module: —

Portability problems fixed by Gnulib:

Portability problems not fixed by Gnulib:

- This function is missing on some platforms: AIX 5.1, HP-UX 11, IRIX 6.5, OSF/1 5.1, Solaris 10, mingw, MSVC 9, BeOS.

12.14 Glibc Extensions to `<errno.h>`

12.14.1 `program_invocation_name`

Gnulib module: —

Portability problems fixed by Gnulib:

Portability problems not fixed by Gnulib:

- This variable is missing on some platforms: Mac OS X 10.5, FreeBSD 6.0, NetBSD 5.0, OpenBSD 3.8, Minix 3.1.8, AIX 5.1, HP-UX 11, IRIX 6.5, OSF/1 5.1, Solaris 11 2011-11, Cygwin 1.7.7, mingw, MSVC 9, Interix 3.5.

12.14.2 `program_invocation_short_name`

Gnulib module: —

Portability problems fixed by Gnulib:

Portability problems not fixed by Gnulib:

- This variable is missing on some platforms: Mac OS X 10.5, FreeBSD 6.0, NetBSD 5.0, OpenBSD 3.8, Minix 3.1.8, AIX 5.1, HP-UX 11, IRIX 6.5, OSF/1 5.1, Solaris 11 2011-11, Cygwin 1.7.7, mingw, MSVC 9, Interix 3.5.

12.15 Glibc `<error.h>`

12.15.1 `error`

Gnulib module: error

Portability problems fixed by Gnulib:

- This function is missing on many non-glibc platforms: Mac OS X 10.5, FreeBSD 6.0, NetBSD 5.0, OpenBSD 3.8, Minix 3.1.8, AIX 5.1, HP-UX 11, IRIX 6.5, OSF/1 5.1, Solaris 11 2011-11, Cygwin 1.7.9, mingw, MSVC 9, Interix 3.5, BeOS.

Portability problems not fixed by Gnulib:

12.15.2 `error_at_line`

Gnulib module: error

Portability problems fixed by Gnulib:

Portability problems not fixed by Gnulib:

- This function is missing on many non-glibc platforms: Mac OS X 10.5, FreeBSD 6.0, NetBSD 5.0, OpenBSD 3.8, Minix 3.1.8, AIX 5.1, HP-UX 11, IRIX 6.5, OSF/1 5.1, Solaris 11 2011-11, Cygwin 1.7.9, mingw, MSVC 9, Interix 3.5, BeOS.

12.15.3 `error_message_count`

Gnulib module: error

Portability problems fixed by Gnulib:

Portability problems not fixed by Gnulib:

- This variable is missing on many non-glibc platforms: Mac OS X 10.5, FreeBSD 6.0, NetBSD 5.0, OpenBSD 3.8, Minix 3.1.8, AIX 5.1, HP-UX 11, IRIX 6.5, OSF/1 5.1, Solaris 11 2011-11, Cygwin 1.7.9, mingw, MSVC 9, Interix 3.5, BeOS.

12.15.4 `error_one_per_line`

Gnulib module: error

Portability problems fixed by Gnulib:

Portability problems not fixed by Gnulib:

- This variable is missing on many non-glibc platforms: Mac OS X 10.5, FreeBSD 6.0, NetBSD 5.0, OpenBSD 3.8, Minix 3.1.8, AIX 5.1, HP-UX 11, IRIX 6.5, OSF/1 5.1, Solaris 11 2011-11, Cygwin 1.7.9, mingw, MSVC 9, Interix 3.5, BeOS.

12.15.5 error_print_progname

Gnulib module: error

Portability problems fixed by Gnulib:

Portability problems not fixed by Gnulib:

- This variable is missing on many non-glibc platforms: Mac OS X 10.5, FreeBSD 6.0, NetBSD 5.0, OpenBSD 3.8, Minix 3.1.8, AIX 5.1, HP-UX 11, IRIX 6.5, OSF/1 5.1, Solaris 11 2011-11, Cygwin 1.7.9, mingw, MSVC 9, Interix 3.5, BeOS.

12.16 Glibc <execinfo.h>

12.16.1 backtrace

Gnulib module: —

Portability problems fixed by Gnulib:

Portability problems not fixed by Gnulib:

- This function is missing on many platforms: Mac OS X 10.4, FreeBSD 6.0, NetBSD 5.0, OpenBSD 3.8, Minix 3.1.8, AIX 5.1, HP-UX 11, IRIX 6.5, OSF/1 5.1, Solaris 10, Cygwin, mingw, MSVC 9, Interix 3.5, BeOS.

12.16.2 backtrace_symbols

Gnulib module: —

Portability problems fixed by Gnulib:

Portability problems not fixed by Gnulib:

- This function is missing on many platforms: Mac OS X 10.4, FreeBSD 6.0, NetBSD 5.0, OpenBSD 3.8, Minix 3.1.8, AIX 5.1, HP-UX 11, IRIX 6.5, OSF/1 5.1, Solaris 10, Cygwin, mingw, MSVC 9, Interix 3.5, BeOS.

12.16.3 backtrace_symbols_fd

Gnulib module: —

Portability problems fixed by Gnulib:

Portability problems not fixed by Gnulib:

- This function is missing on many platforms: Mac OS X 10.4, FreeBSD 6.0, NetBSD 5.0, OpenBSD 3.8, Minix 3.1.8, AIX 5.1, HP-UX 11, IRIX 6.5, OSF/1 5.1, Solaris 10, Cygwin, mingw, MSVC 9, Interix 3.5, BeOS.

12.17 Glibc Extensions to <fcntl.h>

12.17.1 fallocate

Gnulib module: —

Portability problems fixed by Gnulib:

Portability problems not fixed by Gnulib:

- This function is missing on older glibc versions and all non-glibc platforms: Mac OS X 10.5, FreeBSD 6.0, NetBSD 5.0, OpenBSD 3.8, Minix 3.1.8, AIX 5.1, HP-UX 11, IRIX 6.5, OSF/1 5.1, Solaris 11 2011-11, Cygwin, mingw, MSVC 9, Interix 3.5, BeOS.

- On platforms where `off_t` is a 32-bit type, this function may not work correctly across the entire data range of files larger than 2 GB. The fix is to use the `AC_SYS_LARGEFILE` macro.

12.17.2 `name_to_handle_at`

Gnulib module: —

Portability problems fixed by Gnulib:

Portability problems not fixed by Gnulib:

- This function is missing on all non-glibc platforms: glibc 2.13, Mac OS X 10.5, FreeBSD 6.4, NetBSD 5.0, OpenBSD 3.8, Minix 3.1.8, AIX 7.1, HP-UX 11.31, IRIX 6.5, OSF/1 5.1, Solaris 11 2011-11, Cygwin, mingw, MSVC 9, Interix 3.5, BeOS.

12.17.3 `readahead`

Gnulib module: —

Portability problems fixed by Gnulib:

Portability problems not fixed by Gnulib:

- This function is missing on all non-glibc platforms: Mac OS X 10.5, FreeBSD 6.0, NetBSD 5.0, OpenBSD 3.8, Minix 3.1.8, AIX 5.1, HP-UX 11, IRIX 6.5, OSF/1 5.1, Solaris 11 2011-11, Cygwin, mingw, MSVC 9, Interix 3.5, BeOS.

12.17.4 `open_by_handle_at`

Gnulib module: —

Portability problems fixed by Gnulib:

Portability problems not fixed by Gnulib:

- This function is missing on all non-glibc platforms: glibc 2.13, Mac OS X 10.5, FreeBSD 6.4, NetBSD 5.0, OpenBSD 3.8, Minix 3.1.8, AIX 7.1, HP-UX 11.31, IRIX 6.5, OSF/1 5.1, Solaris 11 2011-11, Cygwin, mingw, MSVC 9, Interix 3.5, BeOS.

12.18 Glibc Extensions to `<fenv.h>`

12.18.1 `fedisableexcept`

Gnulib module: —

Portability problems fixed by Gnulib:

Portability problems not fixed by Gnulib:

- This function is missing on some platforms: Mac OS X 10.5, FreeBSD 5.2.1, NetBSD 5.0, OpenBSD 3.8, Minix 3.1.8, AIX 5.1, HP-UX 11, IRIX 6.5, OSF/1 5.1, Solaris 11 2011-11, Cygwin 1.7.7, mingw, MSVC 9, Interix 3.5, BeOS.

12.18.2 `feenableexcept`

Gnulib module: —

Portability problems fixed by Gnulib:

Portability problems not fixed by Gnulib:

- This function is missing on some platforms: Mac OS X 10.5, FreeBSD 5.2.1, NetBSD 5.0, OpenBSD 3.8, Minix 3.1.8, AIX 5.1, HP-UX 11, IRIX 6.5, OSF/1 5.1, Solaris 11 2011-11, Cygwin 1.7.7, mingw, MSVC 9, Interix 3.5, BeOS.

12.18.3 `fegetexcept`

Gnulib module: —

Portability problems fixed by Gnulib:

Portability problems not fixed by Gnulib:

- This function is missing on all non-glibc platforms: Mac OS X 10.5, FreeBSD 6.0, NetBSD 5.0, OpenBSD 3.8, Minix 3.1.8, AIX 5.1, HP-UX 11, IRIX 6.5, OSF/1 5.1, Solaris 11 2011-11, Cygwin 1.7.7, mingw, MSVC 9, Interix 3.5, BeOS.

12.19 Glibc Extensions to `<fmtmsg.h>`

12.19.1 `addseverity`

Gnulib module: —

Portability problems fixed by Gnulib:

Portability problems not fixed by Gnulib:

- This function is missing on some platforms: Mac OS X 10.5, FreeBSD 6.0, NetBSD 5.0, OpenBSD 3.8, Minix 3.1.8, AIX 5.1, HP-UX 11, OSF/1 5.1, Cygwin, mingw, MSVC 9, Interix 3.5, BeOS.

12.20 Glibc `<fstab.h>`

12.20.1 `endfsent`

Gnulib module: —

Portability problems fixed by Gnulib:

Portability problems not fixed by Gnulib:

- This function is missing on some platforms: Minix 3.1.8, IRIX 6.5, Solaris 11 2011-11, Cygwin, mingw, MSVC 9, Interix 3.5, BeOS.

12.20.2 `getfsent`

Gnulib module: —

Portability problems fixed by Gnulib:

Portability problems not fixed by Gnulib:

- This function is missing on some platforms: Minix 3.1.8, IRIX 6.5, Solaris 11 2011-11, Cygwin, mingw, MSVC 9, Interix 3.5, BeOS.

12.20.3 `getfsfile`

Gnulib module: —

Portability problems fixed by Gnulib:

Portability problems not fixed by Gnulib:

- This function is missing on some platforms: Minix 3.1.8, IRIX 6.5, Solaris 11 2011-11, Cygwin, mingw, MSVC 9, Interix 3.5, BeOS.

12.20.4 `getfsspec`

Gnulib module: —

Portability problems fixed by Gnulib:

Portability problems not fixed by Gnulib:

- This function is missing on some platforms: Minix 3.1.8, IRIX 6.5, Solaris 11 2011-11, Cygwin, mingw, MSVC 9, Interix 3.5, BeOS.

12.20.5 `setfsent`

Gnulib module: —

Portability problems fixed by Gnulib:

Portability problems not fixed by Gnulib:

- This function is missing on some platforms: Minix 3.1.8, IRIX 6.5, Solaris 11 2011-11, Cygwin, mingw, MSVC 9, Interix 3.5, BeOS.

12.21 Glibc `<fts.h>`

12.21.1 `fts_children`

Gnulib module: —

Portability problems fixed by Gnulib:

Portability problems not fixed by Gnulib:

- This function is missing on some platforms: AIX 5.1, HP-UX 11, IRIX 6.5, OSF/1 5.1, Solaris 11 2011-11, mingw, MSVC 9, BeOS.
- On platforms where `off_t` is a 32-bit type, this function may not correctly report the size of files or block devices larger than 2 GB and may not work correctly on huge directories larger than 2 GB. Also, on platforms where `ino_t` is a 32-bit type, this function may report inode numbers incorrectly. The fix is to use the `AC_SYS_LARGEFILE` macro (only on Mac OS X systems).

12.21.2 `fts_close`

Gnulib module: —

Portability problems fixed by Gnulib:

Portability problems not fixed by Gnulib:

- This function is missing on some platforms: AIX 5.1, HP-UX 11, IRIX 6.5, OSF/1 5.1, Solaris 11 2011-11, mingw, MSVC 9, BeOS.

12.21.3 fts_open

Gnulib module: —

Portability problems fixed by Gnulib:

Portability problems not fixed by Gnulib:

- This function is missing on some platforms: AIX 5.1, HP-UX 11, IRIX 6.5, OSF/1 5.1, Solaris 11 2011-11, mingw, MSVC 9, BeOS.

12.21.4 fts_read

Gnulib module: —

Portability problems fixed by Gnulib:

Portability problems not fixed by Gnulib:

- This function is missing on some platforms: AIX 5.1, HP-UX 11, IRIX 6.5, OSF/1 5.1, Solaris 11 2011-11, mingw, MSVC 9, BeOS.

- On platforms where off_t is a 32-bit type, this function may not correctly report the size of files or block devices larger than 2 GB and may not work correctly on huge directories larger than 2 GB. Also, on platforms where ino_t is a 32-bit type, this function may report inode numbers incorrectly. The fix is to use the AC_SYS_LARGEFILE macro (only on Mac OS X systems).

12.21.5 fts_set

Gnulib module: —

Portability problems fixed by Gnulib:

Portability problems not fixed by Gnulib:

- This function is missing on some platforms: AIX 5.1, HP-UX 11, IRIX 6.5, OSF/1 5.1, Solaris 11 2011-11, mingw, MSVC 9, BeOS.

12.22 Glibc <getopt.h>

12.22.1 getopt_long

Gnulib module: getopt-gnu

Portability problems fixed by Gnulib:

- This function is missing on some platforms: AIX 5.1, HP-UX 11, IRIX 6.5, OSF/1 5.1, MSVC 9, Interix 3.5.

- The function getopt_long does not obey the combination of '+' and ':' flags in the options string on some platforms: glibc 2.11.

- The use of 'W;' in the optstring argument to does not always allow -W foo to behave synonymously with --foo: glibc 2.11.

- The function getopt_long does not support the '+' flag in the options string on some platforms: Mac OS X 10.5, AIX 5.2, OSF/1 5.1, Solaris 10.

- The value of optind after a missing required argument is wrong on some platforms: Mac OS X 10.5.

- The function `getopt_long` does not obey the '-' flag in the options string when `POSIXLY_CORRECT` is set on some platforms: Cygwin 1.7.0.

- Some implementations fail to reset state, including re-checking `POSIXLY_CORRECT`, when `optind` is set to '0': NetBSD, Cygwin 1.7.0.

- The function `getopt_long` does not support options with optional arguments on some platforms: Mac OS X 10.5, OpenBSD 4.0, AIX 5.2, IRIX 6.5, Solaris 11 2010-11, Cygwin 1.5.x.

- This function crashes if the option string includes `W`; but there are no long options, on some platforms: glibc 2.14.

Portability problems not fixed by Gnulib:

12.22.2 getopt_long_only

Gnulib module: getopt-gnu

Portability problems fixed by Gnulib:

- The function `getopt_long_only` does not obey the combination of '+' and ':' flags in the options string on some platforms: glibc 2.11.

- The use of 'W;' in the optstring argument to does not always allow `-W foo` to behave synonymously with `--foo`: glibc 2.11.

- The function `getopt_long_only` does not support the '+' flag in the options string on some platforms: Mac OS X 10.5, AIX 5.2, OSF/1 5.1, Solaris 10.

- The value of `optind` after a missing required argument is wrong on some platforms: Mac OS X 10.5.

- The function `getopt_long_only` does not obey the '-' flag in the options string when `POSIXLY_CORRECT` is set on some platforms: Cygwin 1.7.0.

- Some implementations fail to reset state, including re-checking `POSIXLY_CORRECT`, when `optind` is set to '0': NetBSD, Cygwin 1.7.0.

- The function `getopt_long_only` does not support options with optional arguments on some platforms: Mac OS X 10.5, OpenBSD 4.0, AIX 5.2, Solaris 11 2010-11, Cygwin 1.5.x.

- This function is missing on some platforms: Mac OS X 10.3, FreeBSD 5.2.1, NetBSD 5.0, Minix 3.1.8, AIX 5.1, HP-UX 11, IRIX 6.5, OSF/1 5.1, mingw, MSVC 9, Interix 3.5.

- This function crashes if the option string includes `W`; but there are no long options, on some platforms: glibc 2.14.

Portability problems not fixed by Gnulib:

- Some implementations return success instead of reporting an ambiguity if user's option is a prefix of two long options with the same outcome: FreeBSD.

- The GNU Coding Standards discourage the use of `getopt_long_only` in new programs.

12.23 Glibc Extensions to `<glob.h>`

12.23.1 glob_pattern_p

Gnulib module: —

Portability problems fixed by Gnulib:

Portability problems not fixed by Gnulib:

- This function is missing on most non-glibc platforms: Mac OS X 10.5, FreeBSD 6.0, NetBSD 5.0, OpenBSD 3.8, Minix 3.1.8, AIX 5.1, HP-UX 11, IRIX 6.5, OSF/1 5.1, Solaris 11 2011-11, Cygwin 1.5.x, mingw, MSVC 9, Interix 3.5, BeOS.

12.24 Glibc Extensions to <gnu/libc-version.h>

12.24.1 gnu_get_libc_release

Gnulib module: —

Portability problems fixed by Gnulib:

Portability problems not fixed by Gnulib:

- This function is missing on some platforms: Mac OS X 10.5, FreeBSD 6.0, NetBSD 5.0, OpenBSD 3.8, Minix 3.1.8, AIX 5.1, HP-UX 11, IRIX 6.5, OSF/1 5.1, Solaris 11 2011-11, Cygwin, mingw, MSVC 9, Interix 3.5.

12.24.2 gnu_get_libc_version

Gnulib module: —

Portability problems fixed by Gnulib:

Portability problems not fixed by Gnulib:

- This function is missing on some platforms: Mac OS X 10.5, FreeBSD 6.0, NetBSD 5.0, OpenBSD 3.8, Minix 3.1.8, AIX 5.1, HP-UX 11, IRIX 6.5, OSF/1 5.1, Solaris 11 2011-11, Cygwin, mingw, MSVC 9, Interix 3.5.

12.25 Glibc Extensions to <grp.h>

12.25.1 fgetgrent

Gnulib module: —

Portability problems fixed by Gnulib:

Portability problems not fixed by Gnulib:

- This function is missing on some platforms: Mac OS X 10.5, FreeBSD 6.0, NetBSD 5.0, OpenBSD 3.8, Minix 3.1.8, Cygwin, mingw, MSVC 9, Interix 3.5, BeOS.

12.25.2 fgetgrent_r

Gnulib module: —

Portability problems fixed by Gnulib:

Portability problems not fixed by Gnulib:

- This function is missing on some platforms: Mac OS X 10.5, FreeBSD 6.0, NetBSD 5.0, OpenBSD 3.8, Minix 3.1.8, HP-UX 11, IRIX 5.3, Cygwin, mingw, MSVC 9, Interix 3.5, BeOS.

12.25.3 getgrent_r

Gnulib module: —

Portability problems fixed by Gnulib:

Portability problems not fixed by Gnulib:

- This function is missing on some platforms: Mac OS X 10.5, OpenBSD 3.8, Minix 3.1.8, HP-UX 11, IRIX 5.3, Cygwin, mingw, MSVC 9, Interix 3.5, BeOS.

12.25.4 getgrouplist

Gnulib module: —

Portability problems fixed by Gnulib:

Portability problems not fixed by Gnulib:

- This function takes `int` instead of `gid_t` parameters on some platforms: OS X 10.11.
- This function is missing on some platforms: Minix 3.1.8, AIX 5.1, HP-UX 11, IRIX 6.5, OSF/1 5.1, Solaris 11 2011-11, Cygwin 1.7.9, mingw, MSVC 9, BeOS.

The Gnulib module `getugroups` provides a similar API.

12.25.5 initgroups

Gnulib module: —

Portability problems fixed by Gnulib:

Portability problems not fixed by Gnulib:

- This function is unsafe to call between `fork` and `exec` if the parent process is multi-threaded. Instead, use `getgroups` or `getgrouplist` (or use the gnulib module `mgetgroups`) before forking, and `setgroups` in the child.
- This function is missing on some platforms: mingw, MSVC 9, Interix 3.5, BeOS.

12.25.6 putgrent

Gnulib module: —

Portability problems fixed by Gnulib:

Portability problems not fixed by Gnulib:

- This function is missing on some platforms: Mac OS X 10.5, FreeBSD 6.0, NetBSD 5.0, OpenBSD 3.8, Minix 3.1.8, HP-UX 11, IRIX 6.5, Solaris 11 2011-11, Cygwin, mingw, MSVC 9, Interix 3.5, BeOS.

12.25.7 setgroups

Gnulib module: —

Portability problems fixed by Gnulib:

Portability problems not fixed by Gnulib:

- This function is missing on some platforms: AIX 5.1, mingw, MSVC 9, Interix 3.5, BeOS.

- On very old systems, this function operated on an array of 'int', even though that was a different size than an array of 'gid_t'; you can use autoconf's AC_TYPE_GETGROUPS to set GETGROUPS_T to the appropriate size (since getgroups and setgroups share the same bug).

12.26 Glibc <gshadow.h>

12.26.1 endsgent

Gnulib module: —

Portability problems fixed by Gnulib:

Portability problems not fixed by Gnulib:

- This function is missing on all non-glibc platforms: glibc 2.9, Mac OS X 10.5, FreeBSD 6.4, NetBSD 5.0, OpenBSD 3.8, Minix 3.1.8, AIX 7.1, HP-UX 11.31, IRIX 6.5, OSF/1 5.1, Solaris 11 2011-11, Cygwin, mingw, MSVC 9, Interix 3.5, BeOS.

12.26.2 fgetsgent

Gnulib module: —

Portability problems fixed by Gnulib:

Portability problems not fixed by Gnulib:

- This function is missing on all non-glibc platforms: glibc 2.9, Mac OS X 10.5, FreeBSD 6.4, NetBSD 5.0, OpenBSD 3.8, Minix 3.1.8, AIX 7.1, HP-UX 11.31, IRIX 6.5, OSF/1 5.1, Solaris 11 2011-11, Cygwin, mingw, MSVC 9, Interix 3.5, BeOS.

12.26.3 fgetsgent_r

Gnulib module: —

Portability problems fixed by Gnulib:

Portability problems not fixed by Gnulib:

- This function is missing on all non-glibc platforms: glibc 2.9, Mac OS X 10.5, FreeBSD 6.4, NetBSD 5.0, OpenBSD 3.8, Minix 3.1.8, AIX 7.1, HP-UX 11.31, IRIX 6.5, OSF/1 5.1, Solaris 11 2011-11, Cygwin, mingw, MSVC 9, Interix 3.5, BeOS.

12.26.4 getsgent

Gnulib module: —

Portability problems fixed by Gnulib:

Portability problems not fixed by Gnulib:

- This function is missing on all non-glibc platforms: glibc 2.9, Mac OS X 10.5, FreeBSD 6.4, NetBSD 5.0, OpenBSD 3.8, Minix 3.1.8, AIX 7.1, HP-UX 11.31, IRIX 6.5, OSF/1 5.1, Solaris 11 2011-11, Cygwin, mingw, MSVC 9, Interix 3.5, BeOS.

12.26.5 getsgent_r

Gnulib module: —

Portability problems fixed by Gnulib:

Portability problems not fixed by Gnulib:

- This function is missing on all non-glibc platforms: glibc 2.9, Mac OS X 10.5, FreeBSD 6.4, NetBSD 5.0, OpenBSD 3.8, Minix 3.1.8, AIX 7.1, HP-UX 11.31, IRIX 6.5, OSF/1 5.1, Solaris 11 2011-11, Cygwin, mingw, MSVC 9, Interix 3.5, BeOS.

12.26.6 getsgnam

Gnulib module: —

Portability problems fixed by Gnulib:

Portability problems not fixed by Gnulib:

- This function is missing on all non-glibc platforms: glibc 2.9, Mac OS X 10.5, FreeBSD 6.4, NetBSD 5.0, OpenBSD 3.8, Minix 3.1.8, AIX 7.1, HP-UX 11.31, IRIX 6.5, OSF/1 5.1, Solaris 11 2011-11, Cygwin, mingw, MSVC 9, Interix 3.5, BeOS.

12.26.7 getsgnam_r

Gnulib module: —

Portability problems fixed by Gnulib:

Portability problems not fixed by Gnulib:

- This function is missing on all non-glibc platforms: glibc 2.9, Mac OS X 10.5, FreeBSD 6.4, NetBSD 5.0, OpenBSD 3.8, Minix 3.1.8, AIX 7.1, HP-UX 11.31, IRIX 6.5, OSF/1 5.1, Solaris 11 2011-11, Cygwin, mingw, MSVC 9, Interix 3.5, BeOS.

12.26.8 putsgent

Gnulib module: —

Portability problems fixed by Gnulib:

Portability problems not fixed by Gnulib:

- This function is missing on all non-glibc platforms: glibc 2.9, Mac OS X 10.5, FreeBSD 6.4, NetBSD 5.0, OpenBSD 3.8, Minix 3.1.8, AIX 7.1, HP-UX 11.31, IRIX 6.5, OSF/1 5.1, Solaris 11 2011-11, Cygwin, mingw, MSVC 9, Interix 3.5, BeOS.

12.26.9 setsgent

Gnulib module: —

Portability problems fixed by Gnulib:

Portability problems not fixed by Gnulib:

- This function is missing on all non-glibc platforms: glibc 2.9, Mac OS X 10.5, FreeBSD 6.4, NetBSD 5.0, OpenBSD 3.8, Minix 3.1.8, AIX 7.1, HP-UX 11.31, IRIX 6.5, OSF/1 5.1, Solaris 11 2011-11, Cygwin, mingw, MSVC 9, Interix 3.5, BeOS.

12.26.10 sgetsgent

Gnulib module: —

Portability problems fixed by Gnulib:

Portability problems not fixed by Gnulib:

- This function is missing on all non-glibc platforms: glibc 2.9, Mac OS X 10.5, FreeBSD 6.4, NetBSD 5.0, OpenBSD 3.8, Minix 3.1.8, AIX 7.1, HP-UX 11.31, IRIX 6.5, OSF/1 5.1, Solaris 11 2011-11, Cygwin, mingw, MSVC 9, Interix 3.5, BeOS.

12.26.11 sgetsgent_r

Gnulib module: —

Portability problems fixed by Gnulib:

Portability problems not fixed by Gnulib:

- This function is missing on all non-glibc platforms: glibc 2.9, Mac OS X 10.5, FreeBSD 6.4, NetBSD 5.0, OpenBSD 3.8, Minix 3.1.8, AIX 7.1, HP-UX 11.31, IRIX 6.5, OSF/1 5.1, Solaris 11 2011-11, Cygwin, mingw, MSVC 9, Interix 3.5, BeOS.

12.27 Glibc <ifaddrs.h>

12.27.1 getifaddrs

Gnulib module: —

Portability problems fixed by Gnulib:

Portability problems not fixed by Gnulib:

- This function is missing on some platforms: AIX 5.1, HP-UX 11, IRIX 6.5, OSF/1 5.1, Solaris 10, Cygwin 1.5.x, mingw, MSVC 9, Interix 3.5, BeOS.

12.27.2 freeifaddrs

Gnulib module: —

Portability problems fixed by Gnulib:

Portability problems not fixed by Gnulib:

- This function is missing on some platforms: AIX 5.1, HP-UX 11, IRIX 6.5, OSF/1 5.1, Solaris 10, Cygwin 1.5.x, mingw, MSVC 9, Interix 3.5, BeOS.

12.28 Glibc <libintl.h>

12.28.1 bind_textdomain_codeset

Gnulib module: —

Portability problems fixed by Gnulib:

Portability problems not fixed by Gnulib:

- This function is missing on some platforms: Mac OS X 10.5, FreeBSD 6.0, OpenBSD 3.8, Minix 3.1.8, AIX 4.3.2, HP-UX 11, IRIX 6.5, OSF/1 5.1, Cygwin, mingw, MSVC 9, Interix 3.5, BeOS.

12.28.2 `bindtextdomain`

Gnulib module: —

Portability problems fixed by Gnulib:

Portability problems not fixed by Gnulib:

- This function is missing on some platforms: Mac OS X 10.5, FreeBSD 6.0, OpenBSD 3.8, Minix 3.1.8, AIX 4.3.2, HP-UX 11, IRIX 6.5, OSF/1 5.1, Cygwin, mingw, MSVC 9, Interix 3.5, BeOS.

12.28.3 `dcgettext`

Gnulib module: —

Portability problems fixed by Gnulib:

Portability problems not fixed by Gnulib:

- This function is missing on some platforms: Mac OS X 10.5, FreeBSD 6.0, OpenBSD 3.8, Minix 3.1.8, AIX 4.3.2, HP-UX 11, IRIX 6.5, OSF/1 5.1, Cygwin, mingw, MSVC 9, Interix 3.5, BeOS.

12.28.4 `dcngettext`

Gnulib module: —

Portability problems fixed by Gnulib:

Portability problems not fixed by Gnulib:

- This function is missing on some platforms: Mac OS X 10.5, FreeBSD 6.0, OpenBSD 3.8, Minix 3.1.8, AIX 4.3.2, HP-UX 11, IRIX 6.5, OSF/1 5.1, Cygwin, mingw, MSVC 9, Interix 3.5, BeOS.

12.28.5 `dgettext`

Gnulib module: —

Portability problems fixed by Gnulib:

Portability problems not fixed by Gnulib:

- This function is missing on some platforms: Mac OS X 10.5, FreeBSD 6.0, OpenBSD 3.8, Minix 3.1.8, AIX 4.3.2, HP-UX 11, IRIX 6.5, OSF/1 5.1, Cygwin, mingw, MSVC 9, Interix 3.5, BeOS.

12.28.6 `dngettext`

Gnulib module: —

Portability problems fixed by Gnulib:

Portability problems not fixed by Gnulib:

- This function is missing on some platforms: Mac OS X 10.5, FreeBSD 6.0, OpenBSD 3.8, Minix 3.1.8, AIX 4.3.2, HP-UX 11, IRIX 6.5, OSF/1 5.1, Cygwin, mingw, MSVC 9, Interix 3.5, BeOS.

12.28.7 `gettext`

Gnulib module: —

Portability problems fixed by Gnulib:

Portability problems not fixed by Gnulib:

- This function is missing on some platforms: Mac OS X 10.5, FreeBSD 6.0, OpenBSD 3.8, Minix 3.1.8, AIX 4.3.2, HP-UX 11, IRIX 6.5, OSF/1 5.1, Cygwin, mingw, MSVC 9, Interix 3.5, BeOS.

12.28.8 `ngettext`

Gnulib module: —

Portability problems fixed by Gnulib:

Portability problems not fixed by Gnulib:

- This function is missing on some platforms: Mac OS X 10.5, FreeBSD 6.0, OpenBSD 3.8, Minix 3.1.8, AIX 4.3.2, HP-UX 11, IRIX 6.5, OSF/1 5.1, Cygwin, mingw, MSVC 9, Interix 3.5, BeOS.

12.28.9 `textdomain`

Gnulib module: —

Portability problems fixed by Gnulib:

Portability problems not fixed by Gnulib:

- This function is missing on some platforms: Mac OS X 10.5, FreeBSD 6.0, OpenBSD 3.8, Minix 3.1.8, AIX 4.3.2, HP-UX 11, IRIX 6.5, OSF/1 5.1, Cygwin, mingw, MSVC 9, Interix 3.5, BeOS.

12.29 Glibc `<link.h>`

12.29.1 `dl_iterate_phdr`

Gnulib module: —

Portability problems fixed by Gnulib:

Portability problems not fixed by Gnulib:

- This function is missing on some platforms: Mac OS X 10.5, FreeBSD 6.0, NetBSD 5.0, Minix 3.1.8, AIX 5.1, HP-UX 11, IRIX 6.5, OSF/1 5.1, Solaris 10, Cygwin, mingw, MSVC 9, Interix 3.5, BeOS.

12.30 Glibc `<malloc.h>`

12.30.1 `mallinfo`

Gnulib module: —

Portability problems fixed by Gnulib:

Portability problems not fixed by Gnulib:

- This function is missing on some platforms: Mac OS X 10.5, FreeBSD 6.0, NetBSD 5.0, OpenBSD 3.8, Minix 3.1.8, IRIX 6.5, Solaris 11 2010-11, mingw, MSVC 9, Interix 3.5, BeOS.

12.30.2 `malloc_get_state`

Gnulib module: —

Portability problems fixed by Gnulib:

Portability problems not fixed by Gnulib:

- This function is missing on all non-glibc platforms: Mac OS X 10.5, FreeBSD 6.0, NetBSD 5.0, OpenBSD 3.8, Minix 3.1.8, AIX 5.1, HP-UX 11, IRIX 6.5, OSF/1 5.1, Solaris 11 2011-11, Cygwin, mingw, MSVC 9, Interix 3.5, BeOS.

12.30.3 `malloc_set_state`

Gnulib module: —

Portability problems fixed by Gnulib:

Portability problems not fixed by Gnulib:

- This function is missing on all non-glibc platforms: Mac OS X 10.5, FreeBSD 6.0, NetBSD 5.0, OpenBSD 3.8, Minix 3.1.8, AIX 5.1, HP-UX 11, IRIX 6.5, OSF/1 5.1, Solaris 11 2011-11, Cygwin, mingw, MSVC 9, Interix 3.5, BeOS.

12.30.4 `malloc_info`

Gnulib module: —

Portability problems fixed by Gnulib:

Portability problems not fixed by Gnulib:

- This function is missing on all non-glibc platforms: glibc 2.9, Mac OS X 10.5, FreeBSD 6.4, NetBSD 5.0, OpenBSD 3.8, Minix 3.1.8, AIX 7.1, HP-UX 11.31, IRIX 6.5, OSF/1 5.1, Solaris 11 2011-11, Cygwin, mingw, MSVC 9, Interix 3.5, BeOS.

12.30.5 `malloc_stats`

Gnulib module: —

Portability problems fixed by Gnulib:

Portability problems not fixed by Gnulib:

- This function is missing on some platforms: Mac OS X 10.5, FreeBSD 6.0, NetBSD 5.0, OpenBSD 3.8, Minix 3.1.8, AIX 5.1, HP-UX 11, IRIX 6.5, OSF/1 5.1, Solaris 11 2011-11, mingw, MSVC 9, Interix 3.5, BeOS.

12.30.6 `malloc_trim`

Gnulib module: —

Portability problems fixed by Gnulib:

Portability problems not fixed by Gnulib:

- This function is missing on some platforms: Mac OS X 10.5, FreeBSD 6.0, NetBSD 5.0, OpenBSD 3.8, Minix 3.1.8, AIX 5.1, HP-UX 11, IRIX 6.5, OSF/1 5.1, Solaris 11 2011-11, mingw, MSVC 9, Interix 3.5, BeOS.

12.30.7 `malloc_usable_size`

Gnulib module: —

Portability problems fixed by Gnulib:

Portability problems not fixed by Gnulib:

- This function is missing on some platforms: Mac OS X 10.5, FreeBSD 6.0, NetBSD 5.0, OpenBSD 3.8, Minix 3.1.8, AIX 5.1, HP-UX 11.00, IRIX 6.5, OSF/1 5.1, Solaris 11 2011-11, mingw, MSVC 9, Interix 3.5, BeOS.

12.30.8 `mallopt`

Gnulib module: —

Portability problems fixed by Gnulib:

Portability problems not fixed by Gnulib:

- This function is missing on some platforms: Mac OS X 10.5, FreeBSD 6.0, NetBSD 5.0, OpenBSD 3.8, Minix 3.1.8, IRIX 6.5, Solaris 11 2010-11, mingw, MSVC 9, Interix 3.5, BeOS.

12.30.9 `memalign`

Gnulib module: —

Portability problems fixed by Gnulib:

Portability problems not fixed by Gnulib:

- This function is missing on some platforms: Mac OS X 10.5, FreeBSD 6.0, NetBSD 5.0, OpenBSD 3.8, Minix 3.1.8, AIX 5.1, HP-UX 11.00, OSF/1 5.1, mingw, MSVC 9, Interix 3.5.

12.30.10 `pvalloc`

Gnulib module: —

Portability problems fixed by Gnulib:

Portability problems not fixed by Gnulib:

- This function is missing on all non-glibc platforms: Mac OS X 10.5, FreeBSD 6.0, NetBSD 5.0, OpenBSD 3.8, Minix 3.1.8, AIX 5.1, HP-UX 11, IRIX 6.5, OSF/1 5.1, Solaris 11 2011-11, Cygwin, mingw, MSVC 9, Interix 3.5, BeOS.

12.31 Glibc Extensions to `<math.h>`

12.31.1 `drem`

Gnulib module: —

Portability problems fixed by Gnulib:

Portability problems not fixed by Gnulib:

- This function is missing on some platforms: Minix 3.1.8, HP-UX 11, Solaris 11 2011-11, mingw, MSVC 9.

12.31.2 `dremf`

Gnulib module: —

Portability problems fixed by Gnulib:

Portability problems not fixed by Gnulib:

- This function is missing on some platforms: Mac OS X 10.5, Minix 3.1.8, AIX 5.1, HP-UX 11, IRIX 6.5, Solaris 11 2011-11, mingw, MSVC 9.

12.31.3 `dreml`

Gnulib module: —

Portability problems fixed by Gnulib:

Portability problems not fixed by Gnulib:

- This function is missing on some platforms: Mac OS X 10.5, FreeBSD 6.0, NetBSD 5.0, OpenBSD 3.8, Minix 3.1.8, AIX 5.1, HP-UX 11, IRIX 6.5, Solaris 11 2011-11, Cygwin, mingw, MSVC 9, Interix 3.5, BeOS.

12.31.4 `exp10`

Gnulib module: —

Portability problems fixed by Gnulib:

Portability problems not fixed by Gnulib:

- This function is missing on some platforms: Mac OS X 10.5, FreeBSD 6.0, NetBSD 5.0, OpenBSD 3.8, Minix 3.1.8, AIX 5.1, HP-UX 11, IRIX 6.5, OSF/1 5.1, Solaris 11 2011-11, Cygwin 1.5.x, mingw, MSVC 9, Interix 3.5.

12.31.5 `exp10f`

Gnulib module: —

Portability problems fixed by Gnulib:

Portability problems not fixed by Gnulib:

- This function is missing on some platforms: Mac OS X 10.5, FreeBSD 6.0, NetBSD 5.0, OpenBSD 3.8, Minix 3.1.8, AIX 5.1, HP-UX 11, IRIX 6.5, OSF/1 5.1, Solaris 11 2011-11, Cygwin 1.5.x, mingw, MSVC 9, Interix 3.5.

12.31.6 `exp10l`

Gnulib module: —

Portability problems fixed by Gnulib:

Portability problems not fixed by Gnulib:

- This function is missing on all non-glibc platforms: Mac OS X 10.5, FreeBSD 6.0, NetBSD 5.0, OpenBSD 3.8, Minix 3.1.8, AIX 5.1, HP-UX 11, IRIX 6.5, OSF/1 5.1, Solaris 11 2011-11, Cygwin, mingw, MSVC 9, Interix 3.5, BeOS.

12.31.7 `finite`

Gnulib module: —

Portability problems fixed by Gnulib:

Portability problems not fixed by Gnulib:

- This function is missing on some platforms: Minix 3.1.8, HP-UX 11, MSVC 9.

12.31.8 `finitef`

Gnulib module: —

Portability problems fixed by Gnulib:

Portability problems not fixed by Gnulib:

- This function is missing on some platforms: Mac OS X 10.5, Minix 3.1.8, AIX 5.1, HP-UX 11, IRIX 6.5, Solaris 11 2011-11, mingw, MSVC 9.

12.31.9 `finitel`

Gnulib module: —

Portability problems fixed by Gnulib:

Portability problems not fixed by Gnulib:

- This function is missing on some platforms: Mac OS X 10.5, FreeBSD 6.0, NetBSD 5.0, OpenBSD 3.8, Minix 3.1.8, AIX 5.1, HP-UX 11, IRIX 6.5, Solaris 11 2011-11, Cygwin, mingw, MSVC 9, Interix 3.5.

12.31.10 `gamma`

Gnulib module: —

Portability problems fixed by Gnulib:

Portability problems not fixed by Gnulib:

- This function is missing on some platforms: Minix 3.1.8, mingw, MSVC 9.

12.31.11 `gammaf`

Gnulib module: —

Portability problems fixed by Gnulib:

Portability problems not fixed by Gnulib:

- This function is missing on some platforms: Mac OS X 10.5, Minix 3.1.8, AIX 5.1, HP-UX 11, IRIX 6.5, mingw, MSVC 9.

12.31.12 `gammal`

Gnulib module: —

Portability problems fixed by Gnulib:

Portability problems not fixed by Gnulib:

- This function is missing on some platforms: Mac OS X 10.5, FreeBSD 6.0, NetBSD 5.0, OpenBSD 3.8, Minix 3.1.8, AIX 5.1, HP-UX 11, IRIX 6.5, Cygwin, mingw, MSVC 9, Interix 3.5, BeOS.

12.31.13 `isinff`

Gnulib module: —

Portability problems fixed by Gnulib:

Portability problems not fixed by Gnulib:

- This function is missing on some platforms: Mac OS X 10.5, FreeBSD 6.0, Minix 3.1.8, AIX 5.1, HP-UX 11, IRIX 6.5, OSF/1 5.1, Solaris 11 2011-11, mingw, MSVC 9.

12.31.14 `isinfl`

Gnulib module: —

Portability problems fixed by Gnulib:

Portability problems not fixed by Gnulib:

- This function is missing on some platforms: Mac OS X 10.5, FreeBSD 6.0, NetBSD 5.0, OpenBSD 3.8, Minix 3.1.8, AIX 5.1, HP-UX 11, IRIX 6.5, OSF/1 5.1, Solaris 11 2011-11, Cygwin, mingw, MSVC 9, Interix 3.5.

12.31.15 `isnanf`

Gnulib module: isnanf

Portability problems fixed by Gnulib:

- This function is missing on some platforms: Mac OS X 10.5, Minix 3.1.8, AIX 5.1, HP-UX 11, MSVC 9.

Portability problems not fixed by Gnulib:

12.31.16 `isnanl`

Gnulib module: isnanl

Portability problems fixed by Gnulib:

- This function is missing on some platforms: Mac OS X 10.5, FreeBSD 6.0, NetBSD 5.0, OpenBSD 3.8, Minix 3.1.8, AIX 5.1, HP-UX 11, IRIX 6.5, Cygwin, MSVC 9, Interix 3.5.

Portability problems not fixed by Gnulib:

12.31.17 `j0f`

Gnulib module: —

Portability problems fixed by Gnulib:

Portability problems not fixed by Gnulib:

- This function is missing on some platforms: Mac OS X 10.5, Minix 3.1.8, AIX 5.1, HP-UX 11, IRIX 6.5, mingw, MSVC 9.

12.31.18 `j0l`

Gnulib module: —

Portability problems fixed by Gnulib:

Portability problems not fixed by Gnulib:

- This function is missing on some platforms: Mac OS X 10.5, FreeBSD 6.0, NetBSD 5.0, OpenBSD 3.8, Minix 3.1.8, AIX 5.1, HP-UX 11, IRIX 6.5, Cygwin, mingw, MSVC 9, Interix 3.5, BeOS.

12.31.19 `j1f`

Gnulib module: —

Portability problems fixed by Gnulib:

Portability problems not fixed by Gnulib:

- This function is missing on some platforms: Mac OS X 10.5, Minix 3.1.8, AIX 5.1, HP-UX 11, IRIX 6.5, mingw, MSVC 9.

12.31.20 `j1l`

Gnulib module: —

Portability problems fixed by Gnulib:

Portability problems not fixed by Gnulib:

- This function is missing on some platforms: Mac OS X 10.5, FreeBSD 6.0, NetBSD 5.0, OpenBSD 3.8, Minix 3.1.8, AIX 5.1, HP-UX 11, IRIX 6.5, Cygwin, mingw, MSVC 9, Interix 3.5, BeOS.

12.31.21 `jnf`

Gnulib module: —

Portability problems fixed by Gnulib:

Portability problems not fixed by Gnulib:

- This function is missing on some platforms: Mac OS X 10.5, Minix 3.1.8, AIX 5.1, HP-UX 11, IRIX 6.5, mingw, MSVC 9.

12.31.22 `jnl`

Gnulib module: —

Portability problems fixed by Gnulib:

Portability problems not fixed by Gnulib:

- This function is missing on some platforms: Mac OS X 10.5, FreeBSD 6.0, NetBSD 5.0, OpenBSD 3.8, Minix 3.1.8, AIX 5.1, HP-UX 11, IRIX 6.5, Cygwin, mingw, MSVC 9, Interix 3.5, BeOS.

12.31.23 lgamma_r

Gnulib module: —

Portability problems fixed by Gnulib:

Portability problems not fixed by Gnulib:

- This function is missing on some platforms: Mac OS X 10.5 x86, Minix 3.1.8, IRIX 6.5, OSF/1 5.1, mingw, MSVC 9.

12.31.24 lgammaf_r

Gnulib module: —

Portability problems fixed by Gnulib:

Portability problems not fixed by Gnulib:

- This function is missing on some platforms: Mac OS X 10.5, Minix 3.1.8, AIX 5.1, HP-UX 11, IRIX 6.5, OSF/1 5.1, mingw, MSVC 9.

12.31.25 lgammal_r

Gnulib module: —

Portability problems fixed by Gnulib:

Portability problems not fixed by Gnulib:

- This function is missing on some platforms: Mac OS X 10.5, FreeBSD 6.0, NetBSD 5.0, OpenBSD 3.8, Minix 3.1.8, HP-UX 11, IRIX 6.5, OSF/1 5.1, Cygwin, mingw, MSVC 9, Interix 3.5, BeOS.

12.31.26 matherr

Gnulib module: —

Portability problems fixed by Gnulib:

Portability problems not fixed by Gnulib:

- This function is missing on some platforms: FreeBSD 6.0, Minix 3.1.8, AIX 5.1, HP-UX 11, OSF/1 5.1, mingw, MSVC 9.

12.31.27 pow10

Gnulib module: —

Portability problems fixed by Gnulib:

Portability problems not fixed by Gnulib:

- This function is missing on some platforms: Mac OS X 10.5, FreeBSD 6.0, NetBSD 5.0, OpenBSD 3.8, Minix 3.1.8, AIX 5.1, HP-UX 11, IRIX 6.5, OSF/1 5.1, Solaris 11 2011-11, Cygwin 1.5.x, mingw, MSVC 9, Interix 3.5.

12.31.28 pow10f

Gnulib module: —

Portability problems fixed by Gnulib:

Portability problems not fixed by Gnulib:

- This function is missing on some platforms: Mac OS X 10.5, FreeBSD 6.0, NetBSD 5.0, OpenBSD 3.8, Minix 3.1.8, AIX 5.1, HP-UX 11, IRIX 6.5, OSF/1 5.1, Solaris 11 2011-11, Cygwin 1.5.x, mingw, MSVC 9, Interix 3.5.

12.31.29 pow10l

Gnulib module: —

Portability problems fixed by Gnulib:

Portability problems not fixed by Gnulib:

- This function is missing on all non-glibc platforms: Mac OS X 10.5, FreeBSD 6.0, NetBSD 5.0, OpenBSD 3.8, Minix 3.1.8, AIX 5.1, HP-UX 11, IRIX 6.5, OSF/1 5.1, Solaris 11 2011-11, Cygwin, mingw, MSVC 9, Interix 3.5, BeOS.

12.31.30 scalbf

Gnulib module: —

Portability problems fixed by Gnulib:

Portability problems not fixed by Gnulib:

- This function is missing on some platforms: Mac OS X 10.5, Minix 3.1.8, AIX 5.1, HP-UX 11, IRIX 6.5, mingw, MSVC 9.

12.31.31 scalbl

Gnulib module: —

Portability problems fixed by Gnulib:

Portability problems not fixed by Gnulib:

- This function is missing on some platforms: Mac OS X 10.5, FreeBSD 6.0, NetBSD 5.0, OpenBSD 3.8, Minix 3.1.8, AIX 5.1, HP-UX 11, IRIX 6.5, Cygwin, mingw, MSVC 9, Interix 3.5, BeOS.

12.31.32 significand

Gnulib module: —

Portability problems fixed by Gnulib:

Portability problems not fixed by Gnulib:

- This function is missing on some platforms: Minix 3.1.8, AIX 5.1, HP-UX 11, IRIX 6.5, OSF/1 5.1, mingw, MSVC 9.

12.31.33 `significandf`

Gnulib module: —

Portability problems fixed by Gnulib:

Portability problems not fixed by Gnulib:

- This function is missing on some platforms: Mac OS X 10.5, Minix 3.1.8, AIX 5.1, HP-UX 11, IRIX 6.5, OSF/1 5.1, mingw, MSVC 9.

12.31.34 `significandl`

Gnulib module: —

Portability problems fixed by Gnulib:

Portability problems not fixed by Gnulib:

- This function is missing on some platforms: Mac OS X 10.5, FreeBSD 6.0, NetBSD 5.0, OpenBSD 3.8, Minix 3.1.8, AIX 5.1, HP-UX 11, IRIX 6.5, OSF/1 5.1, Cygwin, mingw, MSVC 9, Interix 3.5, BeOS.

12.31.35 `sincos`

Gnulib module: —

Portability problems fixed by Gnulib:

Portability problems not fixed by Gnulib:

- This function is missing on some platforms: Mac OS X 10.5, FreeBSD 6.0, NetBSD 5.0, OpenBSD 3.8, Minix 3.1.8, AIX 5.1, HP-UX 11, IRIX 6.5, mingw, MSVC 9, Interix 3.5.

12.31.36 `sincosf`

Gnulib module: —

Portability problems fixed by Gnulib:

Portability problems not fixed by Gnulib:

- This function is missing on some platforms: Mac OS X 10.5, FreeBSD 6.0, NetBSD 5.0, OpenBSD 3.8, Minix 3.1.8, AIX 5.1, HP-UX 11, IRIX 6.5, mingw, MSVC 9, Interix 3.5.

12.31.37 `sincosl`

Gnulib module: —

Portability problems fixed by Gnulib:

Portability problems not fixed by Gnulib:

- This function is missing on some platforms: Mac OS X 10.5, FreeBSD 6.0, NetBSD 5.0, OpenBSD 3.8, Minix 3.1.8, AIX 5.1, HP-UX 11, IRIX 6.5, Cygwin, mingw, MSVC 9, Interix 3.5, BeOS.

12.31.38 `y0f`

Gnulib module: —

Portability problems fixed by Gnulib:

Portability problems not fixed by Gnulib:

- This function is missing on some platforms: Mac OS X 10.5, Minix 3.1.8, AIX 5.1, HP-UX 11, IRIX 6.5, mingw, MSVC 9.

12.31.39 `y0l`

Gnulib module: —

Portability problems fixed by Gnulib:

Portability problems not fixed by Gnulib:

- This function is missing on some platforms: Mac OS X 10.5, FreeBSD 6.0, NetBSD 5.0, OpenBSD 3.8, Minix 3.1.8, AIX 5.1, HP-UX 11, IRIX 6.5, Cygwin, mingw, MSVC 9, Interix 3.5, BeOS.

12.31.40 `y1f`

Gnulib module: —

Portability problems fixed by Gnulib:

Portability problems not fixed by Gnulib:

- This function is missing on some platforms: Mac OS X 10.5, Minix 3.1.8, AIX 5.1, HP-UX 11, IRIX 6.5, mingw, MSVC 9.

12.31.41 `y1l`

Gnulib module: —

Portability problems fixed by Gnulib:

Portability problems not fixed by Gnulib:

- This function is missing on some platforms: Mac OS X 10.5, FreeBSD 6.0, NetBSD 5.0, OpenBSD 3.8, Minix 3.1.8, AIX 5.1, HP-UX 11, IRIX 6.5, Cygwin, mingw, MSVC 9, Interix 3.5, BeOS.

12.31.42 `ynf`

Gnulib module: —

Portability problems fixed by Gnulib:

Portability problems not fixed by Gnulib:

- This function is missing on some platforms: Mac OS X 10.5, Minix 3.1.8, AIX 5.1, HP-UX 11, IRIX 6.5, mingw, MSVC 9.

12.31.43 ynl

Gnulib module: —

Portability problems fixed by Gnulib:

Portability problems not fixed by Gnulib:

- This function is missing on some platforms: Mac OS X 10.5, FreeBSD 6.0, NetBSD 5.0, OpenBSD 3.8, Minix 3.1.8, AIX 5.1, HP-UX 11, IRIX 6.5, Cygwin, mingw, MSVC 9, Interix 3.5, BeOS.

12.32 Glibc <mcheck.h>

12.32.1 mcheck

Gnulib module: —

Portability problems fixed by Gnulib:

Portability problems not fixed by Gnulib:

- This function is missing on some platforms: Mac OS X 10.5, FreeBSD 6.0, NetBSD 5.0, OpenBSD 3.8, Minix 3.1.8, AIX 5.1, HP-UX 11, IRIX 6.5, OSF/1 5.1, Solaris 11 2011-11, Cygwin, mingw, MSVC 9, Interix 3.5.

12.32.2 mcheck_check_all

Gnulib module: —

Portability problems fixed by Gnulib:

Portability problems not fixed by Gnulib:

- This function is missing on all non-glibc platforms: Mac OS X 10.5, FreeBSD 6.0, NetBSD 5.0, OpenBSD 3.8, Minix 3.1.8, AIX 5.1, HP-UX 11, IRIX 6.5, OSF/1 5.1, Solaris 11 2011-11, Cygwin, mingw, MSVC 9, Interix 3.5, BeOS.

12.32.3 mcheck_pedantic

Gnulib module: —

Portability problems fixed by Gnulib:

Portability problems not fixed by Gnulib:

- This function is missing on all non-glibc platforms: Mac OS X 10.5, FreeBSD 6.0, NetBSD 5.0, OpenBSD 3.8, Minix 3.1.8, AIX 5.1, HP-UX 11, IRIX 6.5, OSF/1 5.1, Solaris 11 2011-11, Cygwin, mingw, MSVC 9, Interix 3.5, BeOS.

12.32.4 mprobe

Gnulib module: —

Portability problems fixed by Gnulib:

Portability problems not fixed by Gnulib:

- This function is missing on some platforms: Mac OS X 10.5, FreeBSD 6.0, NetBSD 5.0, OpenBSD 3.8, Minix 3.1.8, AIX 5.1, HP-UX 11, IRIX 6.5, OSF/1 5.1, Solaris 11 2011-11, Cygwin, mingw, MSVC 9, Interix 3.5.

12.32.5 mtrace

Gnulib module: —

Portability problems fixed by Gnulib:

Portability problems not fixed by Gnulib:

- This function is missing on all non-glibc platforms: Mac OS X 10.5, FreeBSD 6.0, NetBSD 5.0, OpenBSD 3.8, Minix 3.1.8, AIX 5.1, HP-UX 11, IRIX 6.5, OSF/1 5.1, Solaris 11 2011-11, Cygwin, mingw, MSVC 9, Interix 3.5, BeOS.

12.32.6 muntrace

Gnulib module: —

Portability problems fixed by Gnulib:

Portability problems not fixed by Gnulib:

- This function is missing on all non-glibc platforms: Mac OS X 10.5, FreeBSD 6.0, NetBSD 5.0, OpenBSD 3.8, Minix 3.1.8, AIX 5.1, HP-UX 11, IRIX 6.5, OSF/1 5.1, Solaris 11 2011-11, Cygwin, mingw, MSVC 9, Interix 3.5, BeOS.

12.33 Glibc <mntent.h>

12.33.1 addmntent

Gnulib module: —

Portability problems fixed by Gnulib:

Portability problems not fixed by Gnulib:

- This function is missing on some platforms: Mac OS X 10.5, FreeBSD 6.0, NetBSD 5.0, OpenBSD 3.8, Minix 3.1.8, AIX 4.3.2, OSF/1 5.1, Solaris 11 2011-11, Cygwin, mingw, MSVC 9, Interix 3.5, BeOS.

12.33.2 endmntent

Gnulib module: —

Portability problems fixed by Gnulib:

Portability problems not fixed by Gnulib:

- This function is missing on some platforms: Mac OS X 10.5, FreeBSD 6.0, NetBSD 5.0, OpenBSD 3.8, Minix 3.1.8, AIX 4.3.2, OSF/1 5.1, Solaris 11 2011-11, mingw, MSVC 9, Interix 3.5, BeOS.

12.33.3 getmntent

Gnulib module: —

Portability problems fixed by Gnulib:

Portability problems not fixed by Gnulib:

- This function is missing on some platforms: Mac OS X 10.5, FreeBSD 6.0, NetBSD 5.0, OpenBSD 3.8, Minix 3.1.8, AIX 4.3.2, OSF/1 5.1, mingw, MSVC 9, BeOS.

12.33.4 `getmntent_r`

Gnulib module: —

Portability problems fixed by Gnulib:

Portability problems not fixed by Gnulib:

- This function is missing on all non-glibc platforms: Mac OS X 10.5, FreeBSD 6.0, NetBSD 5.0, OpenBSD 3.8, Minix 3.1.8, AIX 5.1, HP-UX 11, IRIX 6.5, OSF/1 5.1, Solaris 11 2011-11, Cygwin, mingw, MSVC 9, Interix 3.5, BeOS.

12.33.5 `hasmntopt`

Gnulib module: —

Portability problems fixed by Gnulib:

Portability problems not fixed by Gnulib:

- This function is missing on some platforms: Mac OS X 10.5, FreeBSD 6.0, NetBSD 5.0, OpenBSD 3.8, Minix 3.1.8, AIX 4.3.2, OSF/1 5.1, Cygwin, mingw, MSVC 9, BeOS.

12.33.6 `setmntent`

Gnulib module: —

Portability problems fixed by Gnulib:

Portability problems not fixed by Gnulib:

- This function is missing on some platforms: Mac OS X 10.5, FreeBSD 6.0, NetBSD 5.0, OpenBSD 3.8, Minix 3.1.8, AIX 4.3.2, OSF/1 5.1, Solaris 11 2011-11, mingw, MSVC 9, Interix 3.5, BeOS.

12.34 Glibc Extensions to `<netdb.h>`

12.34.1 `endnetgrent`

Gnulib module: —

Portability problems fixed by Gnulib:

Portability problems not fixed by Gnulib:

- This function is missing on some platforms: Minix 3.1.8, Cygwin, mingw, MSVC 9, Interix 3.5, BeOS.

12.34.2 `gethostbyaddr_r`

Gnulib module: —

Portability problems fixed by Gnulib:

Portability problems not fixed by Gnulib:

- This function is missing on some platforms: Mac OS X 10.5, FreeBSD 6.0, NetBSD 5.0, OpenBSD 3.8, Minix 3.1.8, HP-UX 11, IRIX 5.3, Cygwin, mingw, MSVC 9, Interix 3.5, BeOS.

12.34.3 gethostbyname2

Gnulib module: —

Portability problems fixed by Gnulib:

Portability problems not fixed by Gnulib:

- This function is missing on some platforms: Minix 3.1.8, HP-UX 11, IRIX 6.5, OSF/1 5.1, Solaris 11 2011-11, Cygwin 1.5.x, mingw, MSVC 9, Interix 3.5, BeOS.

12.34.4 gethostbyname2_r

Gnulib module: —

Portability problems fixed by Gnulib:

Portability problems not fixed by Gnulib:

- This function is missing on all non-glibc platforms: Mac OS X 10.5, FreeBSD 6.0, NetBSD 5.0, OpenBSD 3.8, Minix 3.1.8, AIX 5.1, HP-UX 11, IRIX 6.5, OSF/1 5.1, Solaris 11 2011-11, Cygwin, mingw, MSVC 9, Interix 3.5, BeOS.

12.34.5 gethostbyname_r

Gnulib module: —

Portability problems fixed by Gnulib:

Portability problems not fixed by Gnulib:

- This function is missing on some platforms: Mac OS X 10.5, FreeBSD 6.0, NetBSD 5.0, OpenBSD 3.8, Minix 3.1.8, HP-UX 11, IRIX 5.3, Cygwin, mingw, MSVC 9, Interix 3.5, BeOS.

12.34.6 gethostent_r

Gnulib module: —

Portability problems fixed by Gnulib:

Portability problems not fixed by Gnulib:

- This function is missing on some platforms: Mac OS X 10.5, FreeBSD 6.0, NetBSD 5.0, OpenBSD 3.8, Minix 3.1.8, HP-UX 11, IRIX 5.3, Cygwin, mingw, MSVC 9, Interix 3.5, BeOS.

12.34.7 getnetbyaddr_r

Gnulib module: —

Portability problems fixed by Gnulib:

Portability problems not fixed by Gnulib:

- This function is missing on some platforms: Mac OS X 10.5, FreeBSD 6.0, NetBSD 5.0, OpenBSD 3.8, Minix 3.1.8, HP-UX 11, IRIX 5.3, Cygwin, mingw, MSVC 9, Interix 3.5, BeOS.

12.34.8 getnetbyname_r

Gnulib module: —

Portability problems fixed by Gnulib:

Portability problems not fixed by Gnulib:

- This function is missing on some platforms: Mac OS X 10.5, FreeBSD 6.0, NetBSD 5.0, OpenBSD 3.8, Minix 3.1.8, HP-UX 11, IRIX 5.3, Cygwin, mingw, MSVC 9, Interix 3.5, BeOS.

12.34.9 getnetent_r

Gnulib module: —

Portability problems fixed by Gnulib:

Portability problems not fixed by Gnulib:

- This function is missing on some platforms: Mac OS X 10.5, FreeBSD 6.0, NetBSD 5.0, OpenBSD 3.8, Minix 3.1.8, HP-UX 11, IRIX 5.3, Cygwin, mingw, MSVC 9, Interix 3.5, BeOS.

12.34.10 getnetgrent

Gnulib module: —

Portability problems fixed by Gnulib:

Portability problems not fixed by Gnulib:

- This function is missing on some platforms: Minix 3.1.8, Cygwin, mingw, MSVC 9, Interix 3.5, BeOS.

12.34.11 getnetgrent_r

Gnulib module: —

Portability problems fixed by Gnulib:

Portability problems not fixed by Gnulib:

- This function is missing on some platforms: Mac OS X 10.5, FreeBSD 6.0, NetBSD 5.0, OpenBSD 3.8, Minix 3.1.8, HP-UX 11, IRIX 6.5, OSF/1 5.1, Cygwin, mingw, MSVC 9, Interix 3.5, BeOS.

12.34.12 getprotobyname_r

Gnulib module: —

Portability problems fixed by Gnulib:

Portability problems not fixed by Gnulib:

- This function is missing on some platforms: Mac OS X 10.5, FreeBSD 6.0, Minix 3.1.8, HP-UX 11, IRIX 5.3, Cygwin, mingw, MSVC 9, Interix 3.5, BeOS.

12.34.13 `getprotobynumber_r`

Gnulib module: —

Portability problems fixed by Gnulib:

Portability problems not fixed by Gnulib:

- This function is missing on some platforms: Mac OS X 10.5, FreeBSD 6.0, Minix 3.1.8, HP-UX 11, IRIX 5.3, Cygwin, mingw, MSVC 9, Interix 3.5, BeOS.

12.34.14 `getprotoent_r`

Gnulib module: —

Portability problems fixed by Gnulib:

Portability problems not fixed by Gnulib:

- This function is missing on some platforms: Mac OS X 10.5, FreeBSD 6.0, Minix 3.1.8, HP-UX 11, IRIX 5.3, Cygwin, mingw, MSVC 9, Interix 3.5, BeOS.

12.34.15 `getservbyname_r`

Gnulib module: —

Portability problems fixed by Gnulib:

Portability problems not fixed by Gnulib:

- This function is missing on some platforms: Mac OS X 10.5, FreeBSD 6.0, Minix 3.1.8, HP-UX 11, IRIX 5.3, Cygwin, mingw, MSVC 9, Interix 3.5, BeOS.

12.34.16 `getservbyport_r`

Gnulib module: —

Portability problems fixed by Gnulib:

Portability problems not fixed by Gnulib:

- This function is missing on some platforms: Mac OS X 10.5, FreeBSD 6.0, Minix 3.1.8, HP-UX 11, IRIX 5.3, Cygwin, mingw, MSVC 9, Interix 3.5, BeOS.

12.34.17 `getservent_r`

Gnulib module: —

Portability problems fixed by Gnulib:

Portability problems not fixed by Gnulib:

- This function is missing on some platforms: Mac OS X 10.5, FreeBSD 6.0, Minix 3.1.8, HP-UX 11, IRIX 5.3, Cygwin, mingw, MSVC 9, Interix 3.5, BeOS.

12.34.18 `herror`

Gnulib module: —

Portability problems fixed by Gnulib:

Portability problems not fixed by Gnulib:

- This function is missing on some platforms: Minix 3.1.8, mingw, MSVC 9, Interix 3.5.

12.34.19 hstrerror

Gnulib module: —

Portability problems fixed by Gnulib:

Portability problems not fixed by Gnulib:

- This function is missing on some platforms: Minix 3.1.8, HP-UX 11, mingw, MSVC 9, Interix 3.5, BeOS.

12.34.20 innetgr

Gnulib module: —

Portability problems fixed by Gnulib:

Portability problems not fixed by Gnulib:

- This function is missing on some platforms: Minix 3.1.8, Cygwin, mingw, MSVC 9, Interix 3.5, BeOS.

12.34.21 rcmd

Gnulib module: —

Portability problems fixed by Gnulib:

Portability problems not fixed by Gnulib:

- This function is missing on some platforms: mingw, MSVC 9, BeOS.

12.34.22 rcmd_af

Gnulib module: —

Portability problems fixed by Gnulib:

Portability problems not fixed by Gnulib:

- This function is missing on some platforms: Minix 3.1.8, AIX 5.1, HP-UX 11.11, IRIX 6.5, OSF/1 4.0, Cygwin 1.5.x, mingw, MSVC 9, Interix 3.5, BeOS.

12.34.23 rexec

Gnulib module: —

Portability problems fixed by Gnulib:

Portability problems not fixed by Gnulib:

- This function is missing on some platforms: Mac OS X 10.5, FreeBSD 6.0, NetBSD 5.0, OpenBSD 3.8, Minix 3.1.8, mingw, MSVC 9, BeOS.

12.34.24 rexec_af

Gnulib module: —

Portability problems fixed by Gnulib:

Portability problems not fixed by Gnulib:

- This function is missing on some platforms: Mac OS X 10.5, FreeBSD 6.0, NetBSD 5.0, OpenBSD 3.8, Minix 3.1.8, AIX 5.1, HP-UX 11.11, IRIX 6.5, OSF/1 4.0, Cygwin, mingw, MSVC 9, Interix 3.5, BeOS.

12.34.25 `rresvport`

Gnulib module: —

Portability problems fixed by Gnulib:

Portability problems not fixed by Gnulib:

- This function is missing on some platforms: Minix 3.1.8, mingw, MSVC 9, BeOS.

12.34.26 `rresvport_af`

Gnulib module: —

Portability problems fixed by Gnulib:

Portability problems not fixed by Gnulib:

- This function is missing on some platforms: Minix 3.1.8, AIX 5.1, HP-UX 11.11, IRIX 6.5, OSF/1 4.0, Cygwin 1.5.x, mingw, MSVC 9, Interix 3.5, BeOS.

12.34.27 `ruserok`

Gnulib module: —

Portability problems fixed by Gnulib:

Portability problems not fixed by Gnulib:

- This function is missing on some platforms: Minix 3.1.8, mingw, MSVC 9, BeOS.

12.34.28 `ruserok_af`

Gnulib module: —

Portability problems fixed by Gnulib:

Portability problems not fixed by Gnulib:

- This function is missing on all non-glibc platforms: Mac OS X 10.5, FreeBSD 6.0, NetBSD 5.0, OpenBSD 3.8, Minix 3.1.8, AIX 5.1, HP-UX 11, IRIX 6.5, OSF/1 5.1, Solaris 11 2011-11, Cygwin, mingw, MSVC 9, Interix 3.5, BeOS.

12.34.29 `setnetgrent`

Gnulib module: —

Portability problems fixed by Gnulib:

Portability problems not fixed by Gnulib:

- This function is missing on some platforms: Minix 3.1.8, Cygwin, mingw, MSVC 9, Interix 3.5, BeOS.

12.35 Glibc `<netinet/ether.h>`

12.35.1 `ether_aton`

Gnulib module: —

Portability problems fixed by Gnulib:

Portability problems not fixed by Gnulib:

- This function is missing on some platforms: HP-UX 11, Cygwin, mingw, MSVC 9, Interix 3.5, BeOS.

12.35.2 ether_aton_r

Gnulib module: —

Portability problems fixed by Gnulib:

Portability problems not fixed by Gnulib:

- This function is missing on some platforms: Mac OS X 10.5, FreeBSD 6.0, NetBSD 5.0, OpenBSD 3.8, Minix 3.1.8, HP-UX 11, IRIX 6.5, OSF/1 5.1, Solaris 11 2011-11, Cygwin, mingw, MSVC 9, Interix 3.5, BeOS.

12.35.3 ether_hostton

Gnulib module: —

Portability problems fixed by Gnulib:

Portability problems not fixed by Gnulib:

- This function is missing on some platforms: HP-UX 11, Cygwin, mingw, MSVC 9, Interix 3.5, BeOS.

12.35.4 ether_line

Gnulib module: —

Portability problems fixed by Gnulib:

Portability problems not fixed by Gnulib:

- This function is missing on some platforms: HP-UX 11, Cygwin, mingw, MSVC 9, Interix 3.5, BeOS.

12.35.5 ether_ntoa

Gnulib module: —

Portability problems fixed by Gnulib:

Portability problems not fixed by Gnulib:

- This function is missing on some platforms: HP-UX 11, Cygwin, mingw, MSVC 9, Interix 3.5, BeOS.

12.35.6 ether_ntoa_r

Gnulib module: —

Portability problems fixed by Gnulib:

Portability problems not fixed by Gnulib:

- This function is missing on some platforms: Mac OS X 10.5, FreeBSD 6.0, NetBSD 5.0, OpenBSD 3.8, Minix 3.1.8, HP-UX 11, IRIX 6.5, OSF/1 5.1, Solaris 11 2011-11, Cygwin, mingw, MSVC 9, Interix 3.5, BeOS.

12.35.7 `ether_ntohost`

Gnulib module: —

Portability problems fixed by Gnulib:

Portability problems not fixed by Gnulib:

- This function is missing on some platforms: HP-UX 11, Cygwin, mingw, MSVC 9, Interix 3.5, BeOS.

12.36 Glibc Extensions to `<netinet/in.h>`

12.36.1 `bindresvport`

Gnulib module: —

Portability problems fixed by Gnulib:

Portability problems not fixed by Gnulib:

- This function is missing on some platforms: Minix 3.1.8, HP-UX 11, Cygwin 1.5.x, mingw, MSVC 9, BeOS.

12.36.2 `getipv4sourcefilter`

Gnulib module: —

Portability problems fixed by Gnulib:

Portability problems not fixed by Gnulib:

- This function is missing on many platforms: Mac OS X 10.5, FreeBSD 6.0, NetBSD 5.0, OpenBSD 3.8, Minix 3.1.8, AIX 5.1, HP-UX 11.23, IRIX 6.5, OSF/1 5.1, Solaris 10, Cygwin, mingw, MSVC 9, Interix 3.5, BeOS.

12.36.3 `getsourcefilter`

Gnulib module: —

Portability problems fixed by Gnulib:

Portability problems not fixed by Gnulib:

- This function is missing on many platforms: Mac OS X 10.5, FreeBSD 6.0, NetBSD 5.0, OpenBSD 3.8, Minix 3.1.8, AIX 5.1, HP-UX 11.23, IRIX 6.5, OSF/1 5.1, Solaris 10, Cygwin, mingw, MSVC 9, Interix 3.5, BeOS.

12.36.4 `in6addr_any`

Gnulib module: —

Portability problems fixed by Gnulib:

Portability problems not fixed by Gnulib:

- This constant is missing on some platforms: Mac OS X 10.5, Minix 3.1.8, HP-UX 11.00, IRIX 6.5, OSF/1 5.1, Cygwin 1.5.x, mingw, MSVC 9, Interix 3.5, BeOS.

12.36.5 in6addr_loopback

Gnulib module: —

Portability problems fixed by Gnulib:

Portability problems not fixed by Gnulib:

- This constant is missing on some platforms: Mac OS X 10.5, Minix 3.1.8, AIX 4.3.2, HP-UX 11.00, IRIX 6.5, OSF/1 5.1, Cygwin 1.5.x, mingw, MSVC 9, Interix 3.5, BeOS.

12.36.6 inet6_option_alloc

Gnulib module: —

Portability problems fixed by Gnulib:

Portability problems not fixed by Gnulib:

- This function is missing on some platforms: Minix 3.1.8, AIX 5.1, HP-UX 11, IRIX 6.5, OSF/1 5.1, Solaris 11 2011-11, Cygwin, mingw, MSVC 9, Interix 3.5, BeOS.

12.36.7 inet6_option_append

Gnulib module: —

Portability problems fixed by Gnulib:

Portability problems not fixed by Gnulib:

- This function is missing on some platforms: Minix 3.1.8, AIX 5.1, HP-UX 11, IRIX 6.5, OSF/1 5.1, Solaris 11 2011-11, Cygwin, mingw, MSVC 9, Interix 3.5, BeOS.

12.36.8 inet6_option_find

Gnulib module: —

Portability problems fixed by Gnulib:

Portability problems not fixed by Gnulib:

- This function is missing on some platforms: Minix 3.1.8, AIX 5.1, HP-UX 11, IRIX 6.5, OSF/1 5.1, Solaris 11 2011-11, Cygwin, mingw, MSVC 9, Interix 3.5, BeOS.

12.36.9 inet6_option_init

Gnulib module: —

Portability problems fixed by Gnulib:

Portability problems not fixed by Gnulib:

- This function is missing on some platforms: Minix 3.1.8, AIX 5.1, HP-UX 11, IRIX 6.5, OSF/1 5.1, Solaris 11 2011-11, Cygwin, mingw, MSVC 9, Interix 3.5, BeOS.

12.36.10 inet6_option_next

Gnulib module: —

Portability problems fixed by Gnulib:

Portability problems not fixed by Gnulib:

- This function is missing on some platforms: Minix 3.1.8, AIX 5.1, HP-UX 11, IRIX 6.5, OSF/1 5.1, Solaris 11 2011-11, Cygwin, mingw, MSVC 9, Interix 3.5, BeOS.

12.36.11 inet6_option_space

Gnulib module: —

Portability problems fixed by Gnulib:

Portability problems not fixed by Gnulib:

- This function is missing on some platforms: Minix 3.1.8, AIX 5.1, HP-UX 11, IRIX 6.5, OSF/1 5.1, Solaris 11 2011-11, Cygwin, mingw, MSVC 9, Interix 3.5, BeOS.

12.36.12 inet6_opt_append

Gnulib module: —

Portability problems fixed by Gnulib:

Portability problems not fixed by Gnulib:

- This function is missing on many non-glibc platforms: glibc 2.4, Mac OS X 10.5, NetBSD 3.0, OpenBSD 3.8, Minix 3.1.8, AIX 5.2, HP-UX 11.31, IRIX 6.5, OSF/1 5.1, Solaris 9, Cygwin, mingw, MSVC 9, Interix 3.5, BeOS.

12.36.13 inet6_opt_find

Gnulib module: —

Portability problems fixed by Gnulib:

Portability problems not fixed by Gnulib:

- This function is missing on many non-glibc platforms: glibc 2.4, Mac OS X 10.5, NetBSD 3.0, OpenBSD 3.8, Minix 3.1.8, AIX 5.2, HP-UX 11.31, IRIX 6.5, OSF/1 5.1, Solaris 9, Cygwin, mingw, MSVC 9, Interix 3.5, BeOS.

12.36.14 inet6_opt_finish

Gnulib module: —

Portability problems fixed by Gnulib:

Portability problems not fixed by Gnulib:

- This function is missing on many non-glibc platforms: glibc 2.4, Mac OS X 10.5, NetBSD 3.0, OpenBSD 3.8, Minix 3.1.8, AIX 5.2, HP-UX 11.31, IRIX 6.5, OSF/1 5.1, Solaris 9, Cygwin, mingw, MSVC 9, Interix 3.5, BeOS.

12.36.15 inet6_opt_get_val

Gnulib module: —

Portability problems fixed by Gnulib:

Portability problems not fixed by Gnulib:

- This function is missing on many non-glibc platforms: glibc 2.4, Mac OS X 10.5, NetBSD 3.0, OpenBSD 3.8, Minix 3.1.8, AIX 5.2, HP-UX 11.31, IRIX 6.5, OSF/1 5.1, Solaris 9, Cygwin, mingw, MSVC 9, Interix 3.5, BeOS.

12.36.16 `inet6_opt_init`

Gnulib module: —

Portability problems fixed by Gnulib:

Portability problems not fixed by Gnulib:

- This function is missing on many non-glibc platforms: glibc 2.4, Mac OS X 10.5, NetBSD 3.0, OpenBSD 3.8, Minix 3.1.8, AIX 5.2, HP-UX 11.31, IRIX 6.5, OSF/1 5.1, Solaris 9, Cygwin, mingw, MSVC 9, Interix 3.5, BeOS.

12.36.17 `inet6_opt_next`

Gnulib module: —

Portability problems fixed by Gnulib:

Portability problems not fixed by Gnulib:

- This function is missing on many non-glibc platforms: glibc 2.4, Mac OS X 10.5, NetBSD 3.0, OpenBSD 3.8, Minix 3.1.8, AIX 5.2, HP-UX 11.31, IRIX 6.5, OSF/1 5.1, Solaris 9, Cygwin, mingw, MSVC 9, Interix 3.5, BeOS.

12.36.18 `inet6_opt_set_val`

Gnulib module: —

Portability problems fixed by Gnulib:

Portability problems not fixed by Gnulib:

- This function is missing on many non-glibc platforms: glibc 2.4, Mac OS X 10.5, NetBSD 3.0, OpenBSD 3.8, Minix 3.1.8, AIX 5.2, HP-UX 11.31, IRIX 6.5, OSF/1 5.1, Solaris 9, Cygwin, mingw, MSVC 9, Interix 3.5, BeOS.

12.36.19 `inet6_rth_add`

Gnulib module: —

Portability problems fixed by Gnulib:

Portability problems not fixed by Gnulib:

- This function is missing on many non-glibc platforms: glibc 2.4, Mac OS X 10.5, NetBSD 3.0, OpenBSD 3.8, Minix 3.1.8, AIX 5.2, HP-UX 11.31, IRIX 6.5, OSF/1 5.1, Solaris 9, Cygwin, mingw, MSVC 9, Interix 3.5, BeOS.

12.36.20 `inet6_rth_getaddr`

Gnulib module: —

Portability problems fixed by Gnulib:

Portability problems not fixed by Gnulib:

- This function is missing on many non-glibc platforms: glibc 2.4, Mac OS X 10.5, NetBSD 3.0, OpenBSD 3.8, Minix 3.1.8, AIX 5.2, HP-UX 11.31, IRIX 6.5, OSF/1 5.1, Solaris 9, Cygwin, mingw, MSVC 9, Interix 3.5, BeOS.

12.36.21 `inet6_rth_init`

Gnulib module: —

Portability problems fixed by Gnulib:

Portability problems not fixed by Gnulib:

- This function is missing on many non-glibc platforms: glibc 2.4, Mac OS X 10.5, NetBSD 3.0, OpenBSD 3.8, Minix 3.1.8, AIX 5.2, HP-UX 11.31, IRIX 6.5, OSF/1 5.1, Solaris 9, Cygwin, mingw, MSVC 9, Interix 3.5, BeOS.

12.36.22 `inet6_rth_reverse`

Gnulib module: —

Portability problems fixed by Gnulib:

Portability problems not fixed by Gnulib:

- This function is missing on many non-glibc platforms: glibc 2.4, Mac OS X 10.5, NetBSD 3.0, OpenBSD 3.8, Minix 3.1.8, AIX 5.2, HP-UX 11.31, IRIX 6.5, OSF/1 5.1, Solaris 9, Cygwin, mingw, MSVC 9, Interix 3.5, BeOS.

12.36.23 `inet6_rth_segments`

Gnulib module: —

Portability problems fixed by Gnulib:

Portability problems not fixed by Gnulib:

- This function is missing on many non-glibc platforms: glibc 2.4, Mac OS X 10.5, NetBSD 3.0, OpenBSD 3.8, Minix 3.1.8, AIX 5.2, HP-UX 11.31, IRIX 6.5, OSF/1 5.1, Solaris 9, Cygwin, mingw, MSVC 9, Interix 3.5, BeOS.

12.36.24 `inet6_rth_space`

Gnulib module: —

Portability problems fixed by Gnulib:

Portability problems not fixed by Gnulib:

- This function is missing on many non-glibc platforms: glibc 2.4, Mac OS X 10.5, NetBSD 3.0, OpenBSD 3.8, Minix 3.1.8, AIX 5.2, HP-UX 11.31, IRIX 6.5, OSF/1 5.1, Solaris 9, Cygwin, mingw, MSVC 9, Interix 3.5, BeOS.

12.36.25 `setipv4sourcefilter`

Gnulib module: —

Portability problems fixed by Gnulib:

Portability problems not fixed by Gnulib:

- This function is missing on all non-glibc platforms: Mac OS X 10.5, FreeBSD 6.0, NetBSD 5.0, OpenBSD 3.8, Minix 3.1.8, AIX 5.1, HP-UX 11.23, IRIX 6.5, OSF/1 5.1, Solaris 10, Cygwin, mingw, MSVC 9, Interix 3.5, BeOS.

12.36.26 `setsourcefilter`

Gnulib module: —

Portability problems fixed by Gnulib:

Portability problems not fixed by Gnulib:

- This function is missing on all non-glibc platforms: Mac OS X 10.5, FreeBSD 6.0, NetBSD 5.0, OpenBSD 3.8, Minix 3.1.8, AIX 5.1, HP-UX 11.23, IRIX 6.5, OSF/1 5.1, Solaris 10, Cygwin, mingw, MSVC 9, Interix 3.5, BeOS.

12.37 Glibc `<obstack.h>`

12.37.1 `obstack_alloc_failed_handler`

Gnulib module: —

Portability problems fixed by Gnulib:

Portability problems not fixed by Gnulib:

- This variable is missing on some platforms: Mac OS X 10.5, FreeBSD 6.0, NetBSD 5.0, OpenBSD 3.8, Minix 3.1.8, AIX 5.1, HP-UX 11, IRIX 6.5, OSF/1 5.1, Solaris 11 2011-11, Cygwin, mingw, MSVC 9, Interix 3.5.

12.37.2 `obstack_exit_failure`

Gnulib module: —

Portability problems fixed by Gnulib:

Portability problems not fixed by Gnulib:

- This variable is missing on some platforms: Mac OS X 10.5, FreeBSD 6.0, NetBSD 5.0, OpenBSD 3.8, Minix 3.1.8, AIX 5.1, HP-UX 11, IRIX 6.5, OSF/1 5.1, Solaris 11 2011-11, Cygwin, mingw, MSVC 9, Interix 3.5.

12.37.3 `obstack_free`

Gnulib module: —

Portability problems fixed by Gnulib:

Portability problems not fixed by Gnulib:

- This function is missing on some platforms: Mac OS X 10.5, FreeBSD 6.0, NetBSD 5.0, OpenBSD 3.8, Minix 3.1.8, AIX 5.1, HP-UX 11, IRIX 6.5, OSF/1 5.1, Solaris 11 2011-11, Cygwin, mingw, MSVC 9, Interix 3.5.

12.37.4 `obstack_printf`

Gnulib module: obstack-printf or obstack-printf-posix

Portability problems fixed by either Gnulib module `obstack-printf` or `obstack-printf-posix`:

- This function is missing on all non-glibc platforms: Mac OS X 10.5, FreeBSD 6.0, NetBSD 5.0, OpenBSD 3.8, Minix 3.1.8, AIX 5.1, HP-UX 11, IRIX 6.5, OSF/1 5.1, Solaris 11 2011-11, Cygwin, mingw, MSVC 9, Interix 3.5, BeOS.

Portability problems fixed by Gnulib module `ostack-printf-posix`:

- This function does not support size specifiers as in C99 (`hh`, `ll`, `j`, `t`, `z`) on some platforms: AIX 5.1, HP-UX 11.23, IRIX 6.5, OSF/1 5.1, Solaris 9, Cygwin 1.5.24, mingw, MSVC 9, BeOS.

- printf of 'long double' numbers is unsupported on some platforms: mingw, MSVC 9, BeOS.

- printf `"%f"`, `"%e"`, `"%g"` of Infinity and NaN yields an incorrect result on some platforms: AIX 5.2, OSF/1 5.1, Solaris 11 2011-11, mingw, MSVC 9.

- This function does not support the 'a' and 'A' directives on some platforms: glibc-2.3.6, Mac OS X 10.5, NetBSD 5.0, OpenBSD 4.0, AIX 5.2, HP-UX 11, IRIX 6.5, OSF/1 5.1, Solaris 11 2011-11, Cygwin 1.5.x, mingw, MSVC 9, BeOS.

- This function does not support the 'F' directive on some platforms: NetBSD 3.0, AIX 5.1, HP-UX 11.23, IRIX 6.5, OSF/1 5.1, Solaris 9, Cygwin 1.5.x, mingw, MSVC 9, BeOS.

- This function does not support the 'n' directive on some platforms: MSVC 9.

- This function does not support the 'ls' directive on some platforms: OpenBSD 4.0, IRIX 6.5, Solaris 2.6, Cygwin 1.5.x, Haiku.

- This function does not support precisions in the 'ls' directive correctly on some platforms: Solaris 11 2011-11.

- This function does not support format directives that access arguments in an arbitrary order, such as `"%2$s"`, on some platforms: NetBSD 3.0, mingw, MSVC 9, BeOS.

- This function doesn't support the ' flag on some platforms: NetBSD 3.0, Cygwin 1.5.24, mingw, MSVC 9.

- This function behaves incorrectly when a '-' flag and a negative width are specified together, on some platforms: HP-UX 10.20.

- printf `"%010f"` of NaN and Infinity yields an incorrect result (padded with zeroes) on some platforms: Mac OS X 10.5, FreeBSD 6.0, NetBSD 5.0, AIX 5.2, IRIX 6.5, OSF/1 5.1, Solaris 11 2011-11, Cygwin 1.5.x, mingw, MSVC 9.

- This function does not support precisions larger than 512 or 1024 in integer, floating-point and pointer output on some platforms: Solaris 10/x86, mingw, MSVC 9, BeOS.

- This function can crash in out-of-memory conditions on some platforms: Mac OS X 10.3, FreeBSD 6.0, NetBSD 5.0.

- This function does not fully support the 'n' directive on some platforms: HP-UX 11, mingw, MSVC 9.

Portability problems not fixed by Gnulib:

12.37.5 `obstack_vprintf`

Gnulib module: obstack-printf or obstack-printf-posix

Portability problems fixed by either Gnulib module `obstack-printf` or `obstack-printf-posix`:

- This function is missing on all non-glibc platforms: Mac OS X 10.5, FreeBSD 6.0, NetBSD 5.0, OpenBSD 3.8, Minix 3.1.8, AIX 5.1, HP-UX 11, IRIX 6.5, OSF/1 5.1, Solaris 11 2011-11, Cygwin, mingw, MSVC 9, Interix 3.5, BeOS.

Portability problems fixed by Gnulib module `ostack-printf-posix`:

- This function does not support size specifiers as in C99 (`hh`, `ll`, `j`, `t`, `z`) on some platforms: AIX 5.1, HP-UX 11.23, IRIX 6.5, OSF/1 5.1, Solaris 9, Cygwin 1.5.24, mingw, MSVC 9, BeOS.

- printf of '`long double`' numbers is unsupported on some platforms: mingw, MSVC 9, BeOS.

- printf `"%f"`, `"%e"`, `"%g"` of Infinity and NaN yields an incorrect result on some platforms: AIX 5.2, OSF/1 5.1, Solaris 11 2011-11, mingw, MSVC 9.

- This function does not support the '`a`' and '`A`' directives on some platforms: glibc-2.3.6, Mac OS X 10.5, NetBSD 5.0, OpenBSD 4.0, AIX 5.2, HP-UX 11, IRIX 6.5, OSF/1 5.1, Solaris 11 2011-11, Cygwin 1.5.x, mingw, MSVC 9, BeOS.

- This function does not support the '`F`' directive on some platforms: NetBSD 3.0, AIX 5.1, HP-UX 11.23, IRIX 6.5, OSF/1 5.1, Solaris 9, Cygwin 1.5.x, mingw, MSVC 9, BeOS.

- This function does not support the '`n`' directive on some platforms: MSVC 9.

- This function does not support the '`ls`' directive on some platforms: OpenBSD 4.0, IRIX 6.5, Solaris 2.6, Cygwin 1.5.x, Haiku.

- This function does not support precisions in the '`ls`' directive correctly on some platforms: Solaris 11 2011-11.

- This function does not support format directives that access arguments in an arbitrary order, such as `"%2$s"`, on some platforms: NetBSD 3.0, mingw, MSVC 9, BeOS.

- This function doesn't support the ' flag on some platforms: NetBSD 3.0, Cygwin 1.5.24, mingw, MSVC 9.

- This function behaves incorrectly when a '`-`' flag and a negative width are specified together, on some platforms: HP-UX 10.20.

- printf `"%010f"` of NaN and Infinity yields an incorrect result (padded with zeroes) on some platforms: Mac OS X 10.5, FreeBSD 6.0, NetBSD 5.0, AIX 5.2, IRIX 6.5, OSF/1 5.1, Solaris 11 2011-11, Cygwin 1.5.x, mingw, MSVC 9.

- This function does not support precisions larger than 512 or 1024 in integer, floating-point and pointer output on some platforms: Solaris 10/x86, mingw, MSVC 9, BeOS.

- This function can crash in out-of-memory conditions on some platforms: Mac OS X 10.3, FreeBSD 6.0, NetBSD 5.0.

- This function does not fully support the '`n`' directive on some platforms: HP-UX 11, mingw, MSVC 9.

Portability problems not fixed by Gnulib:

12.38 Glibc <printf.h>

12.38.1 parse_printf_format

Gnulib module: —

Portability problems fixed by Gnulib:

Portability problems not fixed by Gnulib:

- This function is missing on all non-glibc platforms: Mac OS X 10.5, FreeBSD 6.0, NetBSD 5.0, OpenBSD 3.8, Minix 3.1.8, AIX 5.1, HP-UX 11, IRIX 6.5, OSF/1 5.1, Solaris 11 2011-11, Cygwin, mingw, MSVC 9, Interix 3.5, BeOS.

12.38.2 printf_size

Gnulib module: —

Portability problems fixed by Gnulib:

Portability problems not fixed by Gnulib:

- This function is missing on all non-glibc platforms: Mac OS X 10.5, FreeBSD 6.0, NetBSD 5.0, OpenBSD 3.8, Minix 3.1.8, AIX 5.1, HP-UX 11, IRIX 6.5, OSF/1 5.1, Solaris 11 2011-11, Cygwin, mingw, MSVC 9, Interix 3.5, BeOS.

12.38.3 printf_size_info

Gnulib module: —

Portability problems fixed by Gnulib:

Portability problems not fixed by Gnulib:

- This function is missing on all non-glibc platforms: Mac OS X 10.5, FreeBSD 6.0, NetBSD 5.0, OpenBSD 3.8, Minix 3.1.8, AIX 5.1, HP-UX 11, IRIX 6.5, OSF/1 5.1, Solaris 11 2011-11, Cygwin, mingw, MSVC 9, Interix 3.5, BeOS.

12.38.4 register_printf_function

Gnulib module: —

Portability problems fixed by Gnulib:

Portability problems not fixed by Gnulib:

- This function is missing on all non-glibc platforms: Mac OS X 10.5, FreeBSD 6.0, NetBSD 5.0, OpenBSD 3.8, Minix 3.1.8, AIX 5.1, HP-UX 11, IRIX 6.5, OSF/1 5.1, Solaris 11 2011-11, Cygwin, mingw, MSVC 9, Interix 3.5, BeOS.

12.38.5 register_printf_modifier

Gnulib module: —

Portability problems fixed by Gnulib:

Portability problems not fixed by Gnulib:

- This function is missing on all non-glibc platforms: glibc 2.9, Mac OS X 10.5, FreeBSD 6.4, NetBSD 5.0, OpenBSD 3.8, Minix 3.1.8, AIX 7.1, HP-UX 11.31, IRIX 6.5, OSF/1 5.1, Solaris 11 2011-11, Cygwin, mingw, MSVC 9, Interix 3.5, BeOS.

12.38.6 register_printf_specifier

Gnulib module: —

Portability problems fixed by Gnulib:

Portability problems not fixed by Gnulib:

- This function is missing on all non-glibc platforms: glibc 2.9, Mac OS X 10.5, FreeBSD 6.4, NetBSD 5.0, OpenBSD 3.8, Minix 3.1.8, AIX 7.1, HP-UX 11.31, IRIX 6.5, OSF/1 5.1, Solaris 11 2011-11, Cygwin, mingw, MSVC 9, Interix 3.5, BeOS.

12.38.7 `register_printf_type`

Gnulib module: —

Portability problems fixed by Gnulib:

Portability problems not fixed by Gnulib:

- This function is missing on all non-glibc platforms: glibc 2.9, Mac OS X 10.5, FreeBSD 6.4, NetBSD 5.0, OpenBSD 3.8, Minix 3.1.8, AIX 7.1, HP-UX 11.31, IRIX 6.5, OSF/1 5.1, Solaris 11 2011-11, Cygwin, mingw, MSVC 9, Interix 3.5, BeOS.

12.39 Glibc Extensions to `<pthread.h>`

12.39.1 `pthread_attr_getaffinity_np`

Gnulib module: —

Portability problems fixed by Gnulib:

Portability problems not fixed by Gnulib:

- This function is missing on all non-glibc platforms: glibc 2.3.2, Mac OS X 10.5, FreeBSD 6.4, NetBSD 5.0, OpenBSD 3.8, Minix 3.1.8, AIX 7.1, HP-UX 11.31, IRIX 6.5, OSF/1 5.1, Solaris 11 2011-11, Cygwin, mingw, MSVC 9, Interix 3.5, BeOS.
- This function has a different signature on some platforms: glibc 2.3.3.

12.39.2 `pthread_attr_setaffinity_np`

Gnulib module: —

Portability problems fixed by Gnulib:

Portability problems not fixed by Gnulib:

- This function is missing on all non-glibc platforms: glibc 2.3.2, Mac OS X 10.5, FreeBSD 6.4, NetBSD 5.0, OpenBSD 3.8, Minix 3.1.8, AIX 7.1, HP-UX 11.31, IRIX 6.5, OSF/1 5.1, Solaris 11 2011-11, Cygwin, mingw, MSVC 9, Interix 3.5, BeOS.
- This function has a different signature on some platforms: glibc 2.3.3.

12.39.3 `pthread_getaffinity_np`

Gnulib module: —

Portability problems fixed by Gnulib:

Portability problems not fixed by Gnulib:

- This function is missing on many non-glibc platforms: glibc 2.3.2, Mac OS X 10.5, FreeBSD 6.4, NetBSD 3.0, OpenBSD 3.8, Minix 3.1.8, AIX 7.1, HP-UX 11.31, IRIX 6.5, OSF/1 5.1, Solaris 11 2011-11, Cygwin, mingw, MSVC 9, Interix 3.5, BeOS.
- This function has a different signature on some platforms: glibc 2.3.3.
- The third parameter has a different type on some platforms: FreeBSD 7.2, NetBSD 5.0.

12.39.4 pthread_getattr_np

Gnulib module: —

Portability problems fixed by Gnulib:

Portability problems not fixed by Gnulib:

- This function is missing on many non-glibc platforms: Mac OS X 10.5, FreeBSD 6.0, NetBSD 5.0, OpenBSD 3.8, Minix 3.1.8, AIX 5.1, HP-UX 11, IRIX 6.5, OSF/1 5.1, Solaris 11 2011-11, Cygwin 1.7.9, mingw, MSVC 9, Interix 3.5, BeOS.

12.39.5 pthread_getname_np

Gnulib module: —

Portability problems fixed by Gnulib:

Portability problems not fixed by Gnulib:

- This function is missing on many non-glibc platforms: glibc 2.11, Mac OS X 10.5, FreeBSD 6.4, OpenBSD 3.8, Minix 3.1.8, AIX 7.1, HP-UX 11.31, IRIX 6.5, Solaris 11 2011-11, Cygwin, mingw, MSVC 9, Interix 3.5, BeOS.

12.39.6 pthread_kill_other_threads_np

Gnulib module: —

Portability problems fixed by Gnulib:

Portability problems not fixed by Gnulib:

- This function is missing on all non-glibc platforms: Mac OS X 10.5, FreeBSD 6.0, NetBSD 5.0, OpenBSD 3.8, Minix 3.1.8, AIX 5.1, HP-UX 11, IRIX 6.5, OSF/1 5.1, Solaris 11 2011-11, Cygwin, mingw, MSVC 9, Interix 3.5, BeOS.

12.39.7 pthread_mutex_consistent_np

Gnulib module: —

Portability problems fixed by Gnulib:

Portability problems not fixed by Gnulib:

- This function is missing on many non-glibc platforms: glibc 2.3.6, Mac OS X 10.5, FreeBSD 6.4, NetBSD 5.0, OpenBSD 3.8, Minix 3.1.8, AIX 7.1, HP-UX 11.31, IRIX 6.5, OSF/1 5.1, Solaris 7, Cygwin, mingw, MSVC 9, Interix 3.5, BeOS.

12.39.8 pthread_mutexattr_getrobust_np

Gnulib module: —

Portability problems fixed by Gnulib:

Portability problems not fixed by Gnulib:

- This function is missing on many non-glibc platforms: glibc 2.3.6, Mac OS X 10.5, FreeBSD 6.4, NetBSD 5.0, OpenBSD 3.8, Minix 3.1.8, AIX 7.1, HP-UX 11.31, IRIX 6.5, OSF/1 5.1, Solaris 7, Cygwin, mingw, MSVC 9, Interix 3.5, BeOS.

This function has now been standardized by POSIX under the name pthread_mutexattr_getrobust.

12.39.9 pthread_mutexattr_setrobust_np

Gnulib module: —

Portability problems fixed by Gnulib:

Portability problems not fixed by Gnulib:

- This function is missing on many non-glibc platforms: glibc 2.3.6, Mac OS X 10.5, FreeBSD 6.4, NetBSD 5.0, OpenBSD 3.8, Minix 3.1.8, AIX 7.1, HP-UX 11.31, IRIX 6.5, OSF/1 5.1, Solaris 7, Cygwin, mingw, MSVC 9, Interix 3.5, BeOS.

This function has now been standardized by POSIX under the name pthread_mutexattr_setrobust.

12.39.10 pthread_rwlockattr_getkind_np

Gnulib module: —

Portability problems fixed by Gnulib:

Portability problems not fixed by Gnulib:

- This function is missing on all non-glibc platforms: Mac OS X 10.5, FreeBSD 6.0, NetBSD 5.0, OpenBSD 3.8, Minix 3.1.8, AIX 5.1, HP-UX 11, IRIX 6.5, OSF/1 5.1, Solaris 11 2011-11, Cygwin, mingw, MSVC 9, Interix 3.5, BeOS.

12.39.11 pthread_rwlockattr_setkind_np

Gnulib module: —

Portability problems fixed by Gnulib:

Portability problems not fixed by Gnulib:

- This function is missing on all non-glibc platforms: Mac OS X 10.5, FreeBSD 6.0, NetBSD 5.0, OpenBSD 3.8, Minix 3.1.8, AIX 5.1, HP-UX 11, IRIX 6.5, OSF/1 5.1, Solaris 11 2011-11, Cygwin, mingw, MSVC 9, Interix 3.5, BeOS.

12.39.12 pthread_setaffinity_np

Gnulib module: —

Portability problems fixed by Gnulib:

Portability problems not fixed by Gnulib:

- This function is missing on many non-glibc platforms: glibc 2.3.2, Mac OS X 10.5, FreeBSD 6.4, NetBSD 3.0, OpenBSD 3.8, Minix 3.1.8, AIX 7.1, HP-UX 11.31, IRIX 6.5, OSF/1 5.1, Solaris 11 2011-11, Cygwin, mingw, MSVC 9, Interix 3.5, BeOS.
- This function has a different signature on some platforms: glibc 2.3.3.
- The third parameter has a different type on some platforms: FreeBSD 7.2, NetBSD 5.0.

12.39.13 pthread_setname_np

Gnulib module: —

Portability problems fixed by Gnulib:

Portability problems not fixed by Gnulib:

- This function is missing on many non-glibc platforms: glibc 2.11, Mac OS X 10.5, FreeBSD 6.4, OpenBSD 3.8, Minix 3.1.8, AIX 7.1, HP-UX 11.31, IRIX 6.5, Solaris 11 2011-11, Cygwin, mingw, MSVC 9, Interix 3.5, BeOS.
- This function has a different signature on some platforms: NetBSD 5.0, OSF/1 5.1. On OSF/1 the third argument must be NULL. On NetBSD the second argument is interpreted as a printf format string, with the third argument as parameter.

12.39.14 pthread_sigqueue

Gnulib module: —

Portability problems fixed by Gnulib:

Portability problems not fixed by Gnulib:

- This function is missing on many non-glibc platforms: glibc 2.10, Mac OS X 10.5, FreeBSD 6.4, NetBSD 5.0, OpenBSD 3.8, Minix 3.1.8, AIX 7.1, HP-UX 11.31, IRIX 6.5, OSF/1 5.1, Solaris 11 2011-11, Cygwin 1.7.9, mingw, MSVC 9, Interix 3.5, BeOS.

12.39.15 pthread_timedjoin_np

Gnulib module: —

Portability problems fixed by Gnulib:

Portability problems not fixed by Gnulib:

- This function is missing on all non-glibc platforms: glibc 2.3.2, Mac OS X 10.5, FreeBSD 6.4, NetBSD 5.0, OpenBSD 3.8, Minix 3.1.8, AIX 7.1, HP-UX 11.31, IRIX 6.5, OSF/1 5.1, Solaris 11 2011-11, Cygwin, mingw, MSVC 9, Interix 3.5, BeOS.
- FreeBSD 6.4 has a function of this name in libthr but not in libpthread, and it also is missing a declaration.

12.39.16 pthread_tryjoin_np

Gnulib module: —

Portability problems fixed by Gnulib:

Portability problems not fixed by Gnulib:

- This function is missing on all non-glibc platforms: glibc 2.3.2, Mac OS X 10.5, FreeBSD 6.4, NetBSD 5.0, OpenBSD 3.8, Minix 3.1.8, AIX 7.1, HP-UX 11.31, IRIX 6.5, OSF/1 5.1, Solaris 11 2011-11, Cygwin, mingw, MSVC 9, Interix 3.5, BeOS.

12.39.17 pthread_yield

Gnulib module: —

Portability problems fixed by Gnulib:

Portability problems not fixed by Gnulib:

- This function is missing on some platforms: Mac OS X 10.5, NetBSD 5.0, Minix 3.1.8, HP-UX 11, IRIX 6.5, Solaris 11 2011-11, Cygwin 1.7.7, mingw, MSVC 9, Interix 3.5, BeOS.

12.40 Glibc <pty.h>

12.40.1 forkpty

Gnulib module: forkpty

Portability problems fixed by Gnulib:

- This function is missing on some platforms: Minix 3.1.8, AIX 5.1, HP-UX 11, IRIX 6.5, Solaris 11 2011-11.
- One some systems (at least including Cygwin, Interix, OSF/1 4 and 5, and Mac OS X) linking with -lutil is not required.
- On glibc, OpenBSD, NetBSD and FreeBSD linking with -lutil is required.
- The function is declared in pty.h on Cygwin, Interix, OSF/1 4 and 5, and glibc. It is declared in util.h on Mac OS X, OpenBSD and NetBSD. It is declared in libutil.h on FreeBSD.
- Some platforms declare the function without marking the last two parameters const. FreeBSD, Cygwin 1.7.1.

Portability problems not fixed by Gnulib:

- This function is missing on some platforms: mingw, MSVC 9.

12.40.2 openpty

Gnulib module: openpty

Portability problems fixed by Gnulib:

- This function is missing on some platforms: AIX 5.1, HP-UX 11, IRIX 6.5, Solaris 11 2011-11.
- One some systems (at least including Cygwin, Interix, OSF/1 4 and 5, and Mac OS X) linking with -lutil is not required.
- On glibc, OpenBSD, NetBSD and FreeBSD linking with -lutil is required.
- The function is declared in pty.h on Cygwin, Interix, OSF/1 4 and 5, and glibc. It is declared in util.h on Mac OS X, OpenBSD and NetBSD. It is declared in libutil.h on FreeBSD.
- Some platforms declare the function without marking the last two parameters const. FreeBSD, Cygwin 1.7.1.

Portability problems not fixed by Gnulib:

- This function is missing on some platforms: mingw, MSVC 9.
- After a successful call to openpty, the application needs to close the master's file descriptor before closing the slave's file descriptor, otherwise the process may hang in a state where it cannot be killed, on some platforms: Mac OS X 10.4.11.

12.41 Glibc Extensions to `<pwd.h>`

12.41.1 `fgetpwent`

Gnulib module: —

Portability problems fixed by Gnulib:

Portability problems not fixed by Gnulib:

- This function is missing on some platforms: Mac OS X 10.5, FreeBSD 6.0, NetBSD 5.0, OpenBSD 3.8, Minix 3.1.8, AIX 4.3.2, Cygwin, mingw, MSVC 9, Interix 3.5, BeOS.

12.41.2 `fgetpwent_r`

Gnulib module: —

Portability problems fixed by Gnulib:

Portability problems not fixed by Gnulib:

- This function is missing on some platforms: Mac OS X 10.5, FreeBSD 6.0, NetBSD 5.0, OpenBSD 3.8, Minix 3.1.8, HP-UX 11, IRIX 5.3, Cygwin, mingw, MSVC 9, Interix 3.5, BeOS.

12.41.3 `getpw`

Gnulib module: —

Portability problems fixed by Gnulib:

Portability problems not fixed by Gnulib:

- This function is missing on some platforms: Mac OS X 10.5, FreeBSD 6.0, NetBSD 5.0, OpenBSD 3.8, Minix 3.1.8, Cygwin, mingw, MSVC 9, Interix 3.5, BeOS.

12.41.4 `getpwent_r`

Gnulib module: —

Portability problems fixed by Gnulib:

Portability problems not fixed by Gnulib:

- This function is missing on some platforms: Mac OS X 10.5, OpenBSD 3.8, Minix 3.1.8, HP-UX 11, IRIX 5.3, Cygwin, mingw, MSVC 9, Interix 3.5, BeOS.

12.41.5 `putpwent`

Gnulib module: —

Portability problems fixed by Gnulib:

Portability problems not fixed by Gnulib:

- This function is missing on some platforms: Mac OS X 10.5, FreeBSD 6.0, NetBSD 5.0, OpenBSD 3.8, Minix 3.1.8, Cygwin, mingw, MSVC 9, Interix 3.5, BeOS.

12.42 Glibc Extensions to <regex.h>

12.42.1 re_comp

Gnulib module: —

Portability problems fixed by Gnulib:

Portability problems not fixed by Gnulib:

- This function is missing on some platforms: Mac OS X 10.5, FreeBSD 6.0, NetBSD 5.0, OpenBSD 3.8, Minix 3.1.8, Cygwin, mingw, MSVC 9, Interix 3.5.

12.42.2 re_compile_fastmap

Gnulib module: —

Portability problems fixed by Gnulib:

Portability problems not fixed by Gnulib:

- This function is missing on some platforms: Mac OS X 10.5, FreeBSD 6.0, NetBSD 5.0, OpenBSD 3.8, Minix 3.1.8, AIX 5.1, HP-UX 11, IRIX 6.5, OSF/1 5.1, Solaris 11 2011-11, Cygwin, mingw, MSVC 9, Interix 3.5.

12.42.3 re_compile_pattern

Gnulib module: —

Portability problems fixed by Gnulib:

Portability problems not fixed by Gnulib:

- This function is missing on some platforms: Mac OS X 10.5, FreeBSD 6.0, NetBSD 5.0, OpenBSD 3.8, Minix 3.1.8, AIX 5.1, HP-UX 11, IRIX 6.5, OSF/1 5.1, Solaris 11 2011-11, Cygwin, mingw, MSVC 9, Interix 3.5.

12.42.4 re_exec

Gnulib module: —

Portability problems fixed by Gnulib:

Portability problems not fixed by Gnulib:

- This function is missing on some platforms: Mac OS X 10.5, FreeBSD 6.0, NetBSD 5.0, OpenBSD 3.8, Minix 3.1.8, Cygwin, mingw, MSVC 9, Interix 3.5.

12.42.5 re_match

Gnulib module: —

Portability problems fixed by Gnulib:

Portability problems not fixed by Gnulib:

- This function is missing on some platforms: Mac OS X 10.5, FreeBSD 6.0, NetBSD 5.0, OpenBSD 3.8, Minix 3.1.8, AIX 5.1, HP-UX 11, IRIX 6.5, OSF/1 5.1, Solaris 11 2011-11, Cygwin, mingw, MSVC 9, Interix 3.5.

12.42.6 `re_match_2`

Gnulib module: —

Portability problems fixed by Gnulib:

Portability problems not fixed by Gnulib:

- This function is missing on some platforms: Mac OS X 10.5, FreeBSD 6.0, NetBSD 5.0, OpenBSD 3.8, Minix 3.1.8, AIX 5.1, HP-UX 11, IRIX 6.5, OSF/1 5.1, Solaris 11 2011-11, Cygwin, mingw, MSVC 9, Interix 3.5.

12.42.7 `re_search`

Gnulib module: —

Portability problems fixed by Gnulib:

Portability problems not fixed by Gnulib:

- This function is missing on some platforms: Mac OS X 10.5, FreeBSD 6.0, NetBSD 5.0, OpenBSD 3.8, Minix 3.1.8, AIX 5.1, HP-UX 11, IRIX 6.5, OSF/1 5.1, Solaris 11 2011-11, Cygwin, mingw, MSVC 9, Interix 3.5.

12.42.8 `re_search_2`

Gnulib module: —

Portability problems fixed by Gnulib:

Portability problems not fixed by Gnulib:

- This function is missing on some platforms: Mac OS X 10.5, FreeBSD 6.0, NetBSD 5.0, OpenBSD 3.8, Minix 3.1.8, AIX 5.1, HP-UX 11, IRIX 6.5, OSF/1 5.1, Solaris 11 2011-11, Cygwin, mingw, MSVC 9, Interix 3.5.

12.42.9 `re_set_registers`

Gnulib module: —

Portability problems fixed by Gnulib:

Portability problems not fixed by Gnulib:

- This function is missing on some platforms: Mac OS X 10.5, FreeBSD 6.0, NetBSD 5.0, OpenBSD 3.8, Minix 3.1.8, AIX 5.1, HP-UX 11, IRIX 6.5, OSF/1 5.1, Solaris 11 2011-11, Cygwin, mingw, MSVC 9, Interix 3.5.

12.42.10 `re_set_syntax`

Gnulib module: —

Portability problems fixed by Gnulib:

Portability problems not fixed by Gnulib:

- This function is missing on some platforms: Mac OS X 10.5, FreeBSD 6.0, NetBSD 5.0, OpenBSD 3.8, Minix 3.1.8, AIX 5.1, HP-UX 11, IRIX 6.5, OSF/1 5.1, Solaris 11 2011-11, Cygwin, mingw, MSVC 9, Interix 3.5.

12.42.11 `re_syntax_options`

Gnulib module: —

Portability problems fixed by Gnulib:

Portability problems not fixed by Gnulib:

- This variable is missing on some platforms: Mac OS X 10.5, FreeBSD 6.0, NetBSD 5.0, OpenBSD 3.8, Minix 3.1.8, AIX 5.1, HP-UX 11, IRIX 6.5, OSF/1 5.1, Solaris 11 2011-11, Cygwin, mingw, MSVC 9, Interix 3.5.

12.43 Glibc `<regexp.h>`

12.43.1 `advance`

Gnulib module: —

Portability problems fixed by Gnulib:

Portability problems not fixed by Gnulib:

- This function is missing on all non-glibc platforms: Mac OS X 10.5, FreeBSD 6.0, NetBSD 5.0, OpenBSD 3.8, Minix 3.1.8, AIX 5.1, HP-UX 11, IRIX 6.5, OSF/1 5.1, Solaris 10, Cygwin, mingw, MSVC 9, Interix 3.5, BeOS.

12.43.2 `loc1`

Gnulib module: —

Portability problems fixed by Gnulib:

Portability problems not fixed by Gnulib:

- This variable is missing on all non-glibc platforms: Mac OS X 10.5, FreeBSD 6.0, NetBSD 5.0, OpenBSD 3.8, Minix 3.1.8, AIX 5.1, HP-UX 11, IRIX 6.5, OSF/1 5.1, Solaris 10, Cygwin, mingw, MSVC 9, Interix 3.5, BeOS.

12.43.3 `loc2`

Gnulib module: —

Portability problems fixed by Gnulib:

Portability problems not fixed by Gnulib:

- This variable is missing on all non-glibc platforms: Mac OS X 10.5, FreeBSD 6.0, NetBSD 5.0, OpenBSD 3.8, Minix 3.1.8, AIX 5.1, HP-UX 11, IRIX 6.5, OSF/1 5.1, Solaris 10, Cygwin, mingw, MSVC 9, Interix 3.5, BeOS.

12.43.4 `locs`

Gnulib module: —

Portability problems fixed by Gnulib:

Portability problems not fixed by Gnulib:

- This variable is missing on all non-glibc platforms: Mac OS X 10.5, FreeBSD 6.0, NetBSD 5.0, OpenBSD 3.8, Minix 3.1.8, AIX 5.1, HP-UX 11, IRIX 6.5, OSF/1 5.1, Solaris 10, Cygwin, mingw, MSVC 9, Interix 3.5, BeOS.

12.43.5 `step`

Gnulib module: —

Portability problems fixed by Gnulib:

Portability problems not fixed by Gnulib:

- This function is missing on all non-glibc platforms: Mac OS X 10.5, FreeBSD 6.0, NetBSD 5.0, OpenBSD 3.8, Minix 3.1.8, AIX 5.1, HP-UX 11, IRIX 6.5, OSF/1 5.1, Solaris 10, Cygwin, mingw, MSVC 9, Interix 3.5, BeOS.

12.44 Glibc `<resolv.h>`

12.44.1 `dn_expand`

Gnulib module: —

Portability problems fixed by Gnulib:

Portability problems not fixed by Gnulib:

- This function is missing on some platforms: Cygwin 1.5.x, mingw, MSVC 9, Interix 3.5.

12.44.2 `res_init`

Gnulib module: —

Portability problems fixed by Gnulib:

Portability problems not fixed by Gnulib:

- This function is missing on some platforms: Cygwin 1.5.x, mingw, MSVC 9, Interix 3.5.

12.44.3 `res_mkquery`

Gnulib module: —

Portability problems fixed by Gnulib:

Portability problems not fixed by Gnulib:

- This function is missing on some platforms: Cygwin 1.5.x, mingw, MSVC 9, Interix 3.5.

12.44.4 `res_query`

Gnulib module: —

Portability problems fixed by Gnulib:

Portability problems not fixed by Gnulib:

- This function is missing on some platforms: Cygwin 1.5.x, mingw, MSVC 9, Interix 3.5.

12.44.5 res_querydomain

Gnulib module: —

Portability problems fixed by Gnulib:

Portability problems not fixed by Gnulib:

- This function is missing on some platforms: Cygwin 1.5.x, mingw, MSVC 9, Interix 3.5.

12.44.6 res_search

Gnulib module: —

Portability problems fixed by Gnulib:

Portability problems not fixed by Gnulib:

- This function is missing on some platforms: Cygwin 1.5.x, mingw, MSVC 9, Interix 3.5.

12.45 Glibc <rpc/auth.h>

12.45.1 authdes_create

Gnulib module: —

Portability problems fixed by Gnulib:

Portability problems not fixed by Gnulib:

- This function is missing on some platforms: Mac OS X 10.5, NetBSD 5.0, OpenBSD 3.8, Minix 3.1.8, IRIX 6.5, OSF/1 5.1, Cygwin, mingw, MSVC 9, Interix 3.5, BeOS.

12.45.2 authdes_pk_create

Gnulib module: —

Portability problems fixed by Gnulib:

Portability problems not fixed by Gnulib:

- This function is missing on all non-glibc platforms: Mac OS X 10.5, FreeBSD 6.0, NetBSD 5.0, OpenBSD 3.8, Minix 3.1.8, AIX 5.1, HP-UX 11, IRIX 6.5, OSF/1 5.1, Solaris 11 2011-11, Cygwin, mingw, MSVC 9, Interix 3.5, BeOS.

12.45.3 authnone_create

Gnulib module: —

Portability problems fixed by Gnulib:

Portability problems not fixed by Gnulib:

- This function is missing on some platforms: Minix 3.1.8, Cygwin, mingw, MSVC 9, BeOS.

12.45.4 `authunix_create`

Gnulib module: —

Portability problems fixed by Gnulib:

Portability problems not fixed by Gnulib:

- This function is missing on some platforms: Minix 3.1.8, HP-UX 11, Solaris 11 2011-11, Cygwin, mingw, MSVC 9, BeOS.

12.45.5 `authunix_create_default`

Gnulib module: —

Portability problems fixed by Gnulib:

Portability problems not fixed by Gnulib:

- This function is missing on some platforms: Minix 3.1.8, HP-UX 11, Solaris 11 2011-11, Cygwin, mingw, MSVC 9, BeOS.

12.45.6 `getnetname`

Gnulib module: —

Portability problems fixed by Gnulib:

Portability problems not fixed by Gnulib:

- This function is missing on some platforms: Mac OS X 10.5, NetBSD 5.0, OpenBSD 3.8, Minix 3.1.8, Cygwin, mingw, MSVC 9, Interix 3.5, BeOS.

12.45.7 `host2netname`

Gnulib module: —

Portability problems fixed by Gnulib:

Portability problems not fixed by Gnulib:

- This function is missing on some platforms: Mac OS X 10.5, NetBSD 5.0, OpenBSD 3.8, Minix 3.1.8, Cygwin, mingw, MSVC 9, Interix 3.5, BeOS.

12.45.8 `key_decryptsession`

Gnulib module: —

Portability problems fixed by Gnulib:

Portability problems not fixed by Gnulib:

- This function is missing on some platforms: Mac OS X 10.5, NetBSD 5.0, OpenBSD 3.8, Minix 3.1.8, IRIX 6.5, Cygwin, mingw, MSVC 9, Interix 3.5, BeOS.

12.45.9 `key_decryptsession_pk`

Gnulib module: —

Portability problems fixed by Gnulib:

Portability problems not fixed by Gnulib:

- This function is missing on some platforms: Mac OS X 10.5, NetBSD 5.0, OpenBSD 3.8, Minix 3.1.8, AIX 5.1, HP-UX 11, IRIX 6.5, OSF/1 5.1, Cygwin, mingw, MSVC 9, Interix 3.5, BeOS.

12.45.10 key_encryptsession

Gnulib module: —

Portability problems fixed by Gnulib:

Portability problems not fixed by Gnulib:

- This function is missing on some platforms: Mac OS X 10.5, NetBSD 5.0, OpenBSD 3.8, Minix 3.1.8, IRIX 6.5, Cygwin, mingw, MSVC 9, Interix 3.5, BeOS.

12.45.11 key_encryptsession_pk

Gnulib module: —

Portability problems fixed by Gnulib:

Portability problems not fixed by Gnulib:

- This function is missing on some platforms: Mac OS X 10.5, NetBSD 5.0, OpenBSD 3.8, Minix 3.1.8, AIX 5.1, HP-UX 11, IRIX 6.5, OSF/1 5.1, Cygwin, mingw, MSVC 9, Interix 3.5, BeOS.

12.45.12 key_gendes

Gnulib module: —

Portability problems fixed by Gnulib:

Portability problems not fixed by Gnulib:

- This function is missing on some platforms: Mac OS X 10.5, NetBSD 5.0, OpenBSD 3.8, Minix 3.1.8, IRIX 6.5, Cygwin, mingw, MSVC 9, Interix 3.5, BeOS.

12.45.13 key_get_conv

Gnulib module: —

Portability problems fixed by Gnulib:

Portability problems not fixed by Gnulib:

- This function is missing on some platforms: Mac OS X 10.5, NetBSD 5.0, OpenBSD 3.8, Minix 3.1.8, IRIX 6.5, OSF/1 5.1, Cygwin, mingw, MSVC 9, Interix 3.5, BeOS.

12.45.14 key_secretkey_is_set

Gnulib module: —

Portability problems fixed by Gnulib:

Portability problems not fixed by Gnulib:

- This function is missing on some platforms: Mac OS X 10.5, NetBSD 5.0, OpenBSD 3.8, Minix 3.1.8, HP-UX 11, IRIX 6.5, OSF/1 5.1, Cygwin, mingw, MSVC 9, Interix 3.5, BeOS.

12.45.15 `key_setsecret`

Gnulib module: —

Portability problems fixed by Gnulib:

Portability problems not fixed by Gnulib:

- This function is missing on some platforms: Mac OS X 10.5, NetBSD 5.0, OpenBSD 3.8, Minix 3.1.8, IRIX 6.5, Cygwin, mingw, MSVC 9, Interix 3.5, BeOS.

12.45.16 `netname2host`

Gnulib module: —

Portability problems fixed by Gnulib:

Portability problems not fixed by Gnulib:

- This function is missing on some platforms: Mac OS X 10.5, NetBSD 5.0, OpenBSD 3.8, Minix 3.1.8, Cygwin, mingw, MSVC 9, Interix 3.5, BeOS.

12.45.17 `netname2user`

Gnulib module: —

Portability problems fixed by Gnulib:

Portability problems not fixed by Gnulib:

- This function is missing on some platforms: Mac OS X 10.5, NetBSD 5.0, OpenBSD 3.8, Minix 3.1.8, Cygwin, mingw, MSVC 9, Interix 3.5, BeOS.

12.45.18 `user2netname`

Gnulib module: —

Portability problems fixed by Gnulib:

Portability problems not fixed by Gnulib:

- This function is missing on some platforms: Mac OS X 10.5, NetBSD 5.0, OpenBSD 3.8, Minix 3.1.8, Cygwin, mingw, MSVC 9, Interix 3.5, BeOS.

12.45.19 `xdr_des_block`

Gnulib module: —

Portability problems fixed by Gnulib:

Portability problems not fixed by Gnulib:

- This function is missing on some platforms: Minix 3.1.8, Cygwin, mingw, MSVC 9, BeOS.

12.45.20 `xdr_opaque_auth`

Gnulib module: —

Portability problems fixed by Gnulib:

Portability problems not fixed by Gnulib:

- This function is missing on some platforms: Minix 3.1.8, Cygwin, mingw, MSVC 9, BeOS.

12.46 Glibc `<rpc/auth_des.h>`

12.46.1 `authdes_getucred`

Gnulib module: —

Portability problems fixed by Gnulib:

Portability problems not fixed by Gnulib:

- This function is missing on some platforms: Mac OS X 10.5, NetBSD 5.0, OpenBSD 3.8, Minix 3.1.8, IRIX 6.5, OSF/1 5.1, Cygwin, mingw, MSVC 9, Interix 3.5, BeOS.

12.46.2 `getpublickey`

Gnulib module: —

Portability problems fixed by Gnulib:

Portability problems not fixed by Gnulib:

- This function is missing on some platforms: Mac OS X 10.5, NetBSD 5.0, OpenBSD 3.8, Minix 3.1.8, IRIX 6.5, OSF/1 5.1, Cygwin, mingw, MSVC 9, Interix 3.5, BeOS.

12.46.3 `getsecretkey`

Gnulib module: —

Portability problems fixed by Gnulib:

Portability problems not fixed by Gnulib:

- This function is missing on some platforms: Mac OS X 10.5, FreeBSD 6.0, NetBSD 5.0, OpenBSD 3.8, Minix 3.1.8, IRIX 6.5, OSF/1 5.1, Cygwin, mingw, MSVC 9, Interix 3.5, BeOS.

12.46.4 `rtime`

Gnulib module: —

Portability problems fixed by Gnulib:

Portability problems not fixed by Gnulib:

- This function is missing on some platforms: Mac OS X 10.5, NetBSD 5.0, OpenBSD 3.8, Minix 3.1.8, HP-UX 11, IRIX 6.5, Solaris 11 2011-11, Cygwin, mingw, MSVC 9, Interix 3.5, BeOS.

12.47 Glibc `<rpc/auth_unix.h>`

12.47.1 `xdr_authunix_parms`

Gnulib module: —

Portability problems fixed by Gnulib:

Portability problems not fixed by Gnulib:

- This function is missing on some platforms: Minix 3.1.8, HP-UX 11, Solaris 11 2011-11, Cygwin, mingw, MSVC 9, BeOS.

12.48 Glibc <rpc/clnt.h>

12.48.1 callrpc

Gnulib module: —

Portability problems fixed by Gnulib:

Portability problems not fixed by Gnulib:

- This function is missing on some platforms: Minix 3.1.8, Cygwin, mingw, MSVC 9, BeOS.

12.48.2 clnt_create

Gnulib module: —

Portability problems fixed by Gnulib:

Portability problems not fixed by Gnulib:

- This function is missing on some platforms: Minix 3.1.8, Cygwin, mingw, MSVC 9, BeOS.

12.48.3 clnt_pcreateerror

Gnulib module: —

Portability problems fixed by Gnulib:

Portability problems not fixed by Gnulib:

- This function is missing on some platforms: Minix 3.1.8, Cygwin, mingw, MSVC 9, BeOS.

12.48.4 clnt_perrno

Gnulib module: —

Portability problems fixed by Gnulib:

Portability problems not fixed by Gnulib:

- This function is missing on some platforms: Minix 3.1.8, Cygwin, mingw, MSVC 9, BeOS.

12.48.5 clnt_perror

Gnulib module: —

Portability problems fixed by Gnulib:

Portability problems not fixed by Gnulib:

- This function is missing on some platforms: Minix 3.1.8, Cygwin, mingw, MSVC 9, BeOS.

12.48.6 clnt_spcreateerror

Gnulib module: —

Portability problems fixed by Gnulib:

Portability problems not fixed by Gnulib:

- This function is missing on some platforms: Minix 3.1.8, Cygwin, mingw, MSVC 9, BeOS.

12.48.7 clnt_sperrno

Gnulib module: —

Portability problems fixed by Gnulib:

Portability problems not fixed by Gnulib:

- This function is missing on some platforms: Minix 3.1.8, Cygwin, mingw, MSVC 9, BeOS.

12.48.8 clnt_sperror

Gnulib module: —

Portability problems fixed by Gnulib:

Portability problems not fixed by Gnulib:

- This function is missing on some platforms: Minix 3.1.8, Cygwin, mingw, MSVC 9, BeOS.

12.48.9 clntraw_create

Gnulib module: —

Portability problems fixed by Gnulib:

Portability problems not fixed by Gnulib:

- This function is missing on some platforms: Minix 3.1.8, Cygwin, mingw, MSVC 9, BeOS.

12.48.10 clnttcp_create

Gnulib module: —

Portability problems fixed by Gnulib:

Portability problems not fixed by Gnulib:

- This function is missing on some platforms: Minix 3.1.8, Cygwin, mingw, MSVC 9, BeOS.

12.48.11 clntudp_bufcreate

Gnulib module: —

Portability problems fixed by Gnulib:

Portability problems not fixed by Gnulib:

- This function is missing on some platforms: Minix 3.1.8, Cygwin, mingw, MSVC 9, BeOS.

12.48.12 clntudp_create

Gnulib module: —

Portability problems fixed by Gnulib:

Portability problems not fixed by Gnulib:

- This function is missing on some platforms: Minix 3.1.8, Cygwin, mingw, MSVC 9, BeOS.

12.48.13 `clntunix_create`

Gnulib module: —

Portability problems fixed by Gnulib:

Portability problems not fixed by Gnulib:

- This function is missing on some platforms: Mac OS X 10.5, NetBSD 5.0, OpenBSD 3.8, Minix 3.1.8, AIX 5.1, HP-UX 11, IRIX 6.5, OSF/1 5.1, Solaris 11 2011-11, Cygwin, mingw, MSVC 9, Interix 3.5, BeOS.

12.48.14 `get_myaddress`

Gnulib module: —

Portability problems fixed by Gnulib:

Portability problems not fixed by Gnulib:

- This function is missing on some platforms: Minix 3.1.8, Cygwin, mingw, MSVC 9, BeOS.

12.48.15 `getrpcport`

Gnulib module: —

Portability problems fixed by Gnulib:

Portability problems not fixed by Gnulib:

- This function is missing on some platforms: Minix 3.1.8, AIX 4.3.2, IRIX 6.5, Cygwin, mingw, MSVC 9, BeOS.

12.48.16 `rpc_createerr`

Gnulib module: —

Portability problems fixed by Gnulib:

Portability problems not fixed by Gnulib:

- This variable is missing on some platforms: Minix 3.1.8, AIX 5.1, IRIX 6.5, OSF/1 5.1, Cygwin, mingw, MSVC 9, BeOS.

12.49 Glibc `<rpc/des_crypt.h>`

12.49.1 `cbc_crypt`

Gnulib module: —

Portability problems fixed by Gnulib:

Portability problems not fixed by Gnulib:

- This function is missing on some platforms: Mac OS X 10.5, NetBSD 5.0, OpenBSD 3.8, Minix 3.1.8, AIX 5.1, HP-UX 11, IRIX 6.5, OSF/1 5.1, Solaris 10, Cygwin, mingw, MSVC 9, Interix 3.5, BeOS.

12.49.2 des_setparity

Gnulib module: —

Portability problems fixed by Gnulib:

Portability problems not fixed by Gnulib:

- This function is missing on some platforms: Mac OS X 10.5, NetBSD 5.0, OpenBSD 3.8, Minix 3.1.8, IRIX 6.5, OSF/1 5.1, Cygwin, mingw, MSVC 9, Interix 3.5, BeOS.

12.49.3 ecb_crypt

Gnulib module: —

Portability problems fixed by Gnulib:

Portability problems not fixed by Gnulib:

- This function is missing on some platforms: Mac OS X 10.5, NetBSD 5.0, OpenBSD 3.8, Minix 3.1.8, AIX 5.1, HP-UX 11, IRIX 6.5, OSF/1 5.1, Solaris 10, Cygwin, mingw, MSVC 9, Interix 3.5, BeOS.

12.50 Glibc <rpc/key_prot.h>

12.50.1 xdr_cryptkeyarg

Gnulib module: —

Portability problems fixed by Gnulib:

Portability problems not fixed by Gnulib:

- This function is missing on some platforms: Mac OS X 10.5, NetBSD 5.0, OpenBSD 3.8, Minix 3.1.8, IRIX 6.5, Cygwin, mingw, MSVC 9, Interix 3.5, BeOS.

12.50.2 xdr_cryptkeyarg2

Gnulib module: —

Portability problems fixed by Gnulib:

Portability problems not fixed by Gnulib:

- This function is missing on some platforms: Mac OS X 10.5, NetBSD 5.0, OpenBSD 3.8, Minix 3.1.8, IRIX 6.5, OSF/1 5.1, Cygwin, mingw, MSVC 9, Interix 3.5, BeOS.

12.50.3 xdr_cryptkeyres

Gnulib module: —

Portability problems fixed by Gnulib:

Portability problems not fixed by Gnulib:

- This function is missing on some platforms: Mac OS X 10.5, NetBSD 5.0, OpenBSD 3.8, Minix 3.1.8, IRIX 6.5, Cygwin, mingw, MSVC 9, Interix 3.5, BeOS.

12.50.4 xdr_getcredres

Gnulib module: —

Portability problems fixed by Gnulib:

Portability problems not fixed by Gnulib:

- This function is missing on some platforms: Mac OS X 10.5, NetBSD 5.0, OpenBSD 3.8, Minix 3.1.8, IRIX 6.5, Cygwin, mingw, MSVC 9, Interix 3.5, BeOS.

12.50.5 xdr_key_netstarg

Gnulib module: —

Portability problems fixed by Gnulib:

Portability problems not fixed by Gnulib:

- This function is missing on some platforms: Mac OS X 10.5, NetBSD 5.0, OpenBSD 3.8, Minix 3.1.8, IRIX 6.5, OSF/1 5.1, Cygwin, mingw, MSVC 9, Interix 3.5, BeOS.

12.50.6 xdr_key_netstres

Gnulib module: —

Portability problems fixed by Gnulib:

Portability problems not fixed by Gnulib:

- This function is missing on some platforms: Mac OS X 10.5, NetBSD 5.0, OpenBSD 3.8, Minix 3.1.8, IRIX 6.5, OSF/1 5.1, Cygwin, mingw, MSVC 9, Interix 3.5, BeOS.

12.50.7 xdr_keybuf

Gnulib module: —

Portability problems fixed by Gnulib:

Portability problems not fixed by Gnulib:

- This function is missing on some platforms: Mac OS X 10.5, NetBSD 5.0, OpenBSD 3.8, Minix 3.1.8, IRIX 6.5, Cygwin, mingw, MSVC 9, Interix 3.5, BeOS.

12.50.8 xdr_keystatus

Gnulib module: —

Portability problems fixed by Gnulib:

Portability problems not fixed by Gnulib:

- This function is missing on some platforms: Mac OS X 10.5, NetBSD 5.0, OpenBSD 3.8, Minix 3.1.8, IRIX 6.5, Cygwin, mingw, MSVC 9, Interix 3.5, BeOS.

12.50.9 xdr_netnamestr

Gnulib module: —

Portability problems fixed by Gnulib:

Portability problems not fixed by Gnulib:

- This function is missing on some platforms: Mac OS X 10.5, NetBSD 5.0, OpenBSD 3.8, Minix 3.1.8, IRIX 6.5, Cygwin, mingw, MSVC 9, Interix 3.5, BeOS.

12.50.10 `xdr_unixcred`

Gnulib module: —

Portability problems fixed by Gnulib:

Portability problems not fixed by Gnulib:

- This function is missing on some platforms: Mac OS X 10.5, NetBSD 5.0, OpenBSD 3.8, Minix 3.1.8, IRIX 6.5, Cygwin, mingw, MSVC 9, Interix 3.5, BeOS.

12.51 Glibc `<rpc/netdb.h>`

12.51.1 `endrpcent`

Gnulib module: —

Portability problems fixed by Gnulib:

Portability problems not fixed by Gnulib:

- This function is missing on some platforms: Minix 3.1.8, Cygwin, mingw, MSVC 9, BeOS.

12.51.2 `getrpcbyname`

Gnulib module: —

Portability problems fixed by Gnulib:

Portability problems not fixed by Gnulib:

- This function is missing on some platforms: Minix 3.1.8, Cygwin, mingw, MSVC 9, BeOS.

12.51.3 `getrpcbyname_r`

Gnulib module: —

Portability problems fixed by Gnulib:

Portability problems not fixed by Gnulib:

- This function is missing on some platforms: Mac OS X 10.5, FreeBSD 6.0, NetBSD 5.0, OpenBSD 3.8, Minix 3.1.8, HP-UX 11, IRIX 5.3, OSF/1 5.1, Cygwin, mingw, MSVC 9, Interix 3.5, BeOS.

12.51.4 `getrpcbynumber`

Gnulib module: —

Portability problems fixed by Gnulib:

Portability problems not fixed by Gnulib:

- This function is missing on some platforms: Minix 3.1.8, Cygwin, mingw, MSVC 9, BeOS.

12.51.5 getrpcbynumber_r

Gnulib module: —

Portability problems fixed by Gnulib:

Portability problems not fixed by Gnulib:

- This function is missing on some platforms: Mac OS X 10.5, FreeBSD 6.0, NetBSD 5.0, OpenBSD 3.8, Minix 3.1.8, HP-UX 11, IRIX 5.3, OSF/1 5.1, Cygwin, mingw, MSVC 9, Interix 3.5, BeOS.

12.51.6 getrpcent

Gnulib module: —

Portability problems fixed by Gnulib:

Portability problems not fixed by Gnulib:

- This function is missing on some platforms: Minix 3.1.8, Cygwin, mingw, MSVC 9, BeOS.

12.51.7 getrpcent_r

Gnulib module: —

Portability problems fixed by Gnulib:

Portability problems not fixed by Gnulib:

- This function is missing on some platforms: Mac OS X 10.5, FreeBSD 6.0, NetBSD 5.0, OpenBSD 3.8, Minix 3.1.8, HP-UX 11, IRIX 5.3, OSF/1 5.1, Cygwin, mingw, MSVC 9, Interix 3.5, BeOS.

12.51.8 setrpcent

Gnulib module: —

Portability problems fixed by Gnulib:

Portability problems not fixed by Gnulib:

- This function is missing on some platforms: Minix 3.1.8, Cygwin, mingw, MSVC 9, BeOS.

12.52 Glibc <rpc/pmap_clnt.h>

12.52.1 clnt_broadcast

Gnulib module: —

Portability problems fixed by Gnulib:

Portability problems not fixed by Gnulib:

- This function is missing on some platforms: Minix 3.1.8, Cygwin, mingw, MSVC 9, BeOS.

12.52.2 `pmap_getmaps`

Gnulib module: —

Portability problems fixed by Gnulib:

Portability problems not fixed by Gnulib:

- This function is missing on some platforms: Minix 3.1.8, Cygwin, mingw, MSVC 9, BeOS.

12.52.3 `pmap_getport`

Gnulib module: —

Portability problems fixed by Gnulib:

Portability problems not fixed by Gnulib:

- This function is missing on some platforms: Minix 3.1.8, Cygwin, mingw, MSVC 9, BeOS.

12.52.4 `pmap_rmtcall`

Gnulib module: —

Portability problems fixed by Gnulib:

Portability problems not fixed by Gnulib:

- This function is missing on some platforms: Minix 3.1.8, Cygwin, mingw, MSVC 9, BeOS.

12.52.5 `pmap_set`

Gnulib module: —

Portability problems fixed by Gnulib:

Portability problems not fixed by Gnulib:

- This function is missing on some platforms: Minix 3.1.8, Cygwin, mingw, MSVC 9, BeOS.

12.52.6 `pmap_unset`

Gnulib module: —

Portability problems fixed by Gnulib:

Portability problems not fixed by Gnulib:

- This function is missing on some platforms: Minix 3.1.8, Cygwin, mingw, MSVC 9, BeOS.

12.53 Glibc `<rpc/pmap_prot.h>`

12.53.1 xdr_pmap

Gnulib module: —

Portability problems fixed by Gnulib:

Portability problems not fixed by Gnulib:

- This function is missing on some platforms: Minix 3.1.8, Cygwin, mingw, MSVC 9, BeOS.

12.53.2 xdr_pmaplist

Gnulib module: —

Portability problems fixed by Gnulib:

Portability problems not fixed by Gnulib:

- This function is missing on some platforms: Minix 3.1.8, Cygwin, mingw, MSVC 9, BeOS.

12.54 Glibc <rpc/pmap_rmt.h>

12.54.1 xdr_rmtcall_args

Gnulib module: —

Portability problems fixed by Gnulib:

Portability problems not fixed by Gnulib:

- This function is missing on some platforms: Minix 3.1.8, HP-UX 11, Solaris 11 2011-11, Cygwin, mingw, MSVC 9, BeOS.

12.54.2 xdr_rmtcallres

Gnulib module: —

Portability problems fixed by Gnulib:

Portability problems not fixed by Gnulib:

- This function is missing on some platforms: Minix 3.1.8, Cygwin, mingw, MSVC 9, BeOS.

12.55 Glibc <rpc/rpc_msg.h>

12.55.1 xdr_callhdr

Gnulib module: —

Portability problems fixed by Gnulib:

Portability problems not fixed by Gnulib:

- This function is missing on some platforms: Minix 3.1.8, Cygwin, mingw, MSVC 9, BeOS.

12.55.2 xdr_callmsg

Gnulib module: —

Portability problems fixed by Gnulib:

Portability problems not fixed by Gnulib:

- This function is missing on some platforms: Minix 3.1.8, Cygwin, mingw, MSVC 9, BeOS.

12.55.3 xdr_replymsg

Gnulib module: —

Portability problems fixed by Gnulib:

Portability problems not fixed by Gnulib:

- This function is missing on some platforms: Minix 3.1.8, Cygwin, mingw, MSVC 9, BeOS.

12.56 Glibc <rpc/svc.h>

12.56.1 svc_exit

Gnulib module: —

Portability problems fixed by Gnulib:

Portability problems not fixed by Gnulib:

- This function is missing on some platforms: Mac OS X 10.5, OpenBSD 3.8, Minix 3.1.8, AIX 5.1, IRIX 6.5, OSF/1 5.1, Cygwin, mingw, MSVC 9, Interix 3.5, BeOS.

12.56.2 svc_fdset

Gnulib module: —

Portability problems fixed by Gnulib:

Portability problems not fixed by Gnulib:

- This variable is missing on some platforms: Minix 3.1.8, AIX 5.1, HP-UX 11, IRIX 6.5, OSF/1 5.1, Cygwin, mingw, MSVC 9, BeOS.

12.56.3 svc_getreq

Gnulib module: —

Portability problems fixed by Gnulib:

Portability problems not fixed by Gnulib:

- This function is missing on some platforms: Minix 3.1.8, Cygwin, mingw, MSVC 9, BeOS.

12.56.4 svc_getreq_common

Gnulib module: —

Portability problems fixed by Gnulib:

Portability problems not fixed by Gnulib:

- This function is missing on some platforms: Mac OS X 10.5, Minix 3.1.8, AIX 5.1, IRIX 6.5, OSF/1 5.1, Cygwin, mingw, MSVC 9, Interix 3.5, BeOS.

12.56.5 svc_getreq_poll

Gnulib module: —

Portability problems fixed by Gnulib:

Portability problems not fixed by Gnulib:

- This function is missing on some platforms: Mac OS X 10.5, Minix 3.1.8, IRIX 6.5, OSF/1 5.1, Cygwin, mingw, MSVC 9, Interix 3.5, BeOS.

12.56.6 svc_getreqset

Gnulib module: —

Portability problems fixed by Gnulib:

Portability problems not fixed by Gnulib:

- This function is missing on some platforms: Minix 3.1.8, Cygwin, mingw, MSVC 9, BeOS.

12.56.7 svc_max_pollfd

Gnulib module: —

Portability problems fixed by Gnulib:

Portability problems not fixed by Gnulib:

- This variable is missing on some platforms: Mac OS X 10.5, FreeBSD 6.0, NetBSD 5.0, Minix 3.1.8, AIX 5.1, HP-UX 11, IRIX 6.5, OSF/1 5.1, Cygwin, mingw, MSVC 9, Interix 3.5, BeOS.

12.56.8 svc_pollfd

Gnulib module: —

Portability problems fixed by Gnulib:

Portability problems not fixed by Gnulib:

- This variable is missing on some platforms: Mac OS X 10.5, FreeBSD 6.0, NetBSD 5.0, Minix 3.1.8, AIX 5.1, HP-UX 11, IRIX 6.5, OSF/1 5.1, Cygwin, mingw, MSVC 9, Interix 3.5, BeOS.

12.56.9 `svc_register`

Gnulib module: —

Portability problems fixed by Gnulib:

Portability problems not fixed by Gnulib:

- This function is missing on some platforms: Minix 3.1.8, Cygwin, mingw, MSVC 9, BeOS.

12.56.10 `svc_run`

Gnulib module: —

Portability problems fixed by Gnulib:

Portability problems not fixed by Gnulib:

- This function is missing on some platforms: Minix 3.1.8, Cygwin, mingw, MSVC 9, BeOS.

12.56.11 `svc_sendreply`

Gnulib module: —

Portability problems fixed by Gnulib:

Portability problems not fixed by Gnulib:

- This function is missing on some platforms: Minix 3.1.8, Cygwin, mingw, MSVC 9, BeOS.

12.56.12 `svc_unregister`

Gnulib module: —

Portability problems fixed by Gnulib:

Portability problems not fixed by Gnulib:

- This function is missing on some platforms: Minix 3.1.8, Cygwin, mingw, MSVC 9, BeOS.

12.56.13 `svcerr_auth`

Gnulib module: —

Portability problems fixed by Gnulib:

Portability problems not fixed by Gnulib:

- This function is missing on some platforms: Minix 3.1.8, Cygwin, mingw, MSVC 9, BeOS.

12.56.14 `svcerr_decode`

Gnulib module: —

Portability problems fixed by Gnulib:

Portability problems not fixed by Gnulib:

- This function is missing on some platforms: Minix 3.1.8, Cygwin, mingw, MSVC 9, BeOS.

12.56.15 svcerr_noproc

Gnulib module: —

Portability problems fixed by Gnulib:

Portability problems not fixed by Gnulib:

- This function is missing on some platforms: Minix 3.1.8, Cygwin, mingw, MSVC 9, BeOS.

12.56.16 svcerr_noprog

Gnulib module: —

Portability problems fixed by Gnulib:

Portability problems not fixed by Gnulib:

- This function is missing on some platforms: Minix 3.1.8, Cygwin, mingw, MSVC 9, BeOS.

12.56.17 svcerr_progvers

Gnulib module: —

Portability problems fixed by Gnulib:

Portability problems not fixed by Gnulib:

- This function is missing on some platforms: Minix 3.1.8, Cygwin, mingw, MSVC 9, BeOS.

12.56.18 svcerr_systemerr

Gnulib module: —

Portability problems fixed by Gnulib:

Portability problems not fixed by Gnulib:

- This function is missing on some platforms: Minix 3.1.8, Cygwin, mingw, MSVC 9, BeOS.

12.56.19 svcerr_weakauth

Gnulib module: —

Portability problems fixed by Gnulib:

Portability problems not fixed by Gnulib:

- This function is missing on some platforms: Minix 3.1.8, Cygwin, mingw, MSVC 9, BeOS.

12.56.20 svcraw_create

Gnulib module: —

Portability problems fixed by Gnulib:

Portability problems not fixed by Gnulib:

- This function is missing on some platforms: Minix 3.1.8, Cygwin, mingw, MSVC 9, BeOS.

12.56.21 svctcp_create

Gnulib module: —

Portability problems fixed by Gnulib:

Portability problems not fixed by Gnulib:

- This function is missing on some platforms: Minix 3.1.8, Cygwin, mingw, MSVC 9, BeOS.

12.56.22 svcudp_bufcreate

Gnulib module: —

Portability problems fixed by Gnulib:

Portability problems not fixed by Gnulib:

- This function is missing on some platforms: Minix 3.1.8, Cygwin, mingw, MSVC 9, BeOS.

12.56.23 svcudp_create

Gnulib module: —

Portability problems fixed by Gnulib:

Portability problems not fixed by Gnulib:

- This function is missing on some platforms: Minix 3.1.8, Cygwin, mingw, MSVC 9, BeOS.

12.56.24 svcunix_create

Gnulib module: —

Portability problems fixed by Gnulib:

Portability problems not fixed by Gnulib:

- This function is missing on some platforms: Mac OS X 10.5, NetBSD 5.0, OpenBSD 3.8, Minix 3.1.8, AIX 5.1, HP-UX 11, IRIX 6.5, OSF/1 5.1, Solaris 11 2011-11, Cygwin, mingw, MSVC 9, Interix 3.5, BeOS.

12.56.25 xprt_register

Gnulib module: —

Portability problems fixed by Gnulib:

Portability problems not fixed by Gnulib:

- This function is missing on some platforms: Minix 3.1.8, Cygwin, mingw, MSVC 9, BeOS.

12.56.26 xprt_unregister

Gnulib module: —

Portability problems fixed by Gnulib:

Portability problems not fixed by Gnulib:

- This function is missing on some platforms: Minix 3.1.8, Cygwin, mingw, MSVC 9, BeOS.

12.57 Glibc `<rpc/xdr.h>`

12.57.1 `xdr_array`

Gnulib module: —

Portability problems fixed by Gnulib:

Portability problems not fixed by Gnulib:

- This function is missing on some platforms: Minix 3.1.8, Cygwin 1.7.4, mingw, MSVC 9, BeOS.

12.57.2 `xdr_bool`

Gnulib module: —

Portability problems fixed by Gnulib:

Portability problems not fixed by Gnulib:

- This function is missing on some platforms: Minix 3.1.8, Cygwin 1.7.4, mingw, MSVC 9, BeOS.

12.57.3 `xdr_bytes`

Gnulib module: —

Portability problems fixed by Gnulib:

Portability problems not fixed by Gnulib:

- This function is missing on some platforms: Minix 3.1.8, Cygwin 1.7.4, mingw, MSVC 9, BeOS.

12.57.4 `xdr_char`

Gnulib module: —

Portability problems fixed by Gnulib:

Portability problems not fixed by Gnulib:

- This function is missing on some platforms: Minix 3.1.8, Cygwin 1.7.4, mingw, MSVC 9, BeOS.

12.57.5 `xdr_double`

Gnulib module: —

Portability problems fixed by Gnulib:

Portability problems not fixed by Gnulib:

- This function is missing on some platforms: Minix 3.1.8, Cygwin 1.7.4, mingw, MSVC 9, BeOS.

12.57.6 `xdr_enum`

Gnulib module: —

Portability problems fixed by Gnulib:

Portability problems not fixed by Gnulib:

- This function is missing on some platforms: Minix 3.1.8, Cygwin 1.7.4, mingw, MSVC 9, BeOS.

12.57.7 `xdr_float`

Gnulib module: —

Portability problems fixed by Gnulib:

Portability problems not fixed by Gnulib:

- This function is missing on some platforms: Minix 3.1.8, Cygwin 1.7.4, mingw, MSVC 9, BeOS.

12.57.8 `xdr_free`

Gnulib module: —

Portability problems fixed by Gnulib:

Portability problems not fixed by Gnulib:

- This function is missing on some platforms: Minix 3.1.8, Cygwin 1.7.4, mingw, MSVC 9, BeOS.

12.57.9 `xdr_hyper`

Gnulib module: —

Portability problems fixed by Gnulib:

Portability problems not fixed by Gnulib:

- This function is missing on some platforms: Mac OS X 10.3, OpenBSD 3.8, Minix 3.1.8, Cygwin 1.7.4, mingw, MSVC 9, Interix 3.5, BeOS.

12.57.10 `xdr_int`

Gnulib module: —

Portability problems fixed by Gnulib:

Portability problems not fixed by Gnulib:

- This function is missing on some platforms: Minix 3.1.8, Cygwin 1.7.4, mingw, MSVC 9, BeOS.

12.57.11 `xdr_int16_t`

Gnulib module: —

Portability problems fixed by Gnulib:

Portability problems not fixed by Gnulib:

- This function is missing on some platforms: Mac OS X 10.3, Minix 3.1.8, AIX 5.1, HP-UX 11, IRIX 6.5, OSF/1 5.1, Cygwin 1.7.4, mingw, MSVC 9, Interix 3.5, BeOS.

12.57.12 xdr_int32_t

Gnulib module: —

Portability problems fixed by Gnulib:

Portability problems not fixed by Gnulib:

- This function is missing on some platforms: Mac OS X 10.3, Minix 3.1.8, AIX 5.1, HP-UX 11, IRIX 6.5, OSF/1 5.1, Cygwin 1.7.4, mingw, MSVC 9, Interix 3.5, BeOS.

12.57.13 xdr_int64_t

Gnulib module: —

Portability problems fixed by Gnulib:

Portability problems not fixed by Gnulib:

- This function is missing on some platforms: Mac OS X 10.3, OpenBSD 3.8, Minix 3.1.8, AIX 5.1, HP-UX 11, IRIX 6.5, OSF/1 5.1, Cygwin 1.7.4, mingw, MSVC 9, Interix 3.5, BeOS.

12.57.14 xdr_int8_t

Gnulib module: —

Portability problems fixed by Gnulib:

Portability problems not fixed by Gnulib:

- This function is missing on some platforms: Mac OS X 10.5, FreeBSD 6.0, NetBSD 5.0, OpenBSD 3.8, Minix 3.1.8, AIX 5.1, HP-UX 11, IRIX 6.5, OSF/1 5.1, Cygwin 1.7.4, mingw, MSVC 9, Interix 3.5, BeOS.

12.57.15 xdr_long

Gnulib module: —

Portability problems fixed by Gnulib:

Portability problems not fixed by Gnulib:

- This function is missing on some platforms: Minix 3.1.8, Cygwin 1.7.4, mingw, MSVC 9, BeOS.

12.57.16 xdr_longlong_t

Gnulib module: —

Portability problems fixed by Gnulib:

Portability problems not fixed by Gnulib:

- This function is missing on some platforms: Mac OS X 10.3, OpenBSD 3.8, Minix 3.1.8, Cygwin 1.7.4, mingw, MSVC 9, Interix 3.5, BeOS.

12.57.17 xdr_netobj

Gnulib module: —

Portability problems fixed by Gnulib:

Portability problems not fixed by Gnulib:

- This function is missing on some platforms: Minix 3.1.8, Cygwin 1.7.4, mingw, MSVC 9, BeOS.

12.57.18 xdr_opaque

Gnulib module: —

Portability problems fixed by Gnulib:

Portability problems not fixed by Gnulib:

- This function is missing on some platforms: Minix 3.1.8, Cygwin 1.7.4, mingw, MSVC 9, BeOS.

12.57.19 xdr_pointer

Gnulib module: —

Portability problems fixed by Gnulib:

Portability problems not fixed by Gnulib:

- This function is missing on some platforms: Minix 3.1.8, Cygwin 1.7.4, mingw, MSVC 9, BeOS.

12.57.20 xdr_quad_t

Gnulib module: —

Portability problems fixed by Gnulib:

Portability problems not fixed by Gnulib:

- This function is missing on all non-glibc platforms: Mac OS X 10.5, FreeBSD 6.0, NetBSD 5.0, OpenBSD 3.8, Minix 3.1.8, AIX 5.1, HP-UX 11, IRIX 6.5, OSF/1 5.1, Solaris 11 2011-11, Cygwin, mingw, MSVC 9, Interix 3.5, BeOS.

12.57.21 xdr_reference

Gnulib module: —

Portability problems fixed by Gnulib:

Portability problems not fixed by Gnulib:

- This function is missing on some platforms: Minix 3.1.8, Cygwin 1.7.4, mingw, MSVC 9, BeOS.

12.57.22 xdr_short

Gnulib module: —

Portability problems fixed by Gnulib:

Portability problems not fixed by Gnulib:

- This function is missing on some platforms: Minix 3.1.8, Cygwin 1.7.4, mingw, MSVC 9, BeOS.

12.57.23 `xdr_sizeof`

Gnulib module: —

Portability problems fixed by Gnulib:

Portability problems not fixed by Gnulib:

- This function is missing on some platforms: Mac OS X 10.3, FreeBSD 6.0, NetBSD 5.0, OpenBSD 3.8, Minix 3.1.8, IRIX 6.5, OSF/1 5.1, Cygwin 1.7.4, mingw, MSVC 9, Interix 3.5, BeOS.

12.57.24 `xdr_string`

Gnulib module: —

Portability problems fixed by Gnulib:

Portability problems not fixed by Gnulib:

- This function is missing on some platforms: Minix 3.1.8, Cygwin 1.7.4, mingw, MSVC 9, BeOS.

12.57.25 `xdr_u_char`

Gnulib module: —

Portability problems fixed by Gnulib:

Portability problems not fixed by Gnulib:

- This function is missing on some platforms: Minix 3.1.8, Cygwin 1.7.4, mingw, MSVC 9, BeOS.

12.57.26 `xdr_u_hyper`

Gnulib module: —

Portability problems fixed by Gnulib:

Portability problems not fixed by Gnulib:

- This function is missing on some platforms: Mac OS X 10.3, OpenBSD 3.8, Minix 3.1.8, IRIX 5.3, Cygwin 1.7.4, mingw, MSVC 9, Interix 3.5, BeOS.

12.57.27 `xdr_u_int`

Gnulib module: —

Portability problems fixed by Gnulib:

Portability problems not fixed by Gnulib:

- This function is missing on some platforms: Minix 3.1.8, Cygwin 1.7.4, mingw, MSVC 9, BeOS.

12.57.28 `xdr_u_long`

Gnulib module: —

Portability problems fixed by Gnulib:

Portability problems not fixed by Gnulib:

- This function is missing on some platforms: Minix 3.1.8, Cygwin 1.7.4, mingw, MSVC 9, BeOS.

12.57.29 xdr_u_longlong_t

Gnulib module: —

Portability problems fixed by Gnulib:

Portability problems not fixed by Gnulib:

- This function is missing on some platforms: Mac OS X 10.3, OpenBSD 3.8, Minix 3.1.8, Cygwin 1.7.4, mingw, MSVC 9, Interix 3.5, BeOS.

12.57.30 xdr_u_quad_t

Gnulib module: —

Portability problems fixed by Gnulib:

Portability problems not fixed by Gnulib:

- This function is missing on all non-glibc platforms: Mac OS X 10.5, FreeBSD 6.0, NetBSD 5.0, OpenBSD 3.8, Minix 3.1.8, AIX 5.1, HP-UX 11, IRIX 6.5, OSF/1 5.1, Solaris 11 2011-11, Cygwin, mingw, MSVC 9, Interix 3.5, BeOS.

12.57.31 xdr_u_short

Gnulib module: —

Portability problems fixed by Gnulib:

Portability problems not fixed by Gnulib:

- This function is missing on some platforms: Minix 3.1.8, Cygwin 1.7.4, mingw, MSVC 9, BeOS.

12.57.32 xdr_uint16_t

Gnulib module: —

Portability problems fixed by Gnulib:

Portability problems not fixed by Gnulib:

- This function is missing on some platforms: Mac OS X 10.5, FreeBSD 6.0, NetBSD 5.0, OpenBSD 3.8, Minix 3.1.8, AIX 5.1, HP-UX 11, IRIX 6.5, OSF/1 5.1, Cygwin 1.7.4, mingw, MSVC 9, Interix 3.5, BeOS.
- This function is not declared in the header on some platforms: Cygwin 1.7.5.

12.57.33 xdr_uint32_t

Gnulib module: —

Portability problems fixed by Gnulib:

Portability problems not fixed by Gnulib:

- This function is missing on some platforms: Mac OS X 10.5, FreeBSD 6.0, NetBSD 5.0, OpenBSD 3.8, Minix 3.1.8, AIX 5.1, HP-UX 11, IRIX 6.5, OSF/1 5.1, Cygwin, mingw, MSVC 9, Interix 3.5, BeOS.
- This function is not declared in the header on some platforms: Cygwin 1.7.5.

12.57.34 xdr_uint64_t

Gnulib module: —

Portability problems fixed by Gnulib:

Portability problems not fixed by Gnulib:

- This function is missing on some platforms: Mac OS X 10.5, FreeBSD 6.0, NetBSD 5.0, OpenBSD 3.8, Minix 3.1.8, AIX 5.1, HP-UX 11, IRIX 6.5, OSF/1 5.1, Cygwin, mingw, MSVC 9, Interix 3.5, BeOS.
- This function is not declared in the header on some platforms: Cygwin 1.7.5.

12.57.35 xdr_uint8_t

Gnulib module: —

Portability problems fixed by Gnulib:

Portability problems not fixed by Gnulib:

- This function is missing on some platforms: Mac OS X 10.5, FreeBSD 6.0, NetBSD 5.0, OpenBSD 3.8, Minix 3.1.8, AIX 5.1, HP-UX 11, IRIX 6.5, OSF/1 5.1, Cygwin, mingw, MSVC 9, Interix 3.5, BeOS.
- This function is not declared in the header on some platforms: Cygwin 1.7.5.

12.57.36 xdr_union

Gnulib module: —

Portability problems fixed by Gnulib:

Portability problems not fixed by Gnulib:

- This function is missing on some platforms: Minix 3.1.8, Cygwin 1.7.4, mingw, MSVC 9, BeOS.

12.57.37 xdr_vector

Gnulib module: —

Portability problems fixed by Gnulib:

Portability problems not fixed by Gnulib:

- This function is missing on some platforms: Minix 3.1.8, Cygwin 1.7.4, mingw, MSVC 9, BeOS.

12.57.38 xdr_void

Gnulib module: —

Portability problems fixed by Gnulib:

Portability problems not fixed by Gnulib:

- This function is missing on some platforms: Minix 3.1.8, Cygwin 1.7.4, mingw, MSVC 9, BeOS.

12.57.39 xdr_wrapstring

Gnulib module: —

Portability problems fixed by Gnulib:

Portability problems not fixed by Gnulib:

- This function is missing on some platforms: Minix 3.1.8, Cygwin 1.7.4, mingw, MSVC 9, BeOS.

12.57.40 xdrmem_create

Gnulib module: —

Portability problems fixed by Gnulib:

Portability problems not fixed by Gnulib:

- This function is missing on some platforms: Minix 3.1.8, Cygwin 1.7.4, mingw, MSVC 9, BeOS.

12.57.41 xdrrec_create

Gnulib module: —

Portability problems fixed by Gnulib:

Portability problems not fixed by Gnulib:

- This function is missing on some platforms: Minix 3.1.8, Cygwin 1.7.4, mingw, MSVC 9, BeOS.

12.57.42 xdrrec_endofrecord

Gnulib module: —

Portability problems fixed by Gnulib:

Portability problems not fixed by Gnulib:

- This function is missing on some platforms: Minix 3.1.8, Cygwin 1.7.4, mingw, MSVC 9, BeOS.

12.57.43 xdrrec_eof

Gnulib module: —

Portability problems fixed by Gnulib:

Portability problems not fixed by Gnulib:

- This function is missing on some platforms: Minix 3.1.8, Cygwin 1.7.4, mingw, MSVC 9, BeOS.

12.57.44 xdrrec_skiprecord

Gnulib module: —

Portability problems fixed by Gnulib:

Portability problems not fixed by Gnulib:

- This function is missing on some platforms: Minix 3.1.8, Cygwin 1.7.4, mingw, MSVC 9, BeOS.

12.57.45 `xdrstdio_create`

Gnulib module: —

Portability problems fixed by Gnulib:

Portability problems not fixed by Gnulib:

- This function is missing on some platforms: Minix 3.1.8, Cygwin 1.7.4, mingw, MSVC 9, BeOS.

12.58 Glibc `<rpcsvc/nislib.h>`

12.58.1 `nis_add`

Gnulib module: —

Portability problems fixed by Gnulib:

Portability problems not fixed by Gnulib:

- This function is missing on some platforms: Mac OS X 10.5, FreeBSD 6.0, NetBSD 5.0, OpenBSD 3.8, Minix 3.1.8, IRIX 6.5, OSF/1 5.1, Solaris 11 2011-11, Cygwin, mingw, MSVC 9, Interix 3.5, BeOS.

12.58.2 `nis_add_entry`

Gnulib module: —

Portability problems fixed by Gnulib:

Portability problems not fixed by Gnulib:

- This function is missing on some platforms: Mac OS X 10.5, FreeBSD 6.0, NetBSD 5.0, OpenBSD 3.8, Minix 3.1.8, IRIX 6.5, OSF/1 5.1, Solaris 11 2011-11, Cygwin, mingw, MSVC 9, Interix 3.5, BeOS.

12.58.3 `nis_addmember`

Gnulib module: —

Portability problems fixed by Gnulib:

Portability problems not fixed by Gnulib:

- This function is missing on some platforms: Mac OS X 10.5, FreeBSD 6.0, NetBSD 5.0, OpenBSD 3.8, Minix 3.1.8, IRIX 6.5, OSF/1 5.1, Solaris 11 2011-11, Cygwin, mingw, MSVC 9, Interix 3.5, BeOS.

12.58.4 `nis_checkpoint`

Gnulib module: —

Portability problems fixed by Gnulib:

Portability problems not fixed by Gnulib:

- This function is missing on some platforms: Mac OS X 10.5, FreeBSD 6.0, NetBSD 5.0, OpenBSD 3.8, Minix 3.1.8, IRIX 6.5, OSF/1 5.1, Solaris 11 2011-11, Cygwin, mingw, MSVC 9, Interix 3.5, BeOS.

12.58.5 nis_clone_object

Gnulib module: —

Portability problems fixed by Gnulib:

Portability problems not fixed by Gnulib:

- This function is missing on some platforms: Mac OS X 10.5, FreeBSD 6.0, NetBSD 5.0, OpenBSD 3.8, Minix 3.1.8, IRIX 6.5, OSF/1 5.1, Cygwin, mingw, MSVC 9, Interix 3.5, BeOS.

12.58.6 nis_creategroup

Gnulib module: —

Portability problems fixed by Gnulib:

Portability problems not fixed by Gnulib:

- This function is missing on some platforms: Mac OS X 10.5, FreeBSD 6.0, NetBSD 5.0, OpenBSD 3.8, Minix 3.1.8, IRIX 6.5, OSF/1 5.1, Solaris 11 2011-11, Cygwin, mingw, MSVC 9, Interix 3.5, BeOS.

12.58.7 nis_destroy_object

Gnulib module: —

Portability problems fixed by Gnulib:

Portability problems not fixed by Gnulib:

- This function is missing on some platforms: Mac OS X 10.5, FreeBSD 6.0, NetBSD 5.0, OpenBSD 3.8, Minix 3.1.8, IRIX 6.5, OSF/1 5.1, Cygwin, mingw, MSVC 9, Interix 3.5, BeOS.

12.58.8 nis_destroygroup

Gnulib module: —

Portability problems fixed by Gnulib:

Portability problems not fixed by Gnulib:

- This function is missing on some platforms: Mac OS X 10.5, FreeBSD 6.0, NetBSD 5.0, OpenBSD 3.8, Minix 3.1.8, IRIX 6.5, OSF/1 5.1, Solaris 11 2011-11, Cygwin, mingw, MSVC 9, Interix 3.5, BeOS.

12.58.9 nis_dir_cmp

Gnulib module: —

Portability problems fixed by Gnulib:

Portability problems not fixed by Gnulib:

- This function is missing on some platforms: Mac OS X 10.5, FreeBSD 6.0, NetBSD 5.0, OpenBSD 3.8, Minix 3.1.8, IRIX 6.5, OSF/1 5.1, Cygwin, mingw, MSVC 9, Interix 3.5, BeOS.

12.58.10 nis_domain_of

Gnulib module: —

Portability problems fixed by Gnulib:

Portability problems not fixed by Gnulib:

- This function is missing on some platforms: Mac OS X 10.5, FreeBSD 6.0, NetBSD 5.0, OpenBSD 3.8, Minix 3.1.8, IRIX 6.5, OSF/1 5.1, Cygwin, mingw, MSVC 9, Interix 3.5, BeOS.

12.58.11 nis_domain_of_r

Gnulib module: —

Portability problems fixed by Gnulib:

Portability problems not fixed by Gnulib:

- This function is missing on all non-glibc platforms: Mac OS X 10.5, FreeBSD 6.0, NetBSD 5.0, OpenBSD 3.8, Minix 3.1.8, AIX 5.1, HP-UX 11, IRIX 6.5, OSF/1 5.1, Solaris 11 2011-11, Cygwin, mingw, MSVC 9, Interix 3.5, BeOS.

12.58.12 nis_first_entry

Gnulib module: —

Portability problems fixed by Gnulib:

Portability problems not fixed by Gnulib:

- This function is missing on some platforms: Mac OS X 10.5, FreeBSD 6.0, NetBSD 5.0, OpenBSD 3.8, Minix 3.1.8, IRIX 6.5, OSF/1 5.1, Solaris 11 2011-11, Cygwin, mingw, MSVC 9, Interix 3.5, BeOS.

12.58.13 nis_freenames

Gnulib module: —

Portability problems fixed by Gnulib:

Portability problems not fixed by Gnulib:

- This function is missing on some platforms: Mac OS X 10.5, FreeBSD 6.0, NetBSD 5.0, OpenBSD 3.8, Minix 3.1.8, IRIX 6.5, OSF/1 5.1, Solaris 11 2011-11, Cygwin, mingw, MSVC 9, Interix 3.5, BeOS.

12.58.14 nis_freeresult

Gnulib module: —

Portability problems fixed by Gnulib:

Portability problems not fixed by Gnulib:

- This function is missing on some platforms: Mac OS X 10.5, FreeBSD 6.0, NetBSD 5.0, OpenBSD 3.8, Minix 3.1.8, IRIX 6.5, OSF/1 5.1, Solaris 11 2011-11, Cygwin, mingw, MSVC 9, Interix 3.5, BeOS.

12.58.15 nis_freeservlist

Gnulib module: —

Portability problems fixed by Gnulib:

Portability problems not fixed by Gnulib:

- This function is missing on some platforms: Mac OS X 10.5, FreeBSD 6.0, NetBSD 5.0, OpenBSD 3.8, Minix 3.1.8, IRIX 6.5, OSF/1 5.1, Solaris 11 2011-11, Cygwin, mingw, MSVC 9, Interix 3.5, BeOS.

12.58.16 nis_freetags

Gnulib module: —

Portability problems fixed by Gnulib:

Portability problems not fixed by Gnulib:

- This function is missing on some platforms: Mac OS X 10.5, FreeBSD 6.0, NetBSD 5.0, OpenBSD 3.8, Minix 3.1.8, IRIX 6.5, OSF/1 5.1, Solaris 11 2011-11, Cygwin, mingw, MSVC 9, Interix 3.5, BeOS.

12.58.17 nis_getnames

Gnulib module: —

Portability problems fixed by Gnulib:

Portability problems not fixed by Gnulib:

- This function is missing on some platforms: Mac OS X 10.5, FreeBSD 6.0, NetBSD 5.0, OpenBSD 3.8, Minix 3.1.8, IRIX 6.5, OSF/1 5.1, Solaris 11 2011-11, Cygwin, mingw, MSVC 9, Interix 3.5, BeOS.

12.58.18 nis_getservlist

Gnulib module: —

Portability problems fixed by Gnulib:

Portability problems not fixed by Gnulib:

- This function is missing on some platforms: Mac OS X 10.5, FreeBSD 6.0, NetBSD 5.0, OpenBSD 3.8, Minix 3.1.8, IRIX 6.5, OSF/1 5.1, Solaris 11 2011-11, Cygwin, mingw, MSVC 9, Interix 3.5, BeOS.

12.58.19 nis_ismember

Gnulib module: —

Portability problems fixed by Gnulib:

Portability problems not fixed by Gnulib:

- This function is missing on some platforms: Mac OS X 10.5, FreeBSD 6.0, NetBSD 5.0, OpenBSD 3.8, Minix 3.1.8, IRIX 6.5, OSF/1 5.1, Solaris 11 2011-11, Cygwin, mingw, MSVC 9, Interix 3.5, BeOS.

12.58.20 `nis_leaf_of`

Gnulib module: —

Portability problems fixed by Gnulib:

Portability problems not fixed by Gnulib:

- This function is missing on some platforms: Mac OS X 10.5, FreeBSD 6.0, NetBSD 5.0, OpenBSD 3.8, Minix 3.1.8, IRIX 6.5, OSF/1 5.1, Cygwin, mingw, MSVC 9, Interix 3.5, BeOS.

12.58.21 `nis_leaf_of_r`

Gnulib module: —

Portability problems fixed by Gnulib:

Portability problems not fixed by Gnulib:

- This function is missing on some platforms: Mac OS X 10.5, FreeBSD 6.0, NetBSD 5.0, OpenBSD 3.8, Minix 3.1.8, AIX 5.1, IRIX 6.5, OSF/1 5.1, Cygwin, mingw, MSVC 9, Interix 3.5, BeOS.

12.58.22 `nis_lerror`

Gnulib module: —

Portability problems fixed by Gnulib:

Portability problems not fixed by Gnulib:

- This function is missing on some platforms: Mac OS X 10.5, FreeBSD 6.0, NetBSD 5.0, OpenBSD 3.8, Minix 3.1.8, IRIX 6.5, OSF/1 5.1, Solaris 11 2011-11, Cygwin, mingw, MSVC 9, Interix 3.5, BeOS.

12.58.23 `nis_list`

Gnulib module: —

Portability problems fixed by Gnulib:

Portability problems not fixed by Gnulib:

- This function is missing on some platforms: Mac OS X 10.5, FreeBSD 6.0, NetBSD 5.0, OpenBSD 3.8, Minix 3.1.8, IRIX 6.5, OSF/1 5.1, Solaris 11 2011-11, Cygwin, mingw, MSVC 9, Interix 3.5, BeOS.

12.58.24 `nis_local_directory`

Gnulib module: —

Portability problems fixed by Gnulib:

Portability problems not fixed by Gnulib:

- This function is missing on some platforms: Mac OS X 10.5, FreeBSD 6.0, NetBSD 5.0, OpenBSD 3.8, Minix 3.1.8, IRIX 6.5, OSF/1 5.1, Cygwin, mingw, MSVC 9, Interix 3.5, BeOS.

12.58.25 `nis_local_group`

Gnulib module: —

Portability problems fixed by Gnulib:

Portability problems not fixed by Gnulib:

- This function is missing on some platforms: Mac OS X 10.5, FreeBSD 6.0, NetBSD 5.0, OpenBSD 3.8, Minix 3.1.8, IRIX 6.5, OSF/1 5.1, Cygwin, mingw, MSVC 9, Interix 3.5, BeOS.

12.58.26 `nis_local_host`

Gnulib module: —

Portability problems fixed by Gnulib:

Portability problems not fixed by Gnulib:

- This function is missing on some platforms: Mac OS X 10.5, FreeBSD 6.0, NetBSD 5.0, OpenBSD 3.8, Minix 3.1.8, IRIX 6.5, OSF/1 5.1, Cygwin, mingw, MSVC 9, Interix 3.5, BeOS.

12.58.27 `nis_local_principal`

Gnulib module: —

Portability problems fixed by Gnulib:

Portability problems not fixed by Gnulib:

- This function is missing on some platforms: Mac OS X 10.5, FreeBSD 6.0, NetBSD 5.0, OpenBSD 3.8, Minix 3.1.8, IRIX 6.5, OSF/1 5.1, Solaris 11 2011-11, Cygwin, mingw, MSVC 9, Interix 3.5, BeOS.

12.58.28 `nis_lookup`

Gnulib module: —

Portability problems fixed by Gnulib:

Portability problems not fixed by Gnulib:

- This function is missing on some platforms: Mac OS X 10.5, FreeBSD 6.0, NetBSD 5.0, OpenBSD 3.8, Minix 3.1.8, IRIX 6.5, OSF/1 5.1, Solaris 11 2011-11, Cygwin, mingw, MSVC 9, Interix 3.5, BeOS.

12.58.29 `nis_mkdir`

Gnulib module: —

Portability problems fixed by Gnulib:

Portability problems not fixed by Gnulib:

- This function is missing on some platforms: Mac OS X 10.5, FreeBSD 6.0, NetBSD 5.0, OpenBSD 3.8, Minix 3.1.8, IRIX 6.5, OSF/1 5.1, Solaris 11 2011-11, Cygwin, mingw, MSVC 9, Interix 3.5, BeOS.

12.58.30 nis_modify

Gnulib module: —

Portability problems fixed by Gnulib:

Portability problems not fixed by Gnulib:

- This function is missing on some platforms: Mac OS X 10.5, FreeBSD 6.0, NetBSD 5.0, OpenBSD 3.8, Minix 3.1.8, IRIX 6.5, OSF/1 5.1, Solaris 11 2011-11, Cygwin, mingw, MSVC 9, Interix 3.5, BeOS.

12.58.31 nis_modify_entry

Gnulib module: —

Portability problems fixed by Gnulib:

Portability problems not fixed by Gnulib:

- This function is missing on some platforms: Mac OS X 10.5, FreeBSD 6.0, NetBSD 5.0, OpenBSD 3.8, Minix 3.1.8, IRIX 6.5, OSF/1 5.1, Solaris 11 2011-11, Cygwin, mingw, MSVC 9, Interix 3.5, BeOS.

12.58.32 nis_name_of

Gnulib module: —

Portability problems fixed by Gnulib:

Portability problems not fixed by Gnulib:

- This function is missing on some platforms: Mac OS X 10.5, FreeBSD 6.0, NetBSD 5.0, OpenBSD 3.8, Minix 3.1.8, IRIX 6.5, OSF/1 5.1, Cygwin, mingw, MSVC 9, Interix 3.5, BeOS.

12.58.33 nis_name_of_r

Gnulib module: —

Portability problems fixed by Gnulib:

Portability problems not fixed by Gnulib:

- This function is missing on some platforms: Mac OS X 10.5, FreeBSD 6.0, NetBSD 5.0, OpenBSD 3.8, Minix 3.1.8, AIX 5.1, IRIX 6.5, OSF/1 5.1, Solaris 11 2011-11, Cygwin, mingw, MSVC 9, Interix 3.5, BeOS.

12.58.34 nis_next_entry

Gnulib module: —

Portability problems fixed by Gnulib:

Portability problems not fixed by Gnulib:

- This function is missing on some platforms: Mac OS X 10.5, FreeBSD 6.0, NetBSD 5.0, OpenBSD 3.8, Minix 3.1.8, IRIX 6.5, OSF/1 5.1, Solaris 11 2011-11, Cygwin, mingw, MSVC 9, Interix 3.5, BeOS.

12.58.35 nis_perror

Gnulib module: —

Portability problems fixed by Gnulib:

Portability problems not fixed by Gnulib:

- This function is missing on some platforms: Mac OS X 10.5, FreeBSD 6.0, NetBSD 5.0, OpenBSD 3.8, Minix 3.1.8, IRIX 6.5, OSF/1 5.1, Solaris 11 2011-11, Cygwin, mingw, MSVC 9, Interix 3.5, BeOS.

12.58.36 nis_ping

Gnulib module: —

Portability problems fixed by Gnulib:

Portability problems not fixed by Gnulib:

- This function is missing on some platforms: Mac OS X 10.5, FreeBSD 6.0, NetBSD 5.0, OpenBSD 3.8, Minix 3.1.8, IRIX 6.5, OSF/1 5.1, Solaris 11 2011-11, Cygwin, mingw, MSVC 9, Interix 3.5, BeOS.

12.58.37 nis_print_directory

Gnulib module: —

Portability problems fixed by Gnulib:

Portability problems not fixed by Gnulib:

- This function is missing on some platforms: Mac OS X 10.5, FreeBSD 6.0, NetBSD 5.0, OpenBSD 3.8, Minix 3.1.8, AIX 5.1, IRIX 6.5, OSF/1 5.1, Solaris 11 2011-11, Cygwin, mingw, MSVC 9, Interix 3.5, BeOS.

12.58.38 nis_print_entry

Gnulib module: —

Portability problems fixed by Gnulib:

Portability problems not fixed by Gnulib:

- This function is missing on some platforms: Mac OS X 10.5, FreeBSD 6.0, NetBSD 5.0, OpenBSD 3.8, Minix 3.1.8, AIX 5.1, IRIX 6.5, OSF/1 5.1, Solaris 11 2011-11, Cygwin, mingw, MSVC 9, Interix 3.5, BeOS.

12.58.39 nis_print_group

Gnulib module: —

Portability problems fixed by Gnulib:

Portability problems not fixed by Gnulib:

- This function is missing on some platforms: Mac OS X 10.5, FreeBSD 6.0, NetBSD 5.0, OpenBSD 3.8, Minix 3.1.8, AIX 5.1, IRIX 6.5, OSF/1 5.1, Solaris 11 2011-11, Cygwin, mingw, MSVC 9, Interix 3.5, BeOS.

12.58.40 `nis_print_group_entry`

Gnulib module: —

Portability problems fixed by Gnulib:

Portability problems not fixed by Gnulib:

- This function is missing on some platforms: Mac OS X 10.5, FreeBSD 6.0, NetBSD 5.0, OpenBSD 3.8, Minix 3.1.8, HP-UX 11, IRIX 6.5, OSF/1 5.1, Solaris 11 2011-11, Cygwin, mingw, MSVC 9, Interix 3.5, BeOS.

12.58.41 `nis_print_link`

Gnulib module: —

Portability problems fixed by Gnulib:

Portability problems not fixed by Gnulib:

- This function is missing on some platforms: Mac OS X 10.5, FreeBSD 6.0, NetBSD 5.0, OpenBSD 3.8, Minix 3.1.8, AIX 5.1, IRIX 6.5, OSF/1 5.1, Solaris 11 2011-11, Cygwin, mingw, MSVC 9, Interix 3.5, BeOS.

12.58.42 `nis_print_object`

Gnulib module: —

Portability problems fixed by Gnulib:

Portability problems not fixed by Gnulib:

- This function is missing on some platforms: Mac OS X 10.5, FreeBSD 6.0, NetBSD 5.0, OpenBSD 3.8, Minix 3.1.8, IRIX 6.5, OSF/1 5.1, Solaris 11 2011-11, Cygwin, mingw, MSVC 9, Interix 3.5, BeOS.

12.58.43 `nis_print_result`

Gnulib module: —

Portability problems fixed by Gnulib:

Portability problems not fixed by Gnulib:

- This function is missing on all non-glibc platforms: Mac OS X 10.5, FreeBSD 6.0, NetBSD 5.0, OpenBSD 3.8, Minix 3.1.8, AIX 5.1, HP-UX 11, IRIX 6.5, OSF/1 5.1, Solaris 11 2011-11, Cygwin, mingw, MSVC 9, Interix 3.5, BeOS.

12.58.44 `nis_print_rights`

Gnulib module: —

Portability problems fixed by Gnulib:

Portability problems not fixed by Gnulib:

- This function is missing on some platforms: Mac OS X 10.5, FreeBSD 6.0, NetBSD 5.0, OpenBSD 3.8, Minix 3.1.8, IRIX 6.5, OSF/1 5.1, Solaris 11 2011-11, Cygwin, mingw, MSVC 9, Interix 3.5, BeOS.

12.58.45 `nis_print_table`

Gnulib module: —

Portability problems fixed by Gnulib:

Portability problems not fixed by Gnulib:

- This function is missing on some platforms: Mac OS X 10.5, FreeBSD 6.0, NetBSD 5.0, OpenBSD 3.8, Minix 3.1.8, AIX 5.1, IRIX 6.5, OSF/1 5.1, Solaris 11 2011-11, Cygwin, mingw, MSVC 9, Interix 3.5, BeOS.

12.58.46 `nis_remove`

Gnulib module: —

Portability problems fixed by Gnulib:

Portability problems not fixed by Gnulib:

- This function is missing on some platforms: Mac OS X 10.5, FreeBSD 6.0, NetBSD 5.0, OpenBSD 3.8, Minix 3.1.8, IRIX 6.5, OSF/1 5.1, Solaris 11 2011-11, Cygwin, mingw, MSVC 9, Interix 3.5, BeOS.

12.58.47 `nis_remove_entry`

Gnulib module: —

Portability problems fixed by Gnulib:

Portability problems not fixed by Gnulib:

- This function is missing on some platforms: Mac OS X 10.5, FreeBSD 6.0, NetBSD 5.0, OpenBSD 3.8, Minix 3.1.8, IRIX 6.5, OSF/1 5.1, Solaris 11 2011-11, Cygwin, mingw, MSVC 9, Interix 3.5, BeOS.

12.58.48 `nis_removemember`

Gnulib module: —

Portability problems fixed by Gnulib:

Portability problems not fixed by Gnulib:

- This function is missing on some platforms: Mac OS X 10.5, FreeBSD 6.0, NetBSD 5.0, OpenBSD 3.8, Minix 3.1.8, IRIX 6.5, OSF/1 5.1, Solaris 11 2011-11, Cygwin, mingw, MSVC 9, Interix 3.5, BeOS.

12.58.49 `nis_rmdir`

Gnulib module: —

Portability problems fixed by Gnulib:

Portability problems not fixed by Gnulib:

- This function is missing on some platforms: Mac OS X 10.5, FreeBSD 6.0, NetBSD 5.0, OpenBSD 3.8, Minix 3.1.8, IRIX 6.5, OSF/1 5.1, Solaris 11 2011-11, Cygwin, mingw, MSVC 9, Interix 3.5, BeOS.

12.58.50 nis_servstate

Gnulib module: —

Portability problems fixed by Gnulib:

Portability problems not fixed by Gnulib:

- This function is missing on some platforms: Mac OS X 10.5, FreeBSD 6.0, NetBSD 5.0, OpenBSD 3.8, Minix 3.1.8, IRIX 6.5, OSF/1 5.1, Solaris 11 2011-11, Cygwin, mingw, MSVC 9, Interix 3.5, BeOS.

12.58.51 nis_sperrno

Gnulib module: —

Portability problems fixed by Gnulib:

Portability problems not fixed by Gnulib:

- This function is missing on some platforms: Mac OS X 10.5, FreeBSD 6.0, NetBSD 5.0, OpenBSD 3.8, Minix 3.1.8, IRIX 6.5, OSF/1 5.1, Solaris 11 2011-11, Cygwin, mingw, MSVC 9, Interix 3.5, BeOS.

12.58.52 nis_sperror

Gnulib module: —

Portability problems fixed by Gnulib:

Portability problems not fixed by Gnulib:

- This function is missing on some platforms: Mac OS X 10.5, FreeBSD 6.0, NetBSD 5.0, OpenBSD 3.8, Minix 3.1.8, IRIX 6.5, OSF/1 5.1, Solaris 11 2011-11, Cygwin, mingw, MSVC 9, Interix 3.5, BeOS.

12.58.53 nis_sperror_r

Gnulib module: —

Portability problems fixed by Gnulib:

Portability problems not fixed by Gnulib:

- This function is missing on some platforms: Mac OS X 10.5, FreeBSD 6.0, NetBSD 5.0, OpenBSD 3.8, Minix 3.1.8, AIX 5.1, IRIX 6.5, OSF/1 5.1, Solaris 11 2011-11, Cygwin, mingw, MSVC 9, Interix 3.5, BeOS.

12.58.54 nis_stats

Gnulib module: —

Portability problems fixed by Gnulib:

Portability problems not fixed by Gnulib:

- This function is missing on some platforms: Mac OS X 10.5, FreeBSD 6.0, NetBSD 5.0, OpenBSD 3.8, Minix 3.1.8, IRIX 6.5, OSF/1 5.1, Solaris 11 2011-11, Cygwin, mingw, MSVC 9, Interix 3.5, BeOS.

12.58.55 `nis_verifygroup`

Gnulib module: —

Portability problems fixed by Gnulib:

Portability problems not fixed by Gnulib:

- This function is missing on some platforms: Mac OS X 10.5, FreeBSD 6.0, NetBSD 5.0, OpenBSD 3.8, Minix 3.1.8, IRIX 6.5, OSF/1 5.1, Solaris 11 2011-11, Cygwin, mingw, MSVC 9, Interix 3.5, BeOS.

12.59 Glibc `<rpcsvc/nis_callback.h>`

12.59.1 `xdr_cback_data`

Gnulib module: —

Portability problems fixed by Gnulib:

Portability problems not fixed by Gnulib:

- This function is missing on some platforms: Mac OS X 10.5, FreeBSD 6.0, NetBSD 5.0, OpenBSD 3.8, Minix 3.1.8, IRIX 6.5, OSF/1 5.1, Solaris 11 2011-11, Cygwin, mingw, MSVC 9, Interix 3.5, BeOS.

12.59.2 `xdr_obj_p`

Gnulib module: —

Portability problems fixed by Gnulib:

Portability problems not fixed by Gnulib:

- This function is missing on some platforms: Mac OS X 10.5, FreeBSD 6.0, NetBSD 5.0, OpenBSD 3.8, Minix 3.1.8, IRIX 6.5, OSF/1 5.1, Solaris 11 2011-11, Cygwin, mingw, MSVC 9, Interix 3.5, BeOS.

12.60 Glibc `<rpcsvc/yp.h>`

12.60.1 `xdr_domainname`

Gnulib module: —

Portability problems fixed by Gnulib:

Portability problems not fixed by Gnulib:

- This function is missing on some platforms: Minix 3.1.8, AIX 5.1, HP-UX 11, IRIX 6.5, OSF/1 5.1, Solaris 11 2011-11, Cygwin, mingw, MSVC 9, Interix 3.5, BeOS.

12.60.2 `xdr_keydat`

Gnulib module: —

Portability problems fixed by Gnulib:

Portability problems not fixed by Gnulib:

- This function is missing on some platforms: NetBSD 5.0, Minix 3.1.8, AIX 5.1, HP-UX 11, IRIX 6.5, OSF/1 5.1, Solaris 11 2011-11, Cygwin, mingw, MSVC 9, Interix 3.5, BeOS.

12.60.3 xdr_mapname

Gnulib module: —

Portability problems fixed by Gnulib:

Portability problems not fixed by Gnulib:

- This function is missing on some platforms: Minix 3.1.8, AIX 5.1, HP-UX 11, IRIX 6.5, OSF/1 5.1, Solaris 11 2011-11, Cygwin, mingw, MSVC 9, Interix 3.5, BeOS.

12.60.4 xdr_peername

Gnulib module: —

Portability problems fixed by Gnulib:

Portability problems not fixed by Gnulib:

- This function is missing on some platforms: Minix 3.1.8, AIX 5.1, HP-UX 11, IRIX 6.5, OSF/1 5.1, Solaris 11 2011-11, Cygwin, mingw, MSVC 9, Interix 3.5, BeOS.

12.60.5 xdr_valdat

Gnulib module: —

Portability problems fixed by Gnulib:

Portability problems not fixed by Gnulib:

- This function is missing on some platforms: NetBSD 5.0, Minix 3.1.8, AIX 5.1, HP-UX 11, IRIX 6.5, OSF/1 5.1, Solaris 11 2011-11, Cygwin, mingw, MSVC 9, Interix 3.5, BeOS.

12.60.6 xdr_ypbind_binding

Gnulib module: —

Portability problems fixed by Gnulib:

Portability problems not fixed by Gnulib:

- This function is missing on some platforms: NetBSD 5.0, Minix 3.1.8, AIX 5.1, HP-UX 11, IRIX 6.5, OSF/1 5.1, Solaris 11 2011-11, Cygwin, mingw, MSVC 9, Interix 3.5, BeOS.

12.60.7 xdr_ypbind_resp

Gnulib module: —

Portability problems fixed by Gnulib:

Portability problems not fixed by Gnulib:

- This function is missing on some platforms: Minix 3.1.8, Cygwin, mingw, MSVC 9, Interix 3.5, BeOS.

12.60.8 xdr_ypbind_resptype

Gnulib module: —

Portability problems fixed by Gnulib:

Portability problems not fixed by Gnulib:

- This function is missing on some platforms: NetBSD 5.0, Minix 3.1.8, AIX 5.1, HP-UX 11, IRIX 6.5, OSF/1 5.1, Cygwin, mingw, MSVC 9, Interix 3.5, BeOS.

12.60.9 xdr_ypbind_setdom

Gnulib module: —

Portability problems fixed by Gnulib:

Portability problems not fixed by Gnulib:

- This function is missing on some platforms: Minix 3.1.8, Cygwin, mingw, MSVC 9, Interix 3.5, BeOS.

12.60.10 xdr_ypmap_parms

Gnulib module: —

Portability problems fixed by Gnulib:

Portability problems not fixed by Gnulib:

- This function is missing on some platforms: Mac OS X 10.5, OpenBSD 3.8, Minix 3.1.8, Cygwin, mingw, MSVC 9, Interix 3.5, BeOS.

12.60.11 xdr_ypmaplist

Gnulib module: —

Portability problems fixed by Gnulib:

Portability problems not fixed by Gnulib:

- This function is missing on some platforms: Minix 3.1.8, Solaris 11 2011-11, Cygwin, mingw, MSVC 9, Interix 3.5, BeOS.

12.60.12 xdr_yppush_status

Gnulib module: —

Portability problems fixed by Gnulib:

Portability problems not fixed by Gnulib:

- This function is missing on some platforms: Mac OS X 10.5, NetBSD 5.0, OpenBSD 3.8, Minix 3.1.8, AIX 5.1, HP-UX 11, IRIX 6.5, OSF/1 5.1, Solaris 11 2011-11, Cygwin, mingw, MSVC 9, Interix 3.5, BeOS.

12.60.13 xdr_yppushresp_xfr

Gnulib module: —

Portability problems fixed by Gnulib:

Portability problems not fixed by Gnulib:

- This function is missing on some platforms: Mac OS X 10.5, OpenBSD 3.8, Minix 3.1.8, Cygwin, mingw, MSVC 9, Interix 3.5, BeOS.

12.60.14 `xdr_ypreq_key`

Gnulib module: —

Portability problems fixed by Gnulib:

Portability problems not fixed by Gnulib:

- This function is missing on some platforms: Minix 3.1.8, Cygwin, mingw, MSVC 9, Interix 3.5, BeOS.

12.60.15 `xdr_ypreq_nokey`

Gnulib module: —

Portability problems fixed by Gnulib:

Portability problems not fixed by Gnulib:

- This function is missing on some platforms: Minix 3.1.8, Cygwin, mingw, MSVC 9, Interix 3.5, BeOS.

12.60.16 `xdr_ypreq_xfr`

Gnulib module: —

Portability problems fixed by Gnulib:

Portability problems not fixed by Gnulib:

- This function is missing on some platforms: Mac OS X 10.5, OpenBSD 3.8, Minix 3.1.8, Cygwin, mingw, MSVC 9, Interix 3.5, BeOS.

12.60.17 `xdr_ypresp_all`

Gnulib module: —

Portability problems fixed by Gnulib:

Portability problems not fixed by Gnulib:

- This function is missing on some platforms: NetBSD 5.0, Minix 3.1.8, AIX 5.1, HP-UX 11, IRIX 6.5, OSF/1 5.1, Solaris 11 2011-11, Cygwin, mingw, MSVC 9, Interix 3.5, BeOS.

12.60.18 `xdr_ypresp_key_val`

Gnulib module: —

Portability problems fixed by Gnulib:

Portability problems not fixed by Gnulib:

- This function is missing on some platforms: Minix 3.1.8, Cygwin, mingw, MSVC 9, Interix 3.5, BeOS.

12.60.19 `xdr_ypresp_maplist`

Gnulib module: —

Portability problems fixed by Gnulib:

Portability problems not fixed by Gnulib:

- This function is missing on some platforms: Minix 3.1.8, Cygwin, mingw, MSVC 9, Interix 3.5, BeOS.

12.60.20 xdr_ypresp_master

Gnulib module: —

Portability problems fixed by Gnulib:

Portability problems not fixed by Gnulib:

- This function is missing on some platforms: Minix 3.1.8, Cygwin, mingw, MSVC 9, Interix 3.5, BeOS.

12.60.21 xdr_ypresp_order

Gnulib module: —

Portability problems fixed by Gnulib:

Portability problems not fixed by Gnulib:

- This function is missing on some platforms: Minix 3.1.8, Cygwin, mingw, MSVC 9, Interix 3.5, BeOS.

12.60.22 xdr_ypresp_val

Gnulib module: —

Portability problems fixed by Gnulib:

Portability problems not fixed by Gnulib:

- This function is missing on some platforms: Minix 3.1.8, Cygwin, mingw, MSVC 9, Interix 3.5, BeOS.

12.60.23 xdr_ypresp_xfr

Gnulib module: —

Portability problems fixed by Gnulib:

Portability problems not fixed by Gnulib:

- This function is missing on some platforms: Mac OS X 10.5, NetBSD 5.0, OpenBSD 3.8, Minix 3.1.8, AIX 5.1, HP-UX 11, IRIX 6.5, OSF/1 5.1, Solaris 11 2011-11, Cygwin, mingw, MSVC 9, Interix 3.5, BeOS.

12.60.24 xdr_ypstat

Gnulib module: —

Portability problems fixed by Gnulib:

Portability problems not fixed by Gnulib:

- This function is missing on some platforms: NetBSD 5.0, Minix 3.1.8, AIX 5.1, HP-UX 11, IRIX 6.5, OSF/1 5.1, Solaris 11 2011-11, Cygwin, mingw, MSVC 9, Interix 3.5, BeOS.

12.60.25 `xdr_ypxfrstat`

Gnulib module: —

Portability problems fixed by Gnulib:

Portability problems not fixed by Gnulib:

- This function is missing on some platforms: Mac OS X 10.5, NetBSD 5.0, OpenBSD 3.8, Minix 3.1.8, AIX 5.1, HP-UX 11, IRIX 6.5, OSF/1 5.1, Solaris 11 2011-11, Cygwin, mingw, MSVC 9, Interix 3.5, BeOS.

12.61 Glibc `<rpcsvc/yp_prot.h>`

12.61.1 `xdr_ypall`

Gnulib module: —

Portability problems fixed by Gnulib:

Portability problems not fixed by Gnulib:

- This function is missing on some platforms: Mac OS X 10.5, FreeBSD 6.0, OpenBSD 3.8, Minix 3.1.8, Cygwin, mingw, MSVC 9, Interix 3.5, BeOS.

12.62 Glibc `<rpcsvc/ypclnt.h>`

12.62.1 `yp_all`

Gnulib module: —

Portability problems fixed by Gnulib:

Portability problems not fixed by Gnulib:

- This function is missing on some platforms: Minix 3.1.8, Cygwin, mingw, MSVC 9, Interix 3.5, BeOS.

12.62.2 `yp_bind`

Gnulib module: —

Portability problems fixed by Gnulib:

Portability problems not fixed by Gnulib:

- This function is missing on some platforms: Minix 3.1.8, Cygwin, mingw, MSVC 9, Interix 3.5, BeOS.

12.62.3 `yp_first`

Gnulib module: —

Portability problems fixed by Gnulib:

Portability problems not fixed by Gnulib:

- This function is missing on some platforms: Minix 3.1.8, Cygwin, mingw, MSVC 9, Interix 3.5, BeOS.

12.62.4 yp_get_default_domain

Gnulib module: —

Portability problems fixed by Gnulib:

Portability problems not fixed by Gnulib:

- This function is missing on some platforms: Minix 3.1.8, HP-UX 11, Cygwin, mingw, MSVC 9, Interix 3.5, BeOS.

12.62.5 yp_master

Gnulib module: —

Portability problems fixed by Gnulib:

Portability problems not fixed by Gnulib:

- This function is missing on some platforms: Minix 3.1.8, Cygwin, mingw, MSVC 9, Interix 3.5, BeOS.

12.62.6 yp_match

Gnulib module: —

Portability problems fixed by Gnulib:

Portability problems not fixed by Gnulib:

- This function is missing on some platforms: Minix 3.1.8, Cygwin, mingw, MSVC 9, Interix 3.5, BeOS.

12.62.7 yp_next

Gnulib module: —

Portability problems fixed by Gnulib:

Portability problems not fixed by Gnulib:

- This function is missing on some platforms: Minix 3.1.8, Cygwin, mingw, MSVC 9, Interix 3.5, BeOS.

12.62.8 yp_order

Gnulib module: —

Portability problems fixed by Gnulib:

Portability problems not fixed by Gnulib:

- This function is missing on some platforms: Minix 3.1.8, Cygwin, mingw, MSVC 9, Interix 3.5, BeOS.

12.62.9 yp_unbind

Gnulib module: —

Portability problems fixed by Gnulib:

Portability problems not fixed by Gnulib:

- This function is missing on some platforms: Minix 3.1.8, Cygwin, mingw, MSVC 9, Interix 3.5, BeOS.

12.62.10 yp_update

Gnulib module: —

Portability problems fixed by Gnulib:

Portability problems not fixed by Gnulib:

- This function is missing on some platforms: Mac OS X 10.5, FreeBSD 6.0, NetBSD 5.0, OpenBSD 3.8, Minix 3.1.8, OSF/1 5.1, Cygwin, mingw, MSVC 9, Interix 3.5, BeOS.

12.62.11 ypbinderr_string

Gnulib module: —

Portability problems fixed by Gnulib:

Portability problems not fixed by Gnulib:

- This function is missing on some platforms: Mac OS X 10.5, NetBSD 5.0, OpenBSD 3.8, Minix 3.1.8, AIX 5.1, HP-UX 11, IRIX 6.5, OSF/1 5.1, Solaris 11 2011-11, Cygwin, mingw, MSVC 9, Interix 3.5, BeOS.

12.62.12 yperr_string

Gnulib module: —

Portability problems fixed by Gnulib:

Portability problems not fixed by Gnulib:

- This function is missing on some platforms: Minix 3.1.8, Cygwin, mingw, MSVC 9, Interix 3.5, BeOS.

12.62.13 ypprot_err

Gnulib module: —

Portability problems fixed by Gnulib:

Portability problems not fixed by Gnulib:

- This function is missing on some platforms: Minix 3.1.8, Cygwin, mingw, MSVC 9, Interix 3.5, BeOS.

12.63 Glibc <rpcsvc/ypupd.h>

12.63.1 xdr_yp_buf

Gnulib module: —

Portability problems fixed by Gnulib:

Portability problems not fixed by Gnulib:

- This function is missing on some platforms: Mac OS X 10.5, FreeBSD 6.0, NetBSD 5.0, OpenBSD 3.8, Minix 3.1.8, Cygwin, mingw, MSVC 9, Interix 3.5, BeOS.

12.63.2 xdr_ypdelete_args

Gnulib module: —

Portability problems fixed by Gnulib:

Portability problems not fixed by Gnulib:

- This function is missing on some platforms: Mac OS X 10.5, FreeBSD 6.0, NetBSD 5.0, OpenBSD 3.8, Minix 3.1.8, Cygwin, mingw, MSVC 9, Interix 3.5, BeOS.

12.63.3 xdr_ypupdate_args

Gnulib module: —

Portability problems fixed by Gnulib:

Portability problems not fixed by Gnulib:

- This function is missing on some platforms: Mac OS X 10.5, FreeBSD 6.0, NetBSD 5.0, OpenBSD 3.8, Minix 3.1.8, Cygwin, mingw, MSVC 9, Interix 3.5, BeOS.

12.64 Glibc Extensions to <sched.h>

12.64.1 clone

Gnulib module: —

Portability problems fixed by Gnulib:

Portability problems not fixed by Gnulib:

- This function is missing on some platforms: Mac OS X 10.5, FreeBSD 6.0, OpenBSD 3.8, Minix 3.1.8, AIX 5.1, HP-UX 11, IRIX 6.5, OSF/1 5.1, Solaris 11 2011-11, Cygwin, mingw, MSVC 9, Interix 3.5, BeOS.

12.64.2 sched_getaffinity

Gnulib module: —

Portability problems fixed by Gnulib:

Portability problems not fixed by Gnulib:

- This function is missing on all non-glibc platforms: Mac OS X 10.5, FreeBSD 6.0, NetBSD 5.0, OpenBSD 3.8, Minix 3.1.8, AIX 5.1, HP-UX 11, IRIX 6.5, OSF/1 5.1, Solaris 11 2011-11, Cygwin, mingw, MSVC 9, Interix 3.5, BeOS.

12.64.3 sched_setaffinity

Gnulib module: —

Portability problems fixed by Gnulib:

Portability problems not fixed by Gnulib:

- This function is missing on all non-glibc platforms: Mac OS X 10.5, FreeBSD 6.0, NetBSD 5.0, OpenBSD 3.8, Minix 3.1.8, AIX 5.1, HP-UX 11, IRIX 6.5, OSF/1 5.1, Solaris 11 2011-11, Cygwin, mingw, MSVC 9, Interix 3.5, BeOS.

12.64.4 `setns`

Gnulib module: —

Portability problems fixed by Gnulib:

Portability problems not fixed by Gnulib:

- This function is missing on all non-glibc platforms: glibc 2.13, Mac OS X 10.5, FreeBSD 6.4, NetBSD 5.0, OpenBSD 3.8, Minix 3.1.8, AIX 7.1, HP-UX 11.31, IRIX 6.5, OSF/1 5.1, Solaris 11 2011-11, Cygwin, mingw, MSVC 9, Interix 3.5, BeOS.

12.65 Glibc Extensions to `<search.h>`

12.65.1 `hcreate_r`

Gnulib module: —

Portability problems fixed by Gnulib:

Portability problems not fixed by Gnulib:

- This function is missing on some platforms: Mac OS X 10.5, FreeBSD 6.0, NetBSD 5.0, OpenBSD 3.8, Minix 3.1.8, HP-UX 11, IRIX 6.5, Solaris 11 2011-11, mingw, MSVC 9, BeOS.

12.65.2 `hdestroy_r`

Gnulib module: —

Portability problems fixed by Gnulib:

Portability problems not fixed by Gnulib:

- This function is missing on some platforms: Mac OS X 10.5, FreeBSD 6.0, NetBSD 5.0, OpenBSD 3.8, Minix 3.1.8, HP-UX 11, IRIX 6.5, Solaris 11 2011-11, mingw, MSVC 9, BeOS.

12.65.3 `hsearch_r`

Gnulib module: —

Portability problems fixed by Gnulib:

Portability problems not fixed by Gnulib:

- This function is missing on some platforms: Mac OS X 10.5, FreeBSD 6.0, NetBSD 5.0, OpenBSD 3.8, Minix 3.1.8, HP-UX 11, IRIX 6.5, Solaris 11 2011-11, mingw, MSVC 9, BeOS.

12.65.4 `tdestroy`

Gnulib module: —

Portability problems fixed by Gnulib:

Portability problems not fixed by Gnulib:

- This function is missing on some platforms: Mac OS X 10.5, FreeBSD 6.0, NetBSD 5.0, OpenBSD 3.8, Minix 3.1.8, AIX 5.1, HP-UX 11, IRIX 6.5, OSF/1 5.1, Solaris 11 2011-11, mingw, MSVC 9, Interix 3.5, BeOS.

12.66 Glibc Extensions to <selinux/selinux.h>

12.66.1 fgetfilecon

Gnulib module: selinux-h

Portability problems fixed by Gnulib:

- This function is missing on some platforms: Mac OS X 10.5, OpenBSD 3.8, Minix 3.1.8, AIX 5.1, HP-UX 11, IRIX 6.5, OSF/1 5.1, Solaris 11 2011-11, mingw, MSVC 9, Interix 3.5, BeOS. On those platforms, this module provides a stub that always sets errno to ENOTSUP and returns '-1'.

- On systems with SELinux support, this module provides a wrapper for the fgetfilecon function that insulates the caller from API-nonconforming behavior. Without this wrapper, fgetfilecon can return '0' and set the context pointer to NULL, and in another scenario can return '10' and set the context pointer to 'unlabeled'. This wrapper returns '-1' in each case and sets errno to ENOTSUP and ENODATA respectively. While the conditions that can provoke such behavior are rare, the average caller does not handle them because the possibility of such behavior is not documented.

Portability problems not fixed by Gnulib:

12.66.2 getfilecon

Gnulib module: selinux-h

Portability problems fixed by Gnulib:

- This function is missing on some platforms: Mac OS X 10.5, OpenBSD 3.8, Minix 3.1.8, AIX 5.1, HP-UX 11, IRIX 6.5, OSF/1 5.1, Solaris 11 2011-11, mingw, MSVC 9, Interix 3.5, BeOS. On those platforms, this module provides a stub that always sets errno to ENOTSUP and returns '-1'.

- On systems with SELinux support, this module provides a wrapper for the getfilecon function that insulates the caller from API-nonconforming behavior. Without this wrapper, getfilecon can return '0' and set the context pointer to NULL, and in another scenario can return '10' and set the context pointer to 'unlabeled'. This wrapper returns '-1' in each case and sets errno to ENOTSUP and ENODATA respectively. While the conditions that can provoke such behavior are rare, the average caller does not handle them because the possibility of such behavior is not documented.

Portability problems not fixed by Gnulib:

12.66.3 lgetfilecon

Gnulib module: selinux-h

Portability problems fixed by Gnulib:

- This function is missing on some platforms: Mac OS X 10.5, OpenBSD 3.8, Minix 3.1.8, AIX 5.1, HP-UX 11, IRIX 6.5, OSF/1 5.1, Solaris 11 2011-11, mingw, MSVC 9, Interix 3.5, BeOS. On those platforms, this module provides a stub that always sets errno to ENOTSUP and returns '-1'.

- On systems with SELinux support, this module provides a wrapper for the lgetfilecon function that insulates the caller from API-nonconforming behavior.

Without this wrapper, `lgetfilecon` can return '0' and set the `context` pointer to NULL, and in another scenario can return '10' and set the `context` pointer to 'unlabeled'. This wrapper returns '-1' in each case and sets `errno` to `ENOTSUP` and `ENODATA` respectively. While the conditions that can provoke such behavior are rare, the average caller does not handle them because the possibility of such behavior is not documented.

Portability problems not fixed by Gnulib:

12.67 Glibc <shadow.h>

12.67.1 endspent

Gnulib module: —

Portability problems fixed by Gnulib:

Portability problems not fixed by Gnulib:

- This function is missing on some platforms: Mac OS X 10.5, FreeBSD 6.0, NetBSD 5.0, OpenBSD 3.8, Minix 3.1.8, AIX 5.1, HP-UX 11, OSF/1 5.1, Cygwin, mingw, MSVC 9, Interix 3.5, BeOS.

12.67.2 fgetspent

Gnulib module: —

Portability problems fixed by Gnulib:

Portability problems not fixed by Gnulib:

- This function is missing on some platforms: Mac OS X 10.5, FreeBSD 6.0, NetBSD 5.0, OpenBSD 3.8, Minix 3.1.8, AIX 5.1, HP-UX 11, OSF/1 5.1, Cygwin, mingw, MSVC 9, Interix 3.5, BeOS.

12.67.3 fgetspent_r

Gnulib module: —

Portability problems fixed by Gnulib:

Portability problems not fixed by Gnulib:

- This function is missing on some platforms: Mac OS X 10.5, FreeBSD 6.0, NetBSD 5.0, OpenBSD 3.8, Minix 3.1.8, AIX 5.1, HP-UX 11, IRIX 5.3, OSF/1 5.1, Cygwin, mingw, MSVC 9, Interix 3.5, BeOS.

12.67.4 getspent

Gnulib module: —

Portability problems fixed by Gnulib:

Portability problems not fixed by Gnulib:

- This function is missing on some platforms: Mac OS X 10.5, FreeBSD 6.0, NetBSD 5.0, OpenBSD 3.8, Minix 3.1.8, AIX 5.1, HP-UX 11, OSF/1 5.1, Cygwin, mingw, MSVC 9, Interix 3.5, BeOS.

12.67.5 getspent_r

Gnulib module: —

Portability problems fixed by Gnulib:

Portability problems not fixed by Gnulib:

- This function is missing on some platforms: Mac OS X 10.5, FreeBSD 6.0, NetBSD 5.0, OpenBSD 3.8, Minix 3.1.8, AIX 5.1, HP-UX 11, IRIX 5.3, OSF/1 5.1, Cygwin, mingw, MSVC 9, Interix 3.5, BeOS.

12.67.6 getspnam

Gnulib module: —

Portability problems fixed by Gnulib:

Portability problems not fixed by Gnulib:

- This function is missing on some platforms: Mac OS X 10.5, FreeBSD 6.0, NetBSD 5.0, OpenBSD 3.8, Minix 3.1.8, AIX 5.1, HP-UX 11, OSF/1 5.1, Cygwin, mingw, MSVC 9, Interix 3.5, BeOS.

12.67.7 getspnam_r

Gnulib module: —

Portability problems fixed by Gnulib:

Portability problems not fixed by Gnulib:

- This function is missing on some platforms: Mac OS X 10.5, FreeBSD 6.0, NetBSD 5.0, OpenBSD 3.8, Minix 3.1.8, AIX 5.1, HP-UX 11, IRIX 5.3, OSF/1 5.1, Cygwin, mingw, MSVC 9, Interix 3.5, BeOS.

12.67.8 lckpwdf

Gnulib module: —

Portability problems fixed by Gnulib:

Portability problems not fixed by Gnulib:

- This function is missing on some platforms: Mac OS X 10.5, FreeBSD 6.0, NetBSD 5.0, OpenBSD 3.8, Minix 3.1.8, AIX 5.1, OSF/1 5.1, Cygwin, mingw, MSVC 9, Interix 3.5, BeOS.

12.67.9 putspent

Gnulib module: —

Portability problems fixed by Gnulib:

Portability problems not fixed by Gnulib:

- This function is missing on some platforms: Mac OS X 10.5, FreeBSD 6.0, NetBSD 5.0, OpenBSD 3.8, Minix 3.1.8, AIX 5.1, HP-UX 11, OSF/1 5.1, Cygwin, mingw, MSVC 9, Interix 3.5, BeOS.

12.67.10 setspent

Gnulib module: —

Portability problems fixed by Gnulib:

Portability problems not fixed by Gnulib:

- This function is missing on some platforms: Mac OS X 10.5, FreeBSD 6.0, NetBSD 5.0, OpenBSD 3.8, Minix 3.1.8, AIX 5.1, HP-UX 11, OSF/1 5.1, Cygwin, mingw, MSVC 9, Interix 3.5, BeOS.

12.67.11 sgetspent

Gnulib module: —

Portability problems fixed by Gnulib:

Portability problems not fixed by Gnulib:

- This function is missing on all non-glibc platforms: Mac OS X 10.5, FreeBSD 6.0, NetBSD 5.0, OpenBSD 3.8, Minix 3.1.8, AIX 5.1, HP-UX 11, IRIX 6.5, OSF/1 5.1, Solaris 11 2011-11, Cygwin, mingw, MSVC 9, Interix 3.5, BeOS.

12.67.12 sgetspent_r

Gnulib module: —

Portability problems fixed by Gnulib:

Portability problems not fixed by Gnulib:

- This function is missing on all non-glibc platforms: Mac OS X 10.5, FreeBSD 6.0, NetBSD 5.0, OpenBSD 3.8, Minix 3.1.8, AIX 5.1, HP-UX 11, IRIX 6.5, OSF/1 5.1, Solaris 11 2011-11, Cygwin, mingw, MSVC 9, Interix 3.5, BeOS.

12.67.13 ulckpwdf

Gnulib module: —

Portability problems fixed by Gnulib:

Portability problems not fixed by Gnulib:

- This function is missing on some platforms: Mac OS X 10.5, FreeBSD 6.0, NetBSD 5.0, OpenBSD 3.8, Minix 3.1.8, AIX 5.1, OSF/1 5.1, Cygwin, mingw, MSVC 9, Interix 3.5, BeOS.

12.68 Glibc Extensions to <signal.h>

12.68.1 gsignal

Gnulib module: —

Portability problems fixed by Gnulib:

Portability problems not fixed by Gnulib:

- This function is missing on some platforms: Mac OS X 10.5, FreeBSD 6.0, NetBSD 5.0, OpenBSD 3.8, Minix 3.1.8, Cygwin, mingw, MSVC 9, Interix 3.5.

12.68.2 `sigandset`

Gnulib module: —

Portability problems fixed by Gnulib:

Portability problems not fixed by Gnulib:

- This function is missing on all non-glibc platforms: Mac OS X 10.5, FreeBSD 6.0, NetBSD 5.0, OpenBSD 3.8, Minix 3.1.8, AIX 5.1, HP-UX 11, IRIX 6.5, OSF/1 5.1, Solaris 11 2011-11, Cygwin, mingw, MSVC 9, Interix 3.5, BeOS.

12.68.3 `sigblock`

Gnulib module: —

Portability problems fixed by Gnulib:

Portability problems not fixed by Gnulib:

- This function is missing on some platforms: Minix 3.1.8, Solaris 11 2011-11, Cygwin, mingw, MSVC 9, BeOS.

12.68.4 `siggetmask`

Gnulib module: —

Portability problems fixed by Gnulib:

Portability problems not fixed by Gnulib:

- This function is missing on some platforms: Mac OS X 10.5, FreeBSD 6.0, NetBSD 5.0, OpenBSD 3.8, Minix 3.1.8, AIX 4.3.2, HP-UX 11, IRIX 6.5, OSF/1 5.1, Solaris 11 2011-11, Cygwin, mingw, MSVC 9, Interix 3.5, BeOS.

12.68.5 `sigisemptyset`

Gnulib module: —

Portability problems fixed by Gnulib:

Portability problems not fixed by Gnulib:

- This function is missing on all non-glibc platforms: Mac OS X 10.5, FreeBSD 6.0, NetBSD 5.0, OpenBSD 3.8, Minix 3.1.8, AIX 5.1, HP-UX 11, IRIX 6.5, OSF/1 5.1, Solaris 11 2011-11, Cygwin, mingw, MSVC 9, Interix 3.5, BeOS.

12.68.6 `sigorset`

Gnulib module: —

Portability problems fixed by Gnulib:

Portability problems not fixed by Gnulib:

- This function is missing on all non-glibc platforms: Mac OS X 10.5, FreeBSD 6.0, NetBSD 5.0, OpenBSD 3.8, Minix 3.1.8, AIX 5.1, HP-UX 11, IRIX 6.5, OSF/1 5.1, Solaris 11 2011-11, Cygwin, mingw, MSVC 9, Interix 3.5, BeOS.

12.68.7 `sigreturn`

Gnulib module: —

Portability problems fixed by Gnulib:

Portability problems not fixed by Gnulib:

- This function is missing on some platforms: AIX 5.1, HP-UX 11, IRIX 6.5, Solaris 11 2011-11, Cygwin, mingw, MSVC 9, Interix 3.5, BeOS.

12.68.8 `sigsetmask`

Gnulib module: —

Portability problems fixed by Gnulib:

Portability problems not fixed by Gnulib:

- This function is missing on some platforms: Minix 3.1.8, Solaris 11 2011-11, Cygwin, mingw, MSVC 9, BeOS.

12.68.9 `sigstack`

Gnulib module: —

Portability problems fixed by Gnulib:

Portability problems not fixed by Gnulib:

- This function is missing on some platforms: Mac OS X 10.5, FreeBSD 6.0, NetBSD 5.0, OpenBSD 3.8, Minix 3.1.8, AIX 5.1, Cygwin, mingw, MSVC 9, Interix 3.5, BeOS.

12.68.10 `sigvec`

Gnulib module: —

Portability problems fixed by Gnulib:

Portability problems not fixed by Gnulib:

- This function is missing on some platforms: Minix 3.1.8, HP-UX 11, Solaris 11 2011-11, Cygwin, mingw, MSVC 9, BeOS.

12.68.11 `ssignal`

Gnulib module: —

Portability problems fixed by Gnulib:

Portability problems not fixed by Gnulib:

- This function is missing on some platforms: Mac OS X 10.5, FreeBSD 6.0, NetBSD 5.0, OpenBSD 3.8, Minix 3.1.8, Cygwin, mingw, MSVC 9, Interix 3.5.

12.68.12 `sys_siglist`

Gnulib module: —

Portability problems fixed by Gnulib:

Portability problems not fixed by Gnulib:

- This constant is missing on some platforms: Mac OS X 10.5, Minix 3.1.8, HP-UX 11, IRIX 6.5, OSF/1 5.1, Solaris 11 2011-11, Cygwin 1.7.9, mingw, MSVC 9, Interix 3.5.

12.68.13 `sysv_signal`

Gnulib module: —

Portability problems fixed by Gnulib:

Portability problems not fixed by Gnulib:

- This function is missing on some platforms: Mac OS X 10.5, FreeBSD 6.0, NetBSD 5.0, OpenBSD 3.8, Minix 3.1.8, AIX 5.1, HP-UX 11, IRIX 6.5, OSF/1 5.1, Solaris 11 2011-11, Cygwin, mingw, MSVC 9, Interix 3.5.

12.69 Glibc Extensions to `<stdio.h>`

12.69.1 `asprintf`

Gnulib module: vasprintf or vasprintf-posix

Portability problems fixed by either Gnulib module `vasprintf` or `vasprintf-posix`:

- This function is missing on some platforms: AIX 5.1, HP-UX 11, IRIX 6.5, OSF/1 5.1, Solaris 10, mingw, MSVC 9, Interix 3.5.

Portability problems fixed by Gnulib module `vasprintf-posix`:

- This function does not support size specifiers as in C99 (`hh`, `ll`, `j`, `t`, `z`) on some platforms: Cygwin 1.5.24, BeOS.
- printf of '`long double`' numbers is unsupported on some platforms: BeOS.
- printf `"%f"`, `"%e"`, `"%g"` of Infinity and NaN yields an incorrect result on some platforms: Solaris 11 2011-11.
- This function does not support the 'a' and 'A' directives on some platforms: glibc-2.3.6, Mac OS X 10.5, NetBSD 5.0, OpenBSD 4.0, Solaris 11 2011-11, Cygwin 1.5.x, BeOS.
- This function does not support the 'F' directive on some platforms: NetBSD 3.0, Cygwin 1.5.x, BeOS.
- This function does not support the 'ls' directive on some platforms: OpenBSD 4.0, Cygwin 1.5.x, Haiku.
- This function does not support precisions in the 'ls' directive correctly on some platforms: Solaris 11 2011-11.
- This function does not support format directives that access arguments in an arbitrary order, such as `"%2$s"`, on some platforms: NetBSD 3.0, BeOS.
- This function doesn't support the ' flag on some platforms: NetBSD 3.0, Cygwin 1.5.24.
- printf `"%010f"` of NaN and Infinity yields an incorrect result (padded with zeroes) on some platforms: Mac OS X 10.5, FreeBSD 6.0, NetBSD 5.0, Solaris 11 2011-11, Cygwin 1.5.x.
- This function does not support precisions larger than 512 or 1024 in integer, floating-point and pointer output on some platforms: BeOS.
- This function can crash in out-of-memory conditions on some platforms: Mac OS X 10.3, FreeBSD 6.0, NetBSD 5.0.

Portability problems not fixed by Gnulib:

12.69.2 `cuserid`

Gnulib module: —

Portability problems fixed by Gnulib:

Portability problems not fixed by Gnulib:

- This function is missing on some platforms: Mac OS X 10.5, FreeBSD 6.0, NetBSD 5.0, OpenBSD 3.8, mingw, MSVC 9.

12.69.3 `clearerr_unlocked`

Gnulib module: —

Portability problems fixed by Gnulib:

Portability problems not fixed by Gnulib:

- This function is missing on some platforms: NetBSD 5.0, OpenBSD 3.8, Minix 3.1.8, AIX 5.1, HP-UX 11, OSF/1 5.1, Solaris 11 2011-11, Cygwin, mingw, MSVC 9, Interix 3.5.

12.69.4 `fcloseall`

Gnulib module: —

Portability problems fixed by Gnulib:

Portability problems not fixed by Gnulib:

- This function is missing on some platforms: Mac OS X 10.5, FreeBSD 6.0, NetBSD 5.0, OpenBSD 3.8, Minix 3.1.8, AIX 5.1, HP-UX 11, IRIX 6.5, OSF/1 5.1, Solaris 10, mingw, Interix 3.5.

12.69.5 `feof_unlocked`

Gnulib module: —

Portability problems fixed by Gnulib:

Portability problems not fixed by Gnulib:

- This function is missing on some platforms: NetBSD 5.0, OpenBSD 3.8, Minix 3.1.8, AIX 5.1, HP-UX 11, OSF/1 5.1, Solaris 11 2011-11, Cygwin, mingw, MSVC 9, Interix 3.5.

12.69.6 `ferror_unlocked`

Gnulib module: —

Portability problems fixed by Gnulib:

Portability problems not fixed by Gnulib:

- This function is missing on some platforms: NetBSD 5.0, OpenBSD 3.8, Minix 3.1.8, AIX 5.1, HP-UX 11, OSF/1 5.1, Solaris 11 2011-11, Cygwin, mingw, MSVC 9, Interix 3.5.

12.69.7 `fflush_unlocked`

Gnulib module: —

Portability problems fixed by Gnulib:

Portability problems not fixed by Gnulib:

- This function is missing on some platforms: Mac OS X 10.5, FreeBSD 6.0, NetBSD 5.0, OpenBSD 3.8, Minix 3.1.8, AIX 5.1, HP-UX 11, IRIX 6.5, Solaris 11 2011-11, Cygwin, mingw, MSVC 9, Interix 3.5.

12.69.8 `fgetc_unlocked`

Gnulib module: —

Portability problems fixed by Gnulib:

Portability problems not fixed by Gnulib:

- This function is missing on all non-glibc platforms: Mac OS X 10.5, FreeBSD 6.0, NetBSD 5.0, OpenBSD 3.8, Minix 3.1.8, AIX 5.1, HP-UX 11, IRIX 6.5, OSF/1 5.1, Solaris 11 2011-11, Cygwin, mingw, MSVC 9, Interix 3.5, BeOS.

12.69.9 `fgets_unlocked`

Gnulib module: —

Portability problems fixed by Gnulib:

Portability problems not fixed by Gnulib:

- This function is missing on some platforms: Mac OS X 10.5, FreeBSD 6.0, NetBSD 5.0, OpenBSD 3.8, Minix 3.1.8, AIX 5.1, HP-UX 11, IRIX 6.5, OSF/1 5.1, Solaris 11 2011-11, Cygwin, mingw, MSVC 9, Interix 3.5.

12.69.10 `fileno_unlocked`

Gnulib module: —

Portability problems fixed by Gnulib:

Portability problems not fixed by Gnulib:

- This function is missing on some platforms: NetBSD 5.0, OpenBSD 3.8, Minix 3.1.8, AIX 5.1, HP-UX 11, OSF/1 5.1, Solaris 11 2011-11, Cygwin, mingw, MSVC 9, Interix 3.5.

12.69.11 `fopencookie`

Gnulib module: —

Portability problems fixed by Gnulib:

Portability problems not fixed by Gnulib:

- This function is missing on many non-glibc platforms: Mac OS X 10.5, FreeBSD 6.0, NetBSD 5.0, OpenBSD 3.8, Minix 3.1.8, AIX 5.1, HP-UX 11, IRIX 6.5, OSF/1 5.1, Solaris 11 2011-11, Cygwin 1.5.x, mingw, MSVC 9, Interix 3.5, BeOS.

12.69.12 `fputc_unlocked`

Gnulib module: —

Portability problems fixed by Gnulib:

Portability problems not fixed by Gnulib:

- This function is missing on some platforms: Mac OS X 10.5, FreeBSD 6.0, NetBSD 5.0, OpenBSD 3.8, Minix 3.1.8, AIX 5.1, HP-UX 11, IRIX 6.5, OSF/1 5.1, Solaris 11 2011-11, Cygwin, mingw, MSVC 9, Interix 3.5.

12.69.13 `fputs_unlocked`

Gnulib module: —

Portability problems fixed by Gnulib:

Portability problems not fixed by Gnulib:

- This function is missing on all non-glibc platforms: Mac OS X 10.5, FreeBSD 6.0, NetBSD 5.0, OpenBSD 3.8, Minix 3.1.8, AIX 5.1, HP-UX 11, IRIX 6.5, OSF/1 5.1, Solaris 11 2011-11, Cygwin, mingw, MSVC 9, Interix 3.5, BeOS.

12.69.14 `fread_unlocked`

Gnulib module: —

Portability problems fixed by Gnulib:

Portability problems not fixed by Gnulib:

- This function is missing on some platforms: Mac OS X 10.5, FreeBSD 6.0, NetBSD 5.0, OpenBSD 3.8, Minix 3.1.8, AIX 5.1, HP-UX 11, IRIX 6.5, Solaris 11 2011-11, Cygwin, mingw, MSVC 9, Interix 3.5.

12.69.15 `fwrite_unlocked`

Gnulib module: —

Portability problems fixed by Gnulib:

Portability problems not fixed by Gnulib:

- This function is missing on some platforms: Mac OS X 10.5, FreeBSD 6.0, NetBSD 5.0, OpenBSD 3.8, Minix 3.1.8, AIX 5.1, HP-UX 11, IRIX 6.5, Solaris 11 2011-11, Cygwin, mingw, MSVC 9, Interix 3.5.

12.69.16 `getw`

Gnulib module: —

Portability problems fixed by Gnulib:

Portability problems not fixed by Gnulib:

- This function is missing on some platforms: BeOS.

12.69.17 `putw`

Gnulib module: —

Portability problems fixed by Gnulib:

Portability problems not fixed by Gnulib:

- This function is missing on some platforms: BeOS.

12.69.18 `setbuffer`

Gnulib module: —

Portability problems fixed by Gnulib:

Portability problems not fixed by Gnulib:

- This function is missing on some platforms: Minix 3.1.8, HP-UX 11, mingw, MSVC 9.

12.69.19 `setlinebuf`

Gnulib module: —

Portability problems fixed by Gnulib:

Portability problems not fixed by Gnulib:

- This function is missing on some platforms: Minix 3.1.8, HP-UX 11.23, mingw, MSVC 9.

12.69.20 `sys_errlist`

Gnulib module: —

Portability problems fixed by Gnulib:

Portability problems not fixed by Gnulib:

- This variable is missing on some platforms: Minix 3.1.8, Mac OS X 10.5, IRIX 6.5, OSF/1 5.1, Cygwin, mingw, Interix 3.5, BeOS.

12.69.21 `sys_nerr`

Gnulib module: —

Portability problems fixed by Gnulib:

Portability problems not fixed by Gnulib:

- This variable is missing on some platforms: Mac OS X 10.5, Minix 3.1.8, IRIX 6.5, OSF/1 5.1, Cygwin, mingw, Interix 3.5, BeOS.

12.69.22 `tmpnam_r`

Gnulib module: —

Portability problems fixed by Gnulib:

Portability problems not fixed by Gnulib:

- This function is missing on some platforms: Mac OS X 10.5, FreeBSD 6.0, NetBSD 5.0, OpenBSD 3.8, Minix 3.1.8, AIX 5.1, HP-UX 11, IRIX 6.5, OSF/1 5.1, Cygwin, mingw, MSVC 9, Interix 3.5, BeOS.

12.69.23 `vasprintf`

Gnulib module: vasprintf or vasprintf-posix

Portability problems fixed by either Gnulib module `vasprintf` or `vasprintf-posix`:

- This function is missing on some platforms: AIX 5.1, HP-UX 11, IRIX 6.5, OSF/1 5.1, Solaris 10, mingw, MSVC 9, Interix 3.5.

Portability problems fixed by Gnulib module `vasprintf-posix`:

- This function does not support size specifiers as in C99 (`hh`, `ll`, `j`, `t`, `z`) on some platforms: Cygwin 1.5.24, BeOS.
- printf of '`long double`' numbers is unsupported on some platforms: BeOS.
- printf "`%f`", "`%e`", "`%g`" of Infinity and NaN yields an incorrect result on some platforms: Solaris 11 2011-11.
- This function does not support the '`a`' and '`A`' directives on some platforms: glibc-2.3.6, Mac OS X 10.5, NetBSD 5.0, OpenBSD 4.0, Solaris 11 2011-11, Cygwin 1.5.x, BeOS.
- This function does not support the '`F`' directive on some platforms: NetBSD 3.0, Cygwin 1.5.x, BeOS.
- This function does not support the '`ls`' directive on some platforms: OpenBSD 4.0, Cygwin 1.5.x, Haiku.
- This function does not support precisions in the '`ls`' directive correctly on some platforms: Solaris 11 2011-11.
- This function does not support format directives that access arguments in an arbitrary order, such as "`%2$s`", on some platforms: NetBSD 3.0, BeOS.
- This function doesn't support the ' flag on some platforms: NetBSD 3.0, Cygwin 1.5.24.
- printf "`%010f`" of NaN and Infinity yields an incorrect result (padded with zeroes) on some platforms: Mac OS X 10.5, FreeBSD 6.0, NetBSD 5.0, Solaris 11 2011-11, Cygwin 1.5.x.
- This function does not support precisions larger than 512 or 1024 in integer, floating-point and pointer output on some platforms: BeOS.
- This function can crash in out-of-memory conditions on some platforms: Mac OS X 10.3, FreeBSD 6.0, NetBSD 5.0.

Portability problems not fixed by Gnulib:

12.70 Glibc Extensions to `<stdlib.h>`

12.70.1 `canonicalize_file_name`

Gnulib module: canonicalize-lgpl

Portability problems fixed by Gnulib:

- This function is missing on many non-glibc platforms: Mac OS X 10.5, FreeBSD 6.0, NetBSD 5.0, OpenBSD 3.8, Minix 3.1.8, AIX 5.1, HP-UX 11, IRIX 6.5, OSF/1 5.1, Solaris 10, Cygwin 1.5.x, mingw, MSVC 9, Interix 3.5, BeOS.
- This function fails to detect trailing slashes on non-directories on some platforms: glibc 2.3.5.

Portability problems not fixed by Gnulib:

12.70.2 cfree

Gnulib module: —

Portability problems fixed by Gnulib:

Portability problems not fixed by Gnulib:

- This function is missing on some platforms: Mac OS X 10.5, FreeBSD 6.0, NetBSD 5.0, Minix 3.1.8, Cygwin, mingw, MSVC 9, Interix 3.5.

12.70.3 clearenv

Gnulib module: —

Portability problems fixed by Gnulib:

Portability problems not fixed by Gnulib:

- This function is missing on some platforms: Mac OS X 10.5, FreeBSD 6.0, NetBSD 5.0, OpenBSD 3.8, Minix 3.1.8, IRIX 6.5, Solaris 10, Cygwin, mingw, MSVC 9, Interix 3.5, BeOS.

12.70.4 drand48_r

Gnulib module: —

Portability problems fixed by Gnulib:

Portability problems not fixed by Gnulib:

- This function is missing on some platforms: Mac OS X 10.5, FreeBSD 6.0, NetBSD 5.0, OpenBSD 3.8, Minix 3.1.8, HP-UX 11, IRIX 6.5, Solaris 11 2011-11, Cygwin, mingw, MSVC 9, Interix 3.5.

12.70.5 ecvt_r

Gnulib module: —

Portability problems fixed by Gnulib:

Portability problems not fixed by Gnulib:

- This function is missing on some platforms: Mac OS X 10.5, FreeBSD 6.0, NetBSD 5.0, OpenBSD 3.8, Minix 3.1.8, HP-UX 11, Solaris 11 2011-11, Cygwin, mingw, MSVC 9, Interix 3.5.

12.70.6 erand48_r

Gnulib module: —

Portability problems fixed by Gnulib:

Portability problems not fixed by Gnulib:

- This function is missing on some platforms: Mac OS X 10.5, FreeBSD 6.0, NetBSD 5.0, OpenBSD 3.8, Minix 3.1.8, HP-UX 11, IRIX 6.5, Solaris 11 2011-11, Cygwin, mingw, MSVC 9, Interix 3.5.

12.70.7 `fcvt_r`

Gnulib module: —

Portability problems fixed by Gnulib:

Portability problems not fixed by Gnulib:

- This function is missing on some platforms: Mac OS X 10.5, FreeBSD 6.0, NetBSD 5.0, OpenBSD 3.8, Minix 3.1.8, HP-UX 11, Solaris 11 2011-11, Cygwin, mingw, MSVC 9, Interix 3.5.

12.70.8 `getloadavg`

Gnulib module: getloadavg

Portability problems fixed by Gnulib:

- This function is missing on some platforms: AIX 5.1, HP-UX 11, IRIX 6.5, OSF/1 5.1, Solaris 2.6, Cygwin, mingw, MSVC 9, Interix 3.5, BeOS.
- This function is declared in `<sys/loadavg.h>`, not `<stdlib.h>`, on some platforms: Solaris 11 2011-11.

Portability problems not fixed by Gnulib:

12.70.9 `getpt`

Gnulib module: —

Portability problems fixed by Gnulib:

Portability problems not fixed by Gnulib:

- This function is missing on many non-glibc platforms: Mac OS X 10.5, FreeBSD 6.0, NetBSD 5.0, OpenBSD 3.8, Minix 3.1.8, AIX 5.1, HP-UX 11, IRIX 6.5, OSF/1 5.1, Solaris 11 2011-11, Cygwin 1.7.9, mingw, MSVC 9, Interix 3.5, BeOS.

12.70.10 `initstate_r`

Gnulib module: random_r

Portability problems fixed by Gnulib:

- This function is missing on some platforms: Mac OS X 10.5, FreeBSD 6.0, NetBSD 5.0, OpenBSD 3.8, Minix 3.1.8, HP-UX 11, IRIX 6.5, Solaris 11 2011-11, Cygwin, mingw, MSVC 9, Interix 3.5.
- This function has an incompatible declaration on some platforms: AIX 7.1, OSF/1 5.1.

Portability problems not fixed by Gnulib:

12.70.11 `jrand48_r`

Gnulib module: —

Portability problems fixed by Gnulib:

Portability problems not fixed by Gnulib:

- This function is missing on some platforms: Mac OS X 10.5, FreeBSD 6.0, NetBSD 5.0, OpenBSD 3.8, Minix 3.1.8, HP-UX 11, IRIX 6.5, Solaris 11 2011-11, Cygwin, mingw, MSVC 9, Interix 3.5.

12.70.12 `lcong48_r`

Gnulib module: —

Portability problems fixed by Gnulib:

Portability problems not fixed by Gnulib:

- This function is missing on some platforms: Mac OS X 10.5, FreeBSD 6.0, NetBSD 5.0, OpenBSD 3.8, Minix 3.1.8, HP-UX 11, IRIX 6.5, Solaris 11 2011-11, Cygwin, mingw, MSVC 9, Interix 3.5.

12.70.13 `lrand48_r`

Gnulib module: —

Portability problems fixed by Gnulib:

Portability problems not fixed by Gnulib:

- This function is missing on some platforms: Mac OS X 10.5, FreeBSD 6.0, NetBSD 5.0, OpenBSD 3.8, Minix 3.1.8, HP-UX 11, IRIX 6.5, Solaris 11 2011-11, Cygwin, mingw, MSVC 9, Interix 3.5.

12.70.14 `mkostemp`

Gnulib module: mkostemp

Portability problems fixed by Gnulib:

- This function is missing on many non-glibc platforms: Mac OS X 10.5, FreeBSD 6.0, NetBSD 5.0, OpenBSD 3.8, Minix 3.1.8, AIX 5.1, HP-UX 11, IRIX 6.5, OSF/1 5.1, Solaris 11 2011-11, Cygwin 1.7.5, mingw, MSVC 9, Interix 3.5, BeOS.
- On platforms where `off_t` is a 32-bit type, `mkostemp` may not work correctly to create files larger than 2 GB. (Cf. `AC_SYS_LARGEFILE`.)

Portability problems not fixed by Gnulib:

The gnulib module `clean-temp` can create temporary files that will not be left behind after signals such as SIGINT.

12.70.15 `mkostemps`

Gnulib module: mkostemps

Portability problems fixed by Gnulib:

- This function is missing on many non-glibc platforms: glibc 2.10, Mac OS X 10.5, FreeBSD 6.0, NetBSD 5.0, OpenBSD 3.8, Minix 3.1.8, AIX 5.1, HP-UX 11, IRIX 6.5, OSF/1 5.1, Solaris 11 2011-11, Cygwin 1.7.5, mingw, MSVC 9, Interix 3.5, BeOS.
- On platforms where `off_t` is a 32-bit type, `mkostemps` may not work correctly to create files larger than 2 GB. (Cf. `AC_SYS_LARGEFILE`.)

Portability problems not fixed by Gnulib:

The gnulib module `clean-temp` can create temporary files that will not be left behind after signals such as SIGINT.

12.70.16 mrand48_r

Gnulib module: —

Portability problems fixed by Gnulib:

Portability problems not fixed by Gnulib:

- This function is missing on some platforms: Mac OS X 10.5, FreeBSD 6.0, NetBSD 5.0, OpenBSD 3.8, Minix 3.1.8, HP-UX 11, IRIX 6.5, Solaris 11 2011-11, Cygwin, mingw, MSVC 9, Interix 3.5.

12.70.17 mkstemps

Gnulib module: mkstemps

Portability problems fixed by Gnulib:

- This function is missing on many non-glibc platforms: glibc 2.10, Minix 3.1.8, AIX 5.1, HP-UX 11, IRIX 6.5, OSF/1 5.1, Solaris 10, Cygwin 1.5.x, mingw, MSVC 9, Interix 3.5, BeOS.
- This function is declared in <unistd.h> instead of <stdlib.h> on some platforms: Mac OS X 10.5.
- On platforms where off_t is a 32-bit type, mkstemps may not work correctly to create files larger than 2 GB. (Cf. AC_SYS_LARGEFILE.)

Portability problems not fixed by Gnulib:

The gnulib module clean-temp can create temporary files that will not be left behind after signals such as SIGINT.

12.70.18 nrand48_r

Gnulib module: —

Portability problems fixed by Gnulib:

Portability problems not fixed by Gnulib:

- This function is missing on some platforms: Mac OS X 10.5, FreeBSD 6.0, NetBSD 5.0, OpenBSD 3.8, Minix 3.1.8, HP-UX 11, IRIX 6.5, Solaris 11 2011-11, Cygwin, mingw, MSVC 9, Interix 3.5.

12.70.19 on_exit

Gnulib module: —

Portability problems fixed by Gnulib:

Portability problems not fixed by Gnulib:

- This function is missing on some platforms: Mac OS X 10.5, FreeBSD 6.0, NetBSD 5.0, OpenBSD 3.8, Minix 3.1.8, AIX 4.3.2, HP-UX 11, IRIX 6.5, OSF/1 5.1, Solaris 11 2011-11, mingw, MSVC 9, Interix 3.5, BeOS.

12.70.20 `ptsname_r`

Gnulib module: ptsname_r

Portability problems fixed by Gnulib:

- This function is missing on some platforms: Mac OS X 10.5, FreeBSD 6.0, NetBSD 5.0, OpenBSD 3.8, Minix 3.1.8, AIX 5.1, HP-UX 11, IRIX 6.5, Solaris 11 2011-11, Cygwin 1.7.9, mingw, MSVC 9, BeOS.
- This function is not declared unless **_REENTRANT** is defined, on some platforms: OSF/1 5.1.
- This function has an incompatible declaration on some platforms: OSF/1 5.1.

Portability problems not fixed by Gnulib:

12.70.21 `qecvt`

Gnulib module: —

Portability problems fixed by Gnulib:

Portability problems not fixed by Gnulib:

- This function is missing on some platforms: Mac OS X 10.5, FreeBSD 6.0, NetBSD 5.0, OpenBSD 3.8, Minix 3.1.8, AIX 5.1, HP-UX 11, IRIX 6.5, OSF/1 5.1, Cygwin, mingw, MSVC 9, Interix 3.5, BeOS.

12.70.22 `qecvt_r`

Gnulib module: —

Portability problems fixed by Gnulib:

Portability problems not fixed by Gnulib:

- This function is missing on all non-glibc platforms: Mac OS X 10.5, FreeBSD 6.0, NetBSD 5.0, OpenBSD 3.8, Minix 3.1.8, AIX 5.1, HP-UX 11, IRIX 6.5, OSF/1 5.1, Solaris 11 2011-11, Cygwin, mingw, MSVC 9, Interix 3.5, BeOS.

12.70.23 `qfcvt`

Gnulib module: —

Portability problems fixed by Gnulib:

Portability problems not fixed by Gnulib:

- This function is missing on some platforms: Mac OS X 10.5, FreeBSD 6.0, NetBSD 5.0, OpenBSD 3.8, Minix 3.1.8, AIX 5.1, HP-UX 11, IRIX 6.5, OSF/1 5.1, Cygwin, mingw, MSVC 9, Interix 3.5, BeOS.

12.70.24 `qfcvt_r`

Gnulib module: —

Portability problems fixed by Gnulib:

Portability problems not fixed by Gnulib:

- This function is missing on all non-glibc platforms: Mac OS X 10.5, FreeBSD 6.0, NetBSD 5.0, OpenBSD 3.8, Minix 3.1.8, AIX 5.1, HP-UX 11, IRIX 6.5, OSF/1 5.1, Solaris 11 2011-11, Cygwin, mingw, MSVC 9, Interix 3.5, BeOS.

12.70.25 `qgcvt`

Gnulib module: —

Portability problems fixed by Gnulib:

Portability problems not fixed by Gnulib:

- This function is missing on some platforms: Mac OS X 10.5, FreeBSD 6.0, NetBSD 5.0, OpenBSD 3.8, Minix 3.1.8, AIX 5.1, HP-UX 11, IRIX 6.5, OSF/1 5.1, Cygwin, mingw, MSVC 9, Interix 3.5, BeOS.

12.70.26 `qsort_r`

Gnulib module: —

Portability problems fixed by Gnulib:

- This function has an incompatible API on some platforms: FreeBSD 10.
- This function is missing on some platforms: glibc 2.7, NetBSD 5.0, OpenBSD 3.8, Minix 3.1.8, AIX 7.1, HP-UX 11.31, IRIX 6.5, OSF/1 5.1, Solaris 11 2011-11, Cygwin, mingw, MSVC 9, Interix 3.5, BeOS.

Portability problems not fixed by Gnulib:

12.70.27 `random_r`

Gnulib module: random_r

Portability problems fixed by Gnulib:

- This function is missing on some platforms: Mac OS X 10.5, FreeBSD 6.0, NetBSD 5.0, OpenBSD 3.8, Minix 3.1.8, HP-UX 11, IRIX 6.5, Solaris 11 2011-11, Cygwin, mingw, MSVC 9, Interix 3.5.
- This function has an incompatible declaration on some platforms: AIX 7.1, OSF/1 5.1.

Portability problems not fixed by Gnulib:

12.70.28 `rpmatch`

Gnulib module: rpmatch

Portability problems fixed by Gnulib:

- This function is missing on some platforms: Mac OS X 10.5, FreeBSD 5.2.1, NetBSD 5.0, OpenBSD 3.8, Minix 3.1.8, HP-UX 11, IRIX 6.5, Solaris 11 2011-11, Cygwin, mingw, MSVC 9, Interix 3.5, BeOS.

Portability problems not fixed by Gnulib:

12.70.29 `secure_getenv`

Gnulib module: secure_getenv

Portability problems fixed by Gnulib:

- This function is missing on some platforms: glibc 2.16, OS X 10.8, FreeBSD 9.1, NetBSD 6.0.1, OpenBSD 5.2, Minix 3.2.0, AIX 7.1, HP-UX 11, IRIX 6.5, Solaris 11, Cygwin, mingw, MSVC 9, Interix 6.1, BeOS.

Portability problems not fixed by Gnulib:

- On platforms other than glibc 2.0 and later, the Gnulib replacement function always returns a null pointer, even when invoked in a non-setuid program.

12.70.30 seed48_r

Gnulib module: —

Portability problems fixed by Gnulib:

Portability problems not fixed by Gnulib:

- This function is missing on some platforms: Mac OS X 10.5, FreeBSD 6.0, NetBSD 5.0, OpenBSD 3.8, Minix 3.1.8, HP-UX 11, IRIX 6.5, Solaris 11 2011-11, Cygwin, mingw, MSVC 9, Interix 3.5.

12.70.31 setstate_r

Gnulib module: random_r

Portability problems fixed by Gnulib:

- This function is missing on some platforms: Mac OS X 10.5, FreeBSD 6.0, NetBSD 5.0, OpenBSD 3.8, Minix 3.1.8, HP-UX 11, IRIX 6.5, Solaris 11 2011-11, Cygwin, mingw, MSVC 9, Interix 3.5.
- This function has an incompatible declaration on some platforms: AIX 7.1, OSF/1 5.1.

Portability problems not fixed by Gnulib:

12.70.32 srand48_r

Gnulib module: —

Portability problems fixed by Gnulib:

Portability problems not fixed by Gnulib:

- This function is missing on some platforms: Mac OS X 10.5, FreeBSD 6.0, NetBSD 5.0, OpenBSD 3.8, Minix 3.1.8, HP-UX 11, IRIX 6.5, Solaris 11 2011-11, Cygwin, mingw, MSVC 9, Interix 3.5.

12.70.33 srandom_r

Gnulib module: random_r

Portability problems fixed by Gnulib:

- This function is missing on some platforms: Mac OS X 10.5, FreeBSD 6.0, NetBSD 5.0, OpenBSD 3.8, Minix 3.1.8, HP-UX 11, IRIX 6.5, Solaris 11 2011-11, Cygwin, mingw, MSVC 9, Interix 3.5.

Portability problems not fixed by Gnulib:

12.70.34 strtod_l

Gnulib module: —

Portability problems fixed by Gnulib:

Portability problems not fixed by Gnulib:

- This function is missing on many platforms: Mac OS X 10.3, FreeBSD 6.0, NetBSD 5.0, OpenBSD 3.8, Minix 3.1.8, AIX 5.1, HP-UX 11, IRIX 6.5, OSF/1 5.1, Solaris 11 2011-11, Cygwin, mingw, MSVC 9, Interix 3.5, BeOS.

12.70.35 strtof_l

Gnulib module: —

Portability problems fixed by Gnulib:

Portability problems not fixed by Gnulib:

- This function is missing on many platforms: Mac OS X 10.3, FreeBSD 6.0, NetBSD 5.0, OpenBSD 3.8, Minix 3.1.8, AIX 5.1, HP-UX 11, IRIX 6.5, OSF/1 5.1, Solaris 11 2011-11, Cygwin, mingw, MSVC 9, Interix 3.5, BeOS.

12.70.36 strtol_l

Gnulib module: —

Portability problems fixed by Gnulib:

Portability problems not fixed by Gnulib:

- This function is missing on many platforms: Mac OS X 10.3, FreeBSD 6.0, NetBSD 5.0, OpenBSD 3.8, Minix 3.1.8, AIX 5.1, HP-UX 11, IRIX 6.5, OSF/1 5.1, Solaris 11 2011-11, Cygwin, mingw, MSVC 9, Interix 3.5, BeOS.

12.70.37 strtold_l

Gnulib module: —

Portability problems fixed by Gnulib:

Portability problems not fixed by Gnulib:

- This function is missing on many platforms: Mac OS X 10.3, FreeBSD 6.0, NetBSD 5.0, OpenBSD 3.8, Minix 3.1.8, AIX 5.1, HP-UX 11, IRIX 6.5, OSF/1 5.1, Solaris 11 2011-11, Cygwin, mingw, MSVC 9, Interix 3.5, BeOS.

12.70.38 strtoll_l

Gnulib module: —

Portability problems fixed by Gnulib:

Portability problems not fixed by Gnulib:

- This function is missing on many platforms: Mac OS X 10.3, FreeBSD 6.0, NetBSD 5.0, OpenBSD 3.8, Minix 3.1.8, AIX 5.1, HP-UX 11, IRIX 6.5, OSF/1 5.1, Solaris 11 2011-11, Cygwin, mingw, MSVC 9, Interix 3.5, BeOS.

12.70.39 strtoq

Gnulib module: —

Portability problems fixed by Gnulib:

Portability problems not fixed by Gnulib:

- This function is missing on some platforms: Minix 3.1.8, AIX 5.1, HP-UX 11, IRIX 6.5, OSF/1 5.1, Solaris 11 2011-11, Cygwin, mingw, MSVC 9.

12.70.40 `strtoul_l`

Gnulib module: —

Portability problems fixed by Gnulib:

Portability problems not fixed by Gnulib:

- This function is missing on many platforms: Mac OS X 10.3, FreeBSD 6.0, NetBSD 5.0, OpenBSD 3.8, Minix 3.1.8, AIX 5.1, HP-UX 11, IRIX 6.5, OSF/1 5.1, Solaris 11 2011-11, Cygwin, mingw, MSVC 9, Interix 3.5, BeOS.

12.70.41 `strtoull_l`

Gnulib module: —

Portability problems fixed by Gnulib:

Portability problems not fixed by Gnulib:

- This function is missing on many platforms: Mac OS X 10.3, FreeBSD 6.0, NetBSD 5.0, OpenBSD 3.8, Minix 3.1.8, AIX 5.1, HP-UX 11, IRIX 6.5, OSF/1 5.1, Solaris 11 2011-11, Cygwin, mingw, MSVC 9, Interix 3.5, BeOS.

12.70.42 `strtouq`

Gnulib module: —

Portability problems fixed by Gnulib:

Portability problems not fixed by Gnulib:

- This function is missing on some platforms: Minix 3.1.8, AIX 5.1, HP-UX 11, IRIX 6.5, OSF/1 5.1, Solaris 11 2011-11, Cygwin, mingw, MSVC 9.

12.70.43 `valloc`

Gnulib module: —

Portability problems fixed by Gnulib:

Portability problems not fixed by Gnulib:

- This function is missing on some platforms: Minix 3.1.8, mingw, MSVC 9, Interix 3.5.

12.71 Glibc Extensions to `<string.h>`

12.71.1 `ffsl`

Gnulib module: ffsl

Portability problems fixed by Gnulib:

- This function is missing on some platforms: Mac OS X 10.4, FreeBSD 5.2.1, NetBSD 5.0, OpenBSD 3.8, Minix 3.1.8, AIX 5.1, HP-UX 11, IRIX 6.5, OSF/1 5.1, Solaris 10, Cygwin, mingw, MSVC 9, Interix 3.5, BeOS.

Portability problems not fixed by Gnulib:

12.71.2 ffsll

Gnulib module: ffsll

Portability problems fixed by Gnulib:

- This function is missing on all non-glibc platforms: Mac OS X 10.5, FreeBSD 6.0, NetBSD 5.0, OpenBSD 3.8, Minix 3.1.8, AIX 5.1, HP-UX 11, IRIX 6.5, OSF/1 5.1, Solaris 10, Cygwin, mingw, MSVC 9, Interix 3.5, BeOS.

Portability problems not fixed by Gnulib:

12.71.3 memfrob

Gnulib module: —

Portability problems fixed by Gnulib:

Portability problems not fixed by Gnulib:

- This function is missing on all non-glibc platforms: Mac OS X 10.5, FreeBSD 6.0, NetBSD 5.0, OpenBSD 3.8, Minix 3.1.8, AIX 5.1, HP-UX 11, IRIX 6.5, OSF/1 5.1, Solaris 11 2011-11, Cygwin, mingw, MSVC 9, Interix 3.5, BeOS.

12.71.4 memmem

Gnulib module: memmem or memmem-simple

Both modules implement the same replacement for the memmem function with the memmem module providing a replacement on more platforms where the existing memmem function has a quadratic worst-case complexity.

Portability problems fixed by either Gnulib module memmem-simple or memmem:

- This function is missing on some platforms: Mac OS X 10.5, FreeBSD 5.2.1, OpenBSD 4.0, Minix 3.1.8, AIX 4.3.2, HP-UX 11, IRIX 6.5, OSF/1 5.1, Solaris 10, mingw, MSVC 9, Interix 3.5, BeOS.
- This function has reversed arguments on some older platforms: Linux libc 5.0.9
- This function can trigger false positives for long periodic needles on some platforms: glibc 2.12, Cygwin 1.7.7.
- This function returns incorrect values in some cases, such as when given an empty needle: glibc <= 2.0, Solaris 11 2011-11, Cygwin 1.5.x.

Performance problems fixed by Gnulib module memmem:

- This function has quadratic instead of linear worst-case complexity on some platforms: glibc 2.8, FreeBSD 6.2, NetBSD 5.0, AIX 5.1, Solaris 11 2011-11, Cygwin 1.5.x. Note for small needles the replacement may be slower.

Portability problems not fixed by Gnulib:

12.71.5 mempcpy

Gnulib module: mempcpy

Portability problems fixed by Gnulib:

- This function is missing on some platforms: Mac OS X 10.5, FreeBSD 6.0, NetBSD 5.0, OpenBSD 3.8, Minix 3.1.8, AIX 5.1, HP-UX 11, IRIX 6.5, OSF/1 5.1, Solaris 11 2011-11, mingw, MSVC 9, Interix 3.5, BeOS.

Portability problems not fixed by Gnulib:

12.71.6 memrchr

Gnulib module: memrchr

Portability problems fixed by Gnulib:

- This function is missing on all non-glibc platforms: Mac OS X 10.5, FreeBSD 6.0, NetBSD 5.0, OpenBSD 3.8, Minix 3.1.8, AIX 5.1, HP-UX 11, IRIX 6.5, OSF/1 5.1, Solaris 11 2011-11, Cygwin, mingw, MSVC 9, Interix 3.5, BeOS.

Portability problems not fixed by Gnulib:

12.71.7 rawmemchr

Gnulib module: rawmemchr

Portability problems fixed by Gnulib:

- This function is missing on all non-glibc platforms: Mac OS X 10.5, FreeBSD 6.0, NetBSD 5.0, OpenBSD 3.8, Minix 3.1.8, AIX 5.1, HP-UX 11, IRIX 6.5, OSF/1 5.1, Solaris 11 2011-11, Cygwin, mingw, MSVC 9, Interix 3.5, BeOS.

Portability problems not fixed by Gnulib:

12.71.8 strcasestr

Gnulib module: strcasestr or strcasestr-simple

Portability problems fixed by either Gnulib module `strcasestr-simple` or `strcasestr`:

- This function is missing on some platforms: AIX 5.1, HP-UX 11, IRIX 6.5, OSF/1 5.1, Solaris 10, Cygwin 1.5.x, mingw, MSVC 9, BeOS.
- This function can trigger memchr bugs on some platforms: glibc 2.10.
- This function can trigger false positives for long periodic needles on some platforms: glibc 2.12, Cygwin 1.7.7.

Portability problems fixed by Gnulib module `strcasestr`:

- This function has quadratic instead of linear worst-case complexity on some platforms: glibc 2.8, FreeBSD 6.2, NetBSD 5.0, OpenBSD 4.0, Solaris 11 2011-11.

Portability problems not fixed by Gnulib:

12.71.9 strchrnul

Gnulib module: strchrnul

Portability problems fixed by Gnulib:

- This function is missing on many non-glibc platforms: Mac OS X 10.5, FreeBSD 6.0, NetBSD 5.0, OpenBSD 3.8, Minix 3.1.8, AIX 5.1, HP-UX 11, IRIX 6.5, OSF/1 5.1, Solaris 10, Cygwin 1.7.8, mingw, MSVC 9, Interix 3.5, BeOS.
- This function crashes when no occurrence is found on some platforms: Cygwin 1.7.9.

Portability problems not fixed by Gnulib:

12.71.10 `strfry`

Gnulib module: —

Portability problems fixed by Gnulib:

Portability problems not fixed by Gnulib:

- This function is missing on all non-glibc platforms: Mac OS X 10.5, FreeBSD 6.0, NetBSD 5.0, OpenBSD 3.8, Minix 3.1.8, AIX 5.1, HP-UX 11, IRIX 6.5, OSF/1 5.1, Solaris 11 2011-11, Cygwin, mingw, MSVC 9, Interix 3.5, BeOS.

12.71.11 `strsep`

Gnulib module: strsep

Portability problems fixed by Gnulib:

- This function is missing on some platforms: AIX 4.3.2, HP-UX 11, IRIX 6.5, OSF/1 5.1, Solaris 10, mingw, MSVC 9, BeOS.

Portability problems not fixed by Gnulib:

12.71.12 `strverscmp`

Gnulib module: strverscmp

Portability problems fixed by Gnulib:

- This function is missing on all non-glibc platforms: Mac OS X 10.5, FreeBSD 6.0, NetBSD 5.0, OpenBSD 3.8, Minix 3.1.8, AIX 5.1, HP-UX 11, IRIX 6.5, OSF/1 5.1, Solaris 11 2011-11, Cygwin, mingw, MSVC 9, Interix 3.5, BeOS.

Portability problems not fixed by Gnulib:

12.72 Glibc `<sys/capability.h>`

12.72.1 `capget`

Gnulib module: —

Portability problems fixed by Gnulib:

Portability problems not fixed by Gnulib:

- This function is missing on all non-glibc platforms: Mac OS X 10.5, FreeBSD 6.0, NetBSD 5.0, OpenBSD 3.8, Minix 3.1.8, AIX 5.1, HP-UX 11, IRIX 6.5, OSF/1 5.1, Solaris 11 2011-11, Cygwin, mingw, MSVC 9, Interix 3.5, BeOS.

12.72.2 `capset`

Gnulib module: —

Portability problems fixed by Gnulib:

Portability problems not fixed by Gnulib:

- This function is missing on all non-glibc platforms: Mac OS X 10.5, FreeBSD 6.0, NetBSD 5.0, OpenBSD 3.8, Minix 3.1.8, AIX 5.1, HP-UX 11, IRIX 6.5, OSF/1 5.1, Solaris 11 2011-11, Cygwin, mingw, MSVC 9, Interix 3.5, BeOS.

12.73 Glibc `<sys/epoll.h>`

12.73.1 `epoll_create`

Gnulib module: —

Portability problems fixed by Gnulib:

Portability problems not fixed by Gnulib:

- This function is missing on all non-glibc platforms: Mac OS X 10.5, FreeBSD 6.0, NetBSD 5.0, OpenBSD 3.8, Minix 3.1.8, AIX 5.1, HP-UX 11, IRIX 6.5, OSF/1 5.1, Solaris 11 2011-11, Cygwin, mingw, MSVC 9, Interix 3.5, BeOS.

12.73.2 `epoll_ctl`

Gnulib module: —

Portability problems fixed by Gnulib:

Portability problems not fixed by Gnulib:

- This function is missing on all non-glibc platforms: Mac OS X 10.5, FreeBSD 6.0, NetBSD 5.0, OpenBSD 3.8, Minix 3.1.8, AIX 5.1, HP-UX 11, IRIX 6.5, OSF/1 5.1, Solaris 11 2011-11, Cygwin, mingw, MSVC 9, Interix 3.5, BeOS.

12.73.3 `epoll_wait`

Gnulib module: —

Portability problems fixed by Gnulib:

Portability problems not fixed by Gnulib:

- This function is missing on all non-glibc platforms: Mac OS X 10.5, FreeBSD 6.0, NetBSD 5.0, OpenBSD 3.8, Minix 3.1.8, AIX 5.1, HP-UX 11, IRIX 6.5, OSF/1 5.1, Solaris 11 2011-11, Cygwin, mingw, MSVC 9, Interix 3.5, BeOS.

12.74 Glibc `<sys/fanotify.h>`

12.74.1 `fanotify_init`

Gnulib module: —

Portability problems fixed by Gnulib:

Portability problems not fixed by Gnulib:

- This function is missing on all non-glibc platforms: glibc 2.12, Mac OS X 10.5, FreeBSD 6.4, NetBSD 5.0, OpenBSD 3.8, Minix 3.1.8, AIX 7.1, HP-UX 11.31, IRIX 6.5, OSF/1 5.1, Solaris 11 2011-11, Cygwin, mingw, MSVC 9, Interix 3.5, BeOS.

12.74.2 `fanotify_mark`

Gnulib module: —

Portability problems fixed by Gnulib:

Portability problems not fixed by Gnulib:

- This function is missing on all non-glibc platforms: glibc 2.12, Mac OS X 10.5, FreeBSD 6.4, NetBSD 5.0, OpenBSD 3.8, Minix 3.1.8, AIX 7.1, HP-UX 11.31, IRIX 6.5, OSF/1 5.1, Solaris 11 2011-11, Cygwin, mingw, MSVC 9, Interix 3.5, BeOS.

12.75 Glibc `<sys/file.h>`

12.75.1 `flock`

Gnulib module: flock

Portability problems fixed by Gnulib:

- This function is missing on some platforms: mingw, MSVC 9

Portability problems not fixed by Gnulib:

- This function is missing on some platforms: AIX 5.1, HP-UX 11.23, Solaris 11 2011-11, BeOS.

12.76 Glibc `<sys/fsuid.h>`

12.76.1 `setfsgid`

Gnulib module: —

Portability problems fixed by Gnulib:

Portability problems not fixed by Gnulib:

- This function is missing on all non-glibc platforms: Mac OS X 10.5, FreeBSD 6.0, NetBSD 5.0, OpenBSD 3.8, Minix 3.1.8, AIX 5.1, HP-UX 11, IRIX 6.5, OSF/1 5.1, Solaris 11 2011-11, Cygwin, mingw, MSVC 9, Interix 3.5, BeOS.

12.76.2 `setfsuid`

Gnulib module: —

Portability problems fixed by Gnulib:

Portability problems not fixed by Gnulib:

- This function is missing on all non-glibc platforms: Mac OS X 10.5, FreeBSD 6.0, NetBSD 5.0, OpenBSD 3.8, Minix 3.1.8, AIX 5.1, HP-UX 11, IRIX 6.5, OSF/1 5.1, Solaris 11 2011-11, Cygwin, mingw, MSVC 9, Interix 3.5, BeOS.

12.77 Glibc `<sys/gmon.h>`

12.77.1 `monstartup`

Gnulib module: —

Portability problems fixed by Gnulib:

Portability problems not fixed by Gnulib:

- This function is missing on some platforms: Minix 3.1.8, HP-UX 11, IRIX 6.5, OSF/1 5.1, Solaris 11 2011-11, Cygwin, mingw, MSVC 9, Interix 3.5, BeOS.

12.78 Glibc <sys/io.h>, <sys/perm.h>

12.78.1 ioperm

Gnulib module: —

Portability problems fixed by Gnulib:

Portability problems not fixed by Gnulib:

- This function is missing on all non-glibc platforms: Mac OS X 10.5, FreeBSD 6.0, NetBSD 5.0, OpenBSD 3.8, Minix 3.1.8, AIX 5.1, HP-UX 11, IRIX 6.5, OSF/1 5.1, Solaris 11 2011-11, Cygwin, mingw, MSVC 9, Interix 3.5, BeOS.

12.78.2 iopl

Gnulib module: —

Portability problems fixed by Gnulib:

Portability problems not fixed by Gnulib:

- This function is missing on all non-glibc platforms: Mac OS X 10.5, FreeBSD 6.0, NetBSD 5.0, OpenBSD 3.8, Minix 3.1.8, AIX 5.1, HP-UX 11, IRIX 6.5, OSF/1 5.1, Solaris 11 2011-11, Cygwin, mingw, MSVC 9, Interix 3.5, BeOS.

12.79 Glibc <sys/kdaemon.h>

12.79.1 bdflush

Gnulib module: —

Portability problems fixed by Gnulib:

Portability problems not fixed by Gnulib:

- This function is missing on all non-glibc platforms: Mac OS X 10.5, FreeBSD 6.0, NetBSD 5.0, OpenBSD 3.8, Minix 3.1.8, AIX 5.1, HP-UX 11, IRIX 6.5, OSF/1 5.1, Solaris 11 2011-11, Cygwin, mingw, MSVC 9, Interix 3.5, BeOS.

12.80 Glibc <sys/klog.h>

12.80.1 klogctl

Gnulib module: —

Portability problems fixed by Gnulib:

Portability problems not fixed by Gnulib:

- This function is missing on all non-glibc platforms: Mac OS X 10.5, FreeBSD 6.0, NetBSD 5.0, OpenBSD 3.8, Minix 3.1.8, AIX 5.1, HP-UX 11, IRIX 6.5, OSF/1 5.1, Solaris 11 2011-11, Cygwin, mingw, MSVC 9, Interix 3.5, BeOS.

12.81 Glibc Extensions to <sys/mman.h>

12.81.1 madvise

Gnulib module: —

Portability problems fixed by Gnulib:

Portability problems not fixed by Gnulib:

- This function is missing on some platforms: Minix 3.1.8, AIX 5.1, Cygwin 1.7.7, mingw, MSVC 9, BeOS.

12.81.2 mincore

Gnulib module: —

Portability problems fixed by Gnulib:

Portability problems not fixed by Gnulib:

- This function is missing on some platforms: Minix 3.1.8, AIX 5.1, HP-UX 11, IRIX 6.5, OSF/1 5.1, Cygwin, mingw, MSVC 9, Interix 3.5, BeOS.

12.81.3 mremap

Gnulib module: —

Portability problems fixed by Gnulib:

Portability problems not fixed by Gnulib:

- This function is missing on many platforms: Mac OS X 10.5, FreeBSD 6.0, NetBSD 3.0, OpenBSD 3.8, Minix 3.1.8, AIX 5.1, HP-UX 11, IRIX 6.5, OSF/1 5.1, Solaris 11 2011-11, Cygwin, mingw, MSVC 9, Interix 3.5, BeOS.

12.81.4 remap_file_pages

Gnulib module: —

Portability problems fixed by Gnulib:

Portability problems not fixed by Gnulib:

- This function is missing on all non-glibc platforms: Mac OS X 10.5, FreeBSD 6.0, NetBSD 5.0, OpenBSD 3.8, Minix 3.1.8, AIX 5.1, HP-UX 11, IRIX 6.5, OSF/1 5.1, Solaris 11 2011-11, Cygwin, mingw, MSVC 9, Interix 3.5, BeOS.

12.82 Glibc <sys/mount.h>

12.82.1 mount

Gnulib module: —

Portability problems fixed by Gnulib:

Portability problems not fixed by Gnulib:

- This function is missing on some platforms: mingw, MSVC 9, Interix 3.5.

12.82.2 umount

Gnulib module: —

Portability problems fixed by Gnulib:

Portability problems not fixed by Gnulib:

- This function is missing on some platforms: Mac OS X 10.5, FreeBSD 6.0, NetBSD 5.0, OpenBSD 3.8, AIX 5.1, mingw, MSVC 9, Interix 3.5, BeOS.

12.82.3 umount2

Gnulib module: —

Portability problems fixed by Gnulib:

Portability problems not fixed by Gnulib:

- This function is missing on some platforms: Mac OS X 10.5, FreeBSD 6.0, NetBSD 5.0, OpenBSD 3.8, Minix 3.1.8, AIX 5.1, HP-UX 11.23, IRIX 6.5, OSF/1 5.1, Cygwin, mingw, MSVC 9, Interix 3.5, BeOS.

12.83 Glibc <sys/personality.h>

12.83.1 personality

Gnulib module: —

Portability problems fixed by Gnulib:

Portability problems not fixed by Gnulib:

- This function is missing on all non-glibc platforms: Mac OS X 10.5, FreeBSD 6.0, NetBSD 5.0, OpenBSD 3.8, Minix 3.1.8, AIX 5.1, HP-UX 11, IRIX 6.5, OSF/1 5.1, Solaris 11 2011-11, Cygwin, mingw, MSVC 9, Interix 3.5, BeOS.

12.84 Glibc <sys/prctl.h>

12.84.1 prctl

Gnulib module: —

Portability problems fixed by Gnulib:

Portability problems not fixed by Gnulib:

- This function is missing on some platforms: Mac OS X 10.5, FreeBSD 6.0, NetBSD 5.0, OpenBSD 3.8, Minix 3.1.8, AIX 5.1, HP-UX 11, OSF/1 5.1, Solaris 11 2011-11, Cygwin, mingw, MSVC 9, Interix 3.5, BeOS.

12.85 Glibc <sys/profil.h>

12.85.1 sprofil

Gnulib module: —

Portability problems fixed by Gnulib:

Portability problems not fixed by Gnulib:

- This function is missing on some platforms: Mac OS X 10.5, FreeBSD 6.0, NetBSD 5.0, OpenBSD 3.8, Minix 3.1.8, AIX 5.1, HP-UX 11.11, OSF/1 5.1, Solaris 11 2011-11, Cygwin, mingw, MSVC 9, Interix 3.5, BeOS.

12.86 Glibc <sys/ptrace.h>

12.86.1 ptrace

Gnulib module: —

Portability problems fixed by Gnulib:

Portability problems not fixed by Gnulib:

- This function is missing on some platforms: AIX 5.1, Cygwin, mingw, MSVC 9, Interix 3.5, BeOS.

12.87 Glibc <sys/quota.h>

12.87.1 quotactl

Gnulib module: —

Portability problems fixed by Gnulib:

Portability problems not fixed by Gnulib:

- This function is missing on some platforms: Minix 3.1.8, AIX 5.1, Solaris 11 2011-11, Cygwin, mingw, MSVC 9, Interix 3.5, BeOS.

12.88 Glibc <sys/reboot.h>

12.88.1 reboot

Gnulib module: —

Portability problems fixed by Gnulib:

Portability problems not fixed by Gnulib:

- This function is missing on some platforms: AIX 5.1, Cygwin, mingw, MSVC 9, Interix 3.5, BeOS.

12.89 Glibc Extensions to <sys/resource.h>

12.89.1 prlimit

Gnulib module: —

Portability problems fixed by Gnulib:

Portability problems not fixed by Gnulib:

- This function is missing on all non-glibc platforms: glibc 2.12, Mac OS X 10.5, FreeBSD 6.4, NetBSD 5.0, OpenBSD 3.8, Minix 3.1.8, AIX 7.1, HP-UX 11.31, IRIX 6.5, OSF/1 5.1, Solaris 11 2011-11, Cygwin, mingw, MSVC 9, Interix 3.5, BeOS.

12.90 Glibc Extensions to <sys/sem.h>

12.90.1 `semtimedop`

Gnulib module: —

Portability problems fixed by Gnulib:

Portability problems not fixed by Gnulib:

- This function is missing on some platforms: Mac OS X 10.5, FreeBSD 6.0, NetBSD 5.0, OpenBSD 3.8, Minix 3.1.8, AIX 5.1, HP-UX 11.11, IRIX 6.5, OSF/1 5.1, Cygwin, mingw, MSVC 9, Interix 3.5, BeOS.

12.91 Glibc <sys/sendfile.h>

12.91.1 `sendfile`

Gnulib module: —

Portability problems fixed by Gnulib:

Portability problems not fixed by Gnulib:

- This function is missing on some platforms: Mac OS X 10.4, NetBSD 5.0, OpenBSD 3.8, Minix 3.1.8, AIX 5.1, IRIX 6.5, OSF/1 4.0, Solaris 11 2010-11, Cygwin, mingw, MSVC 9, Interix 3.5, BeOS.
- On platforms where `off_t` is a 32-bit type, this function may not work correctly on files larger than 2 GB. The fix is to use the `AC_SYS_LARGEFILE` macro.

12.92 Glibc Extensions to <sys/socket.h>

12.92.1 `accept4`

Gnulib module: accept4

Portability problems fixed by Gnulib:

- This function is missing on many non-glibc platforms: Mac OS X 10.5, FreeBSD 6.0, NetBSD 5.0, OpenBSD 3.8, Minix 3.1.8, AIX 5.1, HP-UX 11, IRIX 6.5, OSF/1 5.1, Solaris 11 2011-11, Cygwin 1.7.1, mingw, MSVC 9, Interix 3.5, BeOS. But the replacement function is not atomic; this matters in multi-threaded programs that spawn child processes.

Portability problems not fixed by Gnulib:

- SOCK_CLOEXEC and SOCK_NONBLOCK may not be defined as they're also significant to the socket() function.

12.92.2 `isfdtype`

Gnulib module: —

Portability problems fixed by Gnulib:

Portability problems not fixed by Gnulib:

- This function is missing on some platforms: Mac OS X 10.5, FreeBSD 6.0, NetBSD 5.0, Minix 3.1.8, AIX 5.1, HP-UX 11, IRIX 6.5, OSF/1 4.0, Solaris 11 2011-11, Cygwin, mingw, MSVC 9, Interix 3.5, BeOS.

12.92.3 `recvmmsg`

Gnulib module: —

Portability problems fixed by Gnulib:

Portability problems not fixed by Gnulib:

- This function is missing on all non-glibc platforms: glibc 2.11, Mac OS X 10.5, FreeBSD 6.4, NetBSD 5.0, OpenBSD 3.8, Minix 3.1.8, AIX 7.1, HP-UX 11.31, IRIX 6.5, OSF/1 5.1, Solaris 11 2011-11, Cygwin, mingw, MSVC 9, Interix 3.5, BeOS.

12.92.4 `sendmmsg`

Gnulib module: —

Portability problems fixed by Gnulib:

Portability problems not fixed by Gnulib:

- This function is missing on all non-glibc platforms: glibc 2.13, Mac OS X 10.5, FreeBSD 6.4, NetBSD 5.0, OpenBSD 3.8, Minix 3.1.8, AIX 7.1, HP-UX 11.31, IRIX 6.5, OSF/1 5.1, Solaris 11 2011-11, Cygwin, mingw, MSVC 9, Interix 3.5, BeOS.

12.93 Glibc Extensions to `<sys/stat.h>`

12.93.1 `lchmod`

Gnulib module: lchmod

Portability problems fixed by Gnulib:

- This function is missing on some platforms: Mac OS X 10.4, OpenBSD 3.8, Minix 3.1.8, AIX 5.1, IRIX 6.5, OSF/1 5.1, Solaris 11 2011-11, Cygwin, mingw, MSVC 9, Interix 3.5, BeOS.

Portability problems not fixed by Gnulib:

12.94 Glibc `<sys/statfs.h>`

12.94.1 `fstatfs`

Gnulib module: —

Portability problems fixed by Gnulib:

Portability problems not fixed by Gnulib:

- This function is missing on some platforms: AIX 5.1, mingw, MSVC 9, Interix 3.5, BeOS.

- On platforms where `f_blocks` in 'struct statfs' is a 32-bit value, this function may not work correctly on files systems larger than 4 TiB. The fix is to use the `AC_SYS_LARGEFILE` macro. This affects Mac OS X.

12.94.2 `statfs`

Gnulib module: —

Portability problems fixed by Gnulib:

Portability problems not fixed by Gnulib:

- This function is missing on some platforms: Minix 3.1.8, AIX 5.1, mingw, MSVC 9, Interix 3.5, BeOS.
- On platforms where `f_blocks` in 'struct statfs' is a 32-bit value, this function may not work correctly on files systems larger than 4 TiB. The fix is to use the `AC_SYS_LARGEFILE` macro. This affects Mac OS X.

12.95 Glibc <sys/swap.h>

12.95.1 swapoff

Gnulib module: —

Portability problems fixed by Gnulib:

Portability problems not fixed by Gnulib:

- This function is missing on some platforms: Mac OS X 10.5, NetBSD 5.0, OpenBSD 3.8, Minix 3.1.8, AIX 5.1, IRIX 6.5, OSF/1 5.1, Solaris 11 2011-11, Cygwin, mingw, MSVC 9, Interix 3.5, BeOS.

12.95.2 swapon

Gnulib module: —

Portability problems fixed by Gnulib:

Portability problems not fixed by Gnulib:

- This function is missing on some platforms: OpenBSD 3.8, Minix 3.1.8, AIX 5.1, IRIX 6.5, Solaris 11 2011-11, Cygwin, mingw, MSVC 9, Interix 3.5, BeOS.

12.96 Glibc <sys/sysctl.h>

12.96.1 sysctl

Gnulib module: —

Portability problems fixed by Gnulib:

Portability problems not fixed by Gnulib:

- This function is missing on some platforms: Minix 3.1.8, AIX 5.1, HP-UX 11, IRIX 5.3, OSF/1 5.1, Solaris 11 2011-11, Cygwin, mingw, MSVC 9, Interix 3.5, BeOS.

12.97 Glibc <sys/sysinfo.h>

12.97.1 get_avphys_pages

Gnulib module: —

Portability problems fixed by Gnulib:

Portability problems not fixed by Gnulib:

- This function is missing on many non-glibc platforms: Mac OS X 10.5, FreeBSD 6.0, NetBSD 5.0, OpenBSD 3.8, Minix 3.1.8, AIX 5.1, HP-UX 11, IRIX 6.5, OSF/1 5.1, Solaris 11 2011-11, Cygwin 1.7.1, mingw, MSVC 9, Interix 3.5, BeOS.

12.97.2 get_nprocs

Gnulib module: —

Portability problems fixed by Gnulib:

Portability problems not fixed by Gnulib:

- This function is missing on many non-glibc platforms: Mac OS X 10.5, FreeBSD 6.0, NetBSD 5.0, OpenBSD 3.8, Minix 3.1.8, AIX 5.1, HP-UX 11, IRIX 6.5, OSF/1 5.1, Solaris 10, Cygwin 1.7.1, mingw, MSVC 9, Interix 3.5, BeOS.

Gnulib provides the module nproc that performs a similar function but is portable to more systems.

12.97.3 get_nprocs_conf

Gnulib module: —

Portability problems fixed by Gnulib:

Portability problems not fixed by Gnulib:

- This function is missing on many non-glibc platforms: Mac OS X 10.5, FreeBSD 6.0, NetBSD 5.0, OpenBSD 3.8, Minix 3.1.8, AIX 5.1, HP-UX 11, IRIX 6.5, OSF/1 5.1, Solaris 10, Cygwin 1.7.1, mingw, MSVC 9, Interix 3.5, BeOS.

12.97.4 get_phys_pages

Gnulib module: —

Portability problems fixed by Gnulib:

Portability problems not fixed by Gnulib:

- This function is missing on many non-glibc platforms: Mac OS X 10.5, FreeBSD 6.0, NetBSD 5.0, OpenBSD 3.8, Minix 3.1.8, AIX 5.1, HP-UX 11, IRIX 6.5, OSF/1 5.1, Solaris 11 2011-11, Cygwin 1.7.1, mingw, MSVC 9, Interix 3.5, BeOS.

12.97.5 sysinfo

Gnulib module: —

Portability problems fixed by Gnulib:

Portability problems not fixed by Gnulib:

- This function is missing on some platforms: Mac OS X 10.5, FreeBSD 6.0, NetBSD 5.0, OpenBSD 3.8, Minix 3.1.8, AIX 5.1, Cygwin 1.7.9, mingw, MSVC 9, Interix 3.5, BeOS.

12.98 Glibc <sys/syslog.h>

12.98.1 vsyslog

Gnulib module: —

Portability problems fixed by Gnulib:

Portability problems not fixed by Gnulib:

- This function is missing on some platforms: Minix 3.1.8, AIX 5.1, HP-UX 11, OSF/1 5.1, mingw, MSVC 9, BeOS.

12.99 Glibc <sys/sysmacros.h>

12.99.1 gnu_dev_major

Gnulib module: —

Portability problems fixed by Gnulib:

Portability problems not fixed by Gnulib:

- This function is missing on all non-glibc platforms: Mac OS X 10.5, FreeBSD 6.0, NetBSD 5.0, OpenBSD 3.8, Minix 3.1.8, AIX 5.1, HP-UX 11, IRIX 6.5, OSF/1 5.1, Solaris 11 2011-11, Cygwin, mingw, MSVC 9, Interix 3.5, BeOS.

12.99.2 gnu_dev_makedev

Gnulib module: —

Portability problems fixed by Gnulib:

Portability problems not fixed by Gnulib:

- This function is missing on all non-glibc platforms: Mac OS X 10.5, FreeBSD 6.0, NetBSD 5.0, OpenBSD 3.8, Minix 3.1.8, AIX 5.1, HP-UX 11, IRIX 6.5, OSF/1 5.1, Solaris 11 2011-11, Cygwin, mingw, MSVC 9, Interix 3.5, BeOS.

12.99.3 gnu_dev_minor

Gnulib module: —

Portability problems fixed by Gnulib:

Portability problems not fixed by Gnulib:

- This function is missing on all non-glibc platforms: Mac OS X 10.5, FreeBSD 6.0, NetBSD 5.0, OpenBSD 3.8, Minix 3.1.8, AIX 5.1, HP-UX 11, IRIX 6.5, OSF/1 5.1, Solaris 11 2011-11, Cygwin, mingw, MSVC 9, Interix 3.5, BeOS.

12.100 Glibc Extensions to <sys/time.h>

12.100.1 adjtime

Gnulib module: —

Portability problems fixed by Gnulib:

Portability problems not fixed by Gnulib:

- This function is missing on some platforms: Minix 3.1.8, AIX 5.1, Cygwin, mingw, MSVC 9, Interix 3.5, BeOS.

12.100.2 `futimes`

Gnulib module: —

Portability problems fixed by Gnulib:

Portability problems not fixed by Gnulib:

- This function is missing on some platforms: Minix 3.1.8, AIX 5.1, HP-UX 11, IRIX 6.5, OSF/1 5.1, Solaris 11 2011-11, mingw, MSVC 9, Interix 3.5, BeOS.
- This function cannot set full timestamp resolution. Use `futimens(fd,times)` instead.

12.100.3 `futimesat`

Gnulib module: —

Portability problems fixed by Gnulib:

Portability problems not fixed by Gnulib:

- This function is missing on some platforms: glibc 2.3.6, Mac OS X 10.5, FreeBSD 6.0, NetBSD 5.0, OpenBSD 3.8, Minix 3.1.8, AIX 5.1, HP-UX 11, IRIX 6.5, OSF/1 5.1, Solaris 8, Cygwin 1.5.x, mingw, MSVC 9, Interix 3.5, BeOS.
- On some platforms, this function mis-handles trailing slash: Solaris 9.
- This function cannot set full timestamp resolution. Use `file ? utimensat(fd,file,times,0)` `: futimens(fd,times)`, or the gnulib module fdutimensat, instead.

12.100.4 `lutimes`

Gnulib module: —

Portability problems fixed by Gnulib:

Portability problems not fixed by Gnulib:

- This function is missing on some platforms: Mac OS X 10.4, OpenBSD 3.8, Minix 3.1.8, AIX 5.1, HP-UX 11, IRIX 6.5, OSF/1 5.1, Solaris 11 2011-11, mingw, MSVC 9, Interix 3.5, BeOS.
- This function cannot set full timestamp resolution. Use `utimensat(AT_FDCWD,file,times,AT_SYMLINK_NOFOLLOW)`, or the gnulib module utimens, instead.
- The mere act of using `lstat` modifies the access time of symlinks on some platforms, so `lutimes` can only effectively change modification time: Cygwin.

12.100.5 `settimeofday`

Gnulib module: —

Portability problems fixed by Gnulib:

Portability problems not fixed by Gnulib:

- This function is missing on some platforms: mingw, MSVC 9, BeOS.

12.101 Glibc <sys/timex.h>

12.101.1 adjtimex

Gnulib module: —

Portability problems fixed by Gnulib:

Portability problems not fixed by Gnulib:

- This function is missing on all non-glibc platforms: Mac OS X 10.5, FreeBSD 6.0, NetBSD 5.0, OpenBSD 3.8, Minix 3.1.8, AIX 5.1, HP-UX 11, IRIX 6.5, OSF/1 5.1, Solaris 11 2011-11, Cygwin, mingw, MSVC 9, Interix 3.5, BeOS.

12.101.2 ntp_adjtime

Gnulib module: —

Portability problems fixed by Gnulib:

Portability problems not fixed by Gnulib:

- This function is missing on some platforms: Mac OS X 10.5, OpenBSD 3.8, Minix 3.1.8, AIX 5.1, HP-UX 11, IRIX 6.5, OSF/1 5.1, Cygwin, mingw, MSVC 9, Interix 3.5, BeOS.

12.101.3 ntp_gettime

Gnulib module: —

Portability problems fixed by Gnulib:

Portability problems not fixed by Gnulib:

- This function is missing on some platforms: Mac OS X 10.5, OpenBSD 3.8, Minix 3.1.8, AIX 5.1, HP-UX 11, IRIX 6.5, OSF/1 5.1, Cygwin, mingw, MSVC 9, Interix 3.5, BeOS.

12.101.4 ntp_gettimex

Gnulib module: —

Portability problems fixed by Gnulib:

Portability problems not fixed by Gnulib:

- This function is missing on all non-glibc platforms: glibc 2.11, Mac OS X 10.5, FreeBSD 6.4, NetBSD 5.0, OpenBSD 3.8, Minix 3.1.8, AIX 7.1, HP-UX 11.31, IRIX 6.5, OSF/1 5.1, Solaris 11 2011-11, Cygwin, mingw, MSVC 9, Interix 3.5, BeOS.

12.102 Glibc Extensions to <sys/uio.h>

12.102.1 preadv

Gnulib module: —

Portability problems fixed by Gnulib:

Portability problems not fixed by Gnulib:

- This function is missing on some platforms: glibc 2.9, Mac OS X 10.5, FreeBSD 5.2.1, Minix 3.1.8, AIX 5.2, HP-UX 11.31, IRIX 6.5, OSF/1 5.1, Solaris 11 2011-11, Cygwin, mingw, MSVC 9, Interix 3.5, BeOS.

- On platforms where `off_t` is a 32-bit type, this function may not work correctly on files larger than 2 GB. The fix is to use the `AC_SYS_LARGEFILE` macro.

12.102.2 `process_vm_readv`

Gnulib module: —

Portability problems fixed by Gnulib:

Portability problems not fixed by Gnulib:

- This function is missing on all non-glibc platforms: glibc 2.14, Mac OS X 10.5, FreeBSD 6.4, NetBSD 5.0, OpenBSD 3.8, Minix 3.1.8, AIX 7.1, HP-UX 11.31, IRIX 6.5, OSF/1 5.1, Solaris 11 2011-11, Cygwin, mingw, MSVC 9, Interix 3.5, BeOS.

12.102.3 `process_vm_writev`

Gnulib module: —

Portability problems fixed by Gnulib:

Portability problems not fixed by Gnulib:

- This function is missing on all non-glibc platforms: glibc 2.14, Mac OS X 10.5, FreeBSD 6.4, NetBSD 5.0, OpenBSD 3.8, Minix 3.1.8, AIX 7.1, HP-UX 11.31, IRIX 6.5, OSF/1 5.1, Solaris 11 2011-11, Cygwin, mingw, MSVC 9, Interix 3.5, BeOS.

12.102.4 `pwritev`

Gnulib module: —

Portability problems fixed by Gnulib:

Portability problems not fixed by Gnulib:

- This function is missing on some platforms: glibc 2.9, Mac OS X 10.5, FreeBSD 5.2.1, Minix 3.1.8, AIX 5.2, HP-UX 11.31, IRIX 6.5, OSF/1 5.1, Solaris 11 2011-11, Cygwin, mingw, MSVC 9, Interix 3.5, BeOS.

- On platforms where `off_t` is a 32-bit type, this function may not work correctly on files larger than 2 GB. The fix is to use the `AC_SYS_LARGEFILE` macro.

12.103 Glibc `<sys/ustat.h>`

12.103.1 `ustat`

Gnulib module: —

Portability problems fixed by Gnulib:

Portability problems not fixed by Gnulib:

- This function is missing on some platforms: Mac OS X 10.5, FreeBSD 6.0, NetBSD 5.0, OpenBSD 3.8, Minix 3.1.8, AIX 5.1, Cygwin, mingw, MSVC 9, Interix 3.5, BeOS.

12.104 Glibc <sys/vlimit.h>

12.104.1 vlimit

Gnulib module: —

Portability problems fixed by Gnulib:

Portability problems not fixed by Gnulib:

- This function is missing on some platforms: Mac OS X 10.5, FreeBSD 6.0, NetBSD 5.0, OpenBSD 3.8, Minix 3.1.8, HP-UX 11, IRIX 6.5, OSF/1 5.1, Solaris 11 2011-11, Cygwin, mingw, MSVC 9, Interix 3.5, BeOS.

12.105 Glibc <sys/vm86.h>

12.105.1 vm86

Gnulib module: —

Portability problems fixed by Gnulib:

Portability problems not fixed by Gnulib:

- This function is missing on all non-glibc platforms: Mac OS X 10.5, FreeBSD 6.0, NetBSD 5.0, OpenBSD 3.8, Minix 3.1.8, AIX 5.1, HP-UX 11, IRIX 6.5, OSF/1 5.1, Solaris 11 2011-11, Cygwin, mingw, MSVC 9, Interix 3.5, BeOS.

12.106 Glibc <sys/vtimes.h>

12.106.1 vtimes

Gnulib module: —

Portability problems fixed by Gnulib:

Portability problems not fixed by Gnulib:

- This function is missing on all non-glibc platforms: Mac OS X 10.5, FreeBSD 6.0, NetBSD 5.0, OpenBSD 3.8, Minix 3.1.8, AIX 5.1, HP-UX 11, IRIX 6.5, OSF/1 5.1, Solaris 11 2011-11, Cygwin, mingw, MSVC 9, Interix 3.5, BeOS.

12.107 Glibc Extensions to <sys/wait.h>

12.107.1 wait3

Gnulib module: —

Portability problems fixed by Gnulib:

Portability problems not fixed by Gnulib:

- This function is missing on some platforms: Minix 3.1.8, mingw, MSVC 9, Interix 3.5, BeOS.

12.107.2 `wait4`

Gnulib module: —

Portability problems fixed by Gnulib:

Portability problems not fixed by Gnulib:

- This function is missing on some platforms: Minix 3.1.8, AIX 4.3.2, HP-UX 11.11, IRIX 6.5, mingw, MSVC 9, Interix 3.5, BeOS.

12.108 Glibc `<sys/xattr.h>`

12.108.1 `fgetxattr`

Gnulib module: —

Portability problems fixed by Gnulib:

Portability problems not fixed by Gnulib:

- This function is missing on many non-glibc platforms: Mac OS X 10.3, FreeBSD 6.0, NetBSD 5.0, OpenBSD 3.8, Minix 3.1.8, AIX 5.1, HP-UX 11, IRIX 6.5, OSF/1 5.1, Solaris 11 2011-11, Cygwin 1.5.x, mingw, MSVC 9, Interix 3.5, BeOS.
- This function has extra `offset` and `options` parameters: Mac OS X 10.4

12.108.2 `flistxattr`

Gnulib module: —

Portability problems fixed by Gnulib:

Portability problems not fixed by Gnulib:

- This function is missing on many non-glibc platforms: Mac OS X 10.3, FreeBSD 6.0, NetBSD 5.0, OpenBSD 3.8, Minix 3.1.8, AIX 5.1, HP-UX 11, IRIX 6.5, OSF/1 5.1, Solaris 11 2011-11, Cygwin 1.5.x, mingw, MSVC 9, Interix 3.5, BeOS.

12.108.3 `fremovexattr`

Gnulib module: —

Portability problems fixed by Gnulib:

Portability problems not fixed by Gnulib:

- This function is missing on many non-glibc platforms: Mac OS X 10.3, FreeBSD 6.0, NetBSD 5.0, OpenBSD 3.8, Minix 3.1.8, AIX 5.1, HP-UX 11, IRIX 6.5, OSF/1 5.1, Solaris 11 2011-11, Cygwin 1.5.x, mingw, MSVC 9, Interix 3.5, BeOS.

12.108.4 `fsetxattr`

Gnulib module: —

Portability problems fixed by Gnulib:

Portability problems not fixed by Gnulib:

- This function is missing on many non-glibc platforms: Mac OS X 10.3, FreeBSD 6.0, NetBSD 5.0, OpenBSD 3.8, Minix 3.1.8, AIX 5.1, HP-UX 11, IRIX 6.5, OSF/1 5.1, Solaris 11 2011-11, Cygwin 1.5.x, mingw, MSVC 9, Interix 3.5, BeOS.

12.108.5 `getxattr`

Gnulib module: —

Portability problems fixed by Gnulib:

Portability problems not fixed by Gnulib:

- This function is missing on many non-glibc platforms: Mac OS X 10.3, FreeBSD 6.0, NetBSD 5.0, OpenBSD 3.8, Minix 3.1.8, AIX 5.1, HP-UX 11, IRIX 6.5, OSF/1 5.1, Solaris 11 2011-11, Cygwin 1.5.x, mingw, MSVC 9, Interix 3.5, BeOS.
- This function has extra `offset` and `options` parameters: Mac OS X 10.4

12.108.6 `lgetxattr`

Gnulib module: —

Portability problems fixed by Gnulib:

Portability problems not fixed by Gnulib:

- This function is missing on many non-glibc platforms: Mac OS X 10.5, FreeBSD 6.0, NetBSD 5.0, OpenBSD 3.8, Minix 3.1.8, AIX 5.1, HP-UX 11, IRIX 6.5, OSF/1 5.1, Solaris 11 2011-11, Cygwin 1.5.x, mingw, MSVC 9, Interix 3.5, BeOS.

12.108.7 `listxattr`

Gnulib module: —

Portability problems fixed by Gnulib:

Portability problems not fixed by Gnulib:

- This function is missing on many non-glibc platforms: Mac OS X 10.3, FreeBSD 6.0, NetBSD 5.0, OpenBSD 3.8, Minix 3.1.8, AIX 5.1, HP-UX 11, IRIX 6.5, OSF/1 5.1, Solaris 11 2011-11, Cygwin 1.5.x, mingw, MSVC 9, Interix 3.5, BeOS.

12.108.8 `llistxattr`

Gnulib module: —

Portability problems fixed by Gnulib:

Portability problems not fixed by Gnulib:

- This function is missing on many non-glibc platforms: Mac OS X 10.5, FreeBSD 6.0, NetBSD 5.0, OpenBSD 3.8, Minix 3.1.8, AIX 5.1, HP-UX 11, IRIX 6.5, OSF/1 5.1, Solaris 11 2011-11, Cygwin 1.5.x, mingw, MSVC 9, Interix 3.5, BeOS.

12.108.9 `lremovexattr`

Gnulib module: —

Portability problems fixed by Gnulib:

Portability problems not fixed by Gnulib:

- This function is missing on many non-glibc platforms: Mac OS X 10.5, FreeBSD 6.0, NetBSD 5.0, OpenBSD 3.8, Minix 3.1.8, AIX 5.1, HP-UX 11, IRIX 6.5, OSF/1 5.1, Solaris 11 2011-11, Cygwin 1.5.x, mingw, MSVC 9, Interix 3.5, BeOS.

12.108.10 lsetxattr

Gnulib module: —

Portability problems fixed by Gnulib:

Portability problems not fixed by Gnulib:

- This function is missing on many non-glibc platforms: Mac OS X 10.5, FreeBSD 6.0, NetBSD 5.0, OpenBSD 3.8, Minix 3.1.8, AIX 5.1, HP-UX 11, IRIX 6.5, OSF/1 5.1, Solaris 11 2011-11, Cygwin 1.5.x, mingw, MSVC 9, Interix 3.5, BeOS.

12.108.11 removexattr

Gnulib module: —

Portability problems fixed by Gnulib:

Portability problems not fixed by Gnulib:

- This function is missing on many non-glibc platforms: Mac OS X 10.3, FreeBSD 6.0, NetBSD 5.0, OpenBSD 3.8, Minix 3.1.8, AIX 5.1, HP-UX 11, IRIX 6.5, OSF/1 5.1, Solaris 11 2011-11, Cygwin 1.5.x, mingw, MSVC 9, Interix 3.5, BeOS.

12.108.12 setxattr

Gnulib module: —

Portability problems fixed by Gnulib:

Portability problems not fixed by Gnulib:

- This function is missing on many non-glibc platforms: Mac OS X 10.3, FreeBSD 6.0, NetBSD 5.0, OpenBSD 3.8, Minix 3.1.8, AIX 5.1, HP-UX 11, IRIX 6.5, OSF/1 5.1, Solaris 11 2011-11, Cygwin 1.5.x, mingw, MSVC 9, Interix 3.5, BeOS.

12.109 Glibc Extensions to <termios.h>

12.109.1 cfmakeraw

Gnulib module: —

Portability problems fixed by Gnulib:

Portability problems not fixed by Gnulib:

- This function is missing on some platforms: Minix 3.1.8, AIX 4.3.2, HP-UX 11, IRIX 6.5, Solaris 11 2011-11, Cygwin 1.5.x, mingw, MSVC 9, Interix 3.5, BeOS.

12.109.2 cfsetspeed

Gnulib module: —

Portability problems fixed by Gnulib:

Portability problems not fixed by Gnulib:

- This function is missing on some platforms: Minix 3.1.8, AIX 4.3.2, HP-UX 11, IRIX 6.5, Solaris 11 2011-11, Cygwin, mingw, MSVC 9, Interix 3.5, BeOS.

12.110 Glibc Extensions to `<time.h>`

12.110.1 `clock_adjtime`

Gnulib module: —

Portability problems fixed by Gnulib:

Portability problems not fixed by Gnulib:

- This function is missing on all non-glibc platforms: glibc 2.13, Mac OS X 10.5, FreeBSD 6.4, NetBSD 5.0, OpenBSD 3.8, Minix 3.1.8, AIX 7.1, HP-UX 11.31, IRIX 6.5, OSF/1 5.1, Solaris 11 2011-11, Cygwin, mingw, MSVC 9, Interix 3.5, BeOS.

12.110.2 `dysize`

Gnulib module: —

Portability problems fixed by Gnulib:

Portability problems not fixed by Gnulib:

- This function is missing on all non-glibc platforms: Mac OS X 10.5, FreeBSD 6.0, NetBSD 5.0, OpenBSD 3.8, Minix 3.1.8, AIX 5.1, HP-UX 11, IRIX 6.5, OSF/1 5.1, Solaris 11 2011-11, Cygwin, mingw, MSVC 9, Interix 3.5, BeOS.

12.110.3 `getdate_r`

Gnulib module: —

Portability problems fixed by Gnulib:

Portability problems not fixed by Gnulib:

- This function is missing on some platforms: Mac OS X 10.5, FreeBSD 6.0, NetBSD 5.0, OpenBSD 3.8, Minix 3.1.8, HP-UX 11, IRIX 6.5, Solaris 11 2011-11, Cygwin, mingw, MSVC 9, Interix 3.5, BeOS.

12.110.4 `stime`

Gnulib module: —

Portability problems fixed by Gnulib:

Portability problems not fixed by Gnulib:

- This function is missing on some platforms: Mac OS X 10.5, FreeBSD 6.0, NetBSD 5.0, OpenBSD 3.8, Cygwin, mingw, MSVC 9, Interix 3.5.

12.110.5 `strptime_l`

Gnulib module: —

Portability problems fixed by Gnulib:

Portability problems not fixed by Gnulib:

- This function is missing on many platforms: Mac OS X 10.3, FreeBSD 6.0, NetBSD 5.0, OpenBSD 3.8, Minix 3.1.8, AIX 5.1, HP-UX 11, IRIX 6.5, OSF/1 5.1, Solaris 11 2011-11, Cygwin, mingw, MSVC 9, Interix 3.5, BeOS.

12.110.6 `timegm`

Gnulib module: timegm

Portability problems fixed by Gnulib:

- This function is missing on some platforms: AIX 5.1, HP-UX 11, IRIX 6.5, OSF/1 5.1, Solaris 11 2011-11, mingw, MSVC 9, Interix 3.5, BeOS.

Portability problems not fixed by Gnulib:

12.110.7 `timelocal`

Gnulib module: —

Portability problems fixed by Gnulib:

Portability problems not fixed by Gnulib:

- This function is missing on some platforms: AIX 5.1, HP-UX 11, IRIX 6.5, OSF/1 5.1, Solaris 11 2011-11, mingw, MSVC 9, Interix 3.5.

12.110.8 `timespec_get`

Gnulib module: —

Portability problems fixed by Gnulib:

Portability problems not fixed by Gnulib:

- This function is missing on all non-glibc platforms: glibc 2.15, Mac OS X 10.5, FreeBSD 6.4, NetBSD 5.0, OpenBSD 3.8, Minix 3.1.8, AIX 7.1, HP-UX 11.31, IRIX 6.5, OSF/1 5.1, Solaris 11 2011-11, Cygwin, mingw, MSVC 9, Interix 3.5, BeOS.

12.111 Glibc `<ttyent.h>`

12.111.1 endttyent

Gnulib module: —

Portability problems fixed by Gnulib:

Portability problems not fixed by Gnulib:

- This function is missing on some platforms: HP-UX 11, IRIX 6.5, Solaris 11 2011-11, Cygwin, mingw, MSVC 9, Interix 3.5, BeOS.

12.111.2 getttyent

Gnulib module: —

Portability problems fixed by Gnulib:

Portability problems not fixed by Gnulib:

- This function is missing on some platforms: HP-UX 11, IRIX 6.5, Solaris 11 2011-11, Cygwin, mingw, MSVC 9, Interix 3.5, BeOS.

12.111.3 `getttynam`

Gnulib module: —

Portability problems fixed by Gnulib:

Portability problems not fixed by Gnulib:

- This function is missing on some platforms: HP-UX 11, IRIX 6.5, Solaris 11 2011-11, Cygwin, mingw, MSVC 9, Interix 3.5, BeOS.

12.111.4 `setttyent`

Gnulib module: —

Portability problems fixed by Gnulib:

Portability problems not fixed by Gnulib:

- This function is missing on some platforms: HP-UX 11, IRIX 6.5, Solaris 11 2011-11, Cygwin, mingw, MSVC 9, Interix 3.5, BeOS.

12.112 Glibc Extensions to `<unistd.h>`

12.112.1 `acct`

Gnulib module: —

Portability problems fixed by Gnulib:

Portability problems not fixed by Gnulib:

- This function is missing on some platforms: Minix 3.1.8, AIX 5.1, Cygwin, mingw, MSVC 9, Interix 3.5, BeOS.

12.112.2 `brk`

Gnulib module: —

Portability problems fixed by Gnulib:

Portability problems not fixed by Gnulib:

- This function is missing on some platforms: AIX 5.1, Cygwin, mingw, MSVC 9.

12.112.3 `chroot`

Gnulib module: —

Portability problems fixed by Gnulib:

Portability problems not fixed by Gnulib:

- This function is missing on some platforms: AIX 5.1, mingw, MSVC 9, BeOS.

12.112.4 `daemon`

Gnulib module: —

Portability problems fixed by Gnulib:

Portability problems not fixed by Gnulib:

- This function is missing on some platforms: Minix 3.1.8, AIX 5.1, HP-UX 11, IRIX 6.5, OSF/1 5.1, mingw, MSVC 9, BeOS.

12.112.5 dup3

Gnulib module: dup3

Portability problems fixed by Gnulib:

- This function is missing on many non-glibc platforms: Mac OS X 10.5, FreeBSD 6.0, NetBSD 5.0, OpenBSD 3.8, Minix 3.1.8, AIX 5.1, HP-UX 11, IRIX 6.5, OSF/1 5.1, Solaris 11 2011-11, Cygwin 1.7.1, mingw, MSVC 9, Interix 3.5, BeOS.

- This function can crash on some platforms: Cygwin 1.7.25.

Portability problems not fixed by Gnulib:

12.112.6 endusershell

Gnulib module: getusershell

Portability problems fixed by Gnulib:

- This function is missing on some platforms: Minix 3.1.8, AIX 4.3.2, IRIX 6.5, mingw, MSVC 9, Interix 3.5, BeOS.

- This function is missing a declaration on some platforms: Solaris 9.

Portability problems not fixed by Gnulib:

12.112.7 euidaccess

Gnulib module: euidaccess

Portability problems fixed by Gnulib:

- This function is missing on many non-glibc platforms: Mac OS X 10.5, FreeBSD 6.0, NetBSD 5.0, OpenBSD 3.8, Minix 3.1.8, AIX 5.1, HP-UX 11, IRIX 6.5, OSF/1 5.1, Solaris 11 2011-11, Cygwin 1.5.x, mingw, MSVC 9, Interix 3.5, BeOS.

Portability problems not fixed by Gnulib:

Other problems of this function:

- There is an inherent race between calling this function and performing some action based on the results; you should think twice before trusting this function, especially in a set-uid or set-gid program.

- This function does not have an option for not following symbolic links (like `stat` versus `lstat`). If you need this option, use the Gnulib module `faccessat` with the `AT_EACCESS` flag.

12.112.8 execvpe

Gnulib module: —

Portability problems fixed by Gnulib:

Portability problems not fixed by Gnulib:

- This function is missing on many non-glibc platforms: glibc 2.10, Mac OS X 10.5, FreeBSD 6.0, NetBSD 5.0, OpenBSD 3.8, Minix 3.1.8, AIX 5.1, HP-UX 11, IRIX 6.5, OSF/1 5.1, Solaris 11 2011-11, Cygwin 1.5.x, mingw, Interix 3.5, BeOS.

12.112.9 get_current_dir_name

Gnulib module: —

Portability problems fixed by Gnulib:

Portability problems not fixed by Gnulib:

- This function is missing on some platforms: Mac OS X 10.5, FreeBSD 6.0, NetBSD 5.0, OpenBSD 3.8, Minix 3.1.8, AIX 4.3.2, HP-UX 11, IRIX 6.5, OSF/1 5.1, Solaris 11 2011-11, Cygwin 1.7.9, mingw, MSVC 9, Interix 3.5, BeOS.

12.112.10 getdomainname

Gnulib module: getdomainname

Portability problems fixed by Gnulib:

- This function is missing on some platforms: Solaris 11 2011-11, mingw, MSVC 9, Interix 3.5, BeOS.
- This function is declared in `netdb.h`, not in `unistd.h`, on some platforms: AIX 7.1.
- This function is declared in `netdb.h` and in `sys/socket.h`, not in `unistd.h`, on some platforms: OSF/1 5.1.
- The second argument is of type `int`, not `size_t`, on some platforms: Mac OS X 10.5, FreeBSD 6.4, AIX 7.1, IRIX 6.5.

Portability problems not fixed by Gnulib:

12.112.11 getdtablesize

Gnulib module: getdtablesize

Portability problems fixed by Gnulib:

- This function is missing on some platforms: Android LP64, mingw, MSVC 9.
- This function is not declared on some platforms: Android LP32.
- This function does not represent the true `RLIMIT_NOFILE` soft limit on some platforms: Android LP32, Cygwin 1.7.25.

Portability problems not fixed by Gnulib:

12.112.12 getpagesize

Gnulib module: getpagesize

Portability problems fixed by Gnulib:

- This function is missing on some platforms: MSVC 9, BeOS.
- This function is broken on some platforms: mingw.

Portability problems not fixed by Gnulib:

12.112.13 getpass

Gnulib module: getpass or getpass-gnu

Portability problems fixed by either Gnulib module `getpass` or `getpass-gnu`:

- This function is missing on some platforms: mingw, MSVC 9, BeOS.

Portability problems fixed by Gnulib module `getpass-gnu`:

- The returned password is truncated to PASS_MAX characters on some platforms: Mac OS X 10.5 (128), FreeBSD 6.2 (128), NetBSD 3.0 (128), OpenBSD 4.0 (128), AIX 5.1 (32), HP-UX 11 (8), IRIX 6.5 (32), OSF/1 5.1 (80), Solaris 11 2010-11 (8, even less than PASS_MAX), Cygwin (128). The gnulib implementation returns the password untruncated.

Portability problems not fixed by Gnulib:

12.112.14 getresgid

Gnulib module: —

Portability problems fixed by Gnulib:

Portability problems not fixed by Gnulib:

- This function is missing on some platforms: Mac OS X 10.5, NetBSD 5.0, Minix 3.1.8, AIX 5.1, HP-UX 11.00, IRIX 6.5, OSF/1 5.1, Solaris 11 2011-11, Cygwin, mingw, MSVC 9, Interix 3.5, BeOS.

12.112.15 getresuid

Gnulib module: —

Portability problems fixed by Gnulib:

Portability problems not fixed by Gnulib:

- This function is missing on some platforms: Mac OS X 10.5, NetBSD 5.0, Minix 3.1.8, AIX 5.1, HP-UX 11.00, IRIX 6.5, OSF/1 5.1, Solaris 11 2011-11, Cygwin, mingw, MSVC 9, Interix 3.5, BeOS.

12.112.16 getusershell

Gnulib module: getusershell

Portability problems fixed by Gnulib:

- This function is missing on some platforms: Minix 3.1.8, AIX 4.3.2, IRIX 6.5, mingw, MSVC 9, Interix 3.5, BeOS.
- This function is missing a declaration on some platforms: Solaris 9.

Portability problems not fixed by Gnulib:

12.112.17 group_member

Gnulib module: group-member

Portability problems fixed by Gnulib:

- This function is missing on all non-glibc platforms: Mac OS X 10.5, FreeBSD 6.0, NetBSD 5.0, OpenBSD 3.8, Minix 3.1.8, AIX 5.1, HP-UX 11, IRIX 6.5, OSF/1 5.1, Solaris 11 2011-11, Cygwin, mingw, MSVC 9, Interix 3.5, BeOS.

Portability problems not fixed by Gnulib:

12.112.18 pipe2

Gnulib module: pipe2

Portability problems fixed by Gnulib:

- This function is missing on many non-glibc platforms: Mac OS X 10.5, FreeBSD 6.0, NetBSD 5.0, OpenBSD 3.8, Minix 3.1.8, AIX 5.1, HP-UX 11, IRIX 6.5, OSF/1 5.1, Solaris 11 2011-11, Cygwin 1.7.1, mingw, MSVC 9, Interix 3.5, BeOS. But the replacement function is not atomic; this matters in multi-threaded programs that spawn child processes.

Portability problems not fixed by Gnulib:

- This function crashes rather than failing with EMFILE if no resources are left on some platforms: Cygwin 1.7.9.

Note: This function portably supports the O_NONBLOCK flag only if the gnulib module nonblocking is also used.

12.112.19 profil

Gnulib module: —

Portability problems fixed by Gnulib:

Portability problems not fixed by Gnulib:

- This function is missing on some platforms: Minix 3.1.8, AIX 5.1, Cygwin, mingw, MSVC 9, Interix 3.5, BeOS.

12.112.20 revoke

Gnulib module: —

Portability problems fixed by Gnulib:

Portability problems not fixed by Gnulib:

- This function is missing on some platforms: Minix 3.1.8, AIX 5.1, HP-UX 11, IRIX 6.5, Solaris 11 2011-11, mingw, MSVC 9, Interix 3.5, BeOS.

12.112.21 sbrk

Gnulib module: —

Portability problems fixed by Gnulib:

Portability problems not fixed by Gnulib:

- This function is missing on some platforms: AIX 5.1, mingw, MSVC 9.

12.112.22 setlogin

Gnulib module: —

Portability problems fixed by Gnulib:

Portability problems not fixed by Gnulib:

- This function is missing on some platforms: Minix 3.1.8, AIX 5.1, HP-UX 11, IRIX 6.5, Solaris 11 2011-11, Cygwin, mingw, MSVC 9, Interix 3.5, BeOS.

12.112.23 setdomainname

Gnulib module: —

Portability problems fixed by Gnulib:

Portability problems not fixed by Gnulib:

- This function is missing on some platforms: Minix 3.1.8, AIX 5.1, Cygwin, mingw, MSVC 9, Interix 3.5, BeOS.

12.112.24 sethostid

Gnulib module: —

Portability problems fixed by Gnulib:

Portability problems not fixed by Gnulib:

- This function is missing on some platforms: Minix 3.1.8, AIX 5.1, HP-UX 11, Solaris 11 2011-11, Cygwin, mingw, MSVC 9, Interix 3.5, BeOS.

12.112.25 sethostname

Gnulib module: sethostname

Portability problems fixed by Gnulib:

- This function is missing on some platforms: Minix 3.1.8, Cygwin, mingw, MSVC 9, Interix 3.5, BeOS. Note that the Gnulib replacement may fail with ENOSYS on some platforms.
- This function is not declared on some platforms: AIX 7.1, OSF/1 5.1, Solaris 10.

Portability problems not fixed by Gnulib:

- On Solaris 11 2010-11, the first argument is char * instead of const char * and the second parameter is int instead of size_t.

12.112.26 setresgid

Gnulib module: —

Portability problems fixed by Gnulib:

Portability problems not fixed by Gnulib:

- This function is missing on some platforms: Mac OS X 10.5, NetBSD 5.0, Minix 3.1.8, AIX 5.1, IRIX 6.5, OSF/1 5.1, Solaris 11 2011-11, Cygwin, mingw, MSVC 9, Interix 3.5, BeOS.

12.112.27 setresuid

Gnulib module: —

Portability problems fixed by Gnulib:

Portability problems not fixed by Gnulib:

- This function is missing on some platforms: Mac OS X 10.5, NetBSD 5.0, Minix 3.1.8, AIX 5.1, IRIX 6.5, OSF/1 5.1, Solaris 11 2011-11, Cygwin, mingw, MSVC 9, Interix 3.5, BeOS.

12.112.28 setusershell

Gnulib module: getusershell

Portability problems fixed by Gnulib:

- This function is missing on some platforms: Minix 3.1.8, AIX 4.3.2, IRIX 6.5, mingw, MSVC 9, Interix 3.5, BeOS.
- This function is missing a declaration on some platforms: Solaris 9.

Portability problems not fixed by Gnulib:

12.112.29 syncfs

Gnulib module: —

Portability problems fixed by Gnulib:

Portability problems not fixed by Gnulib:

- This function is missing on all non-glibc platforms: glibc 2.13, Mac OS X 10.5, FreeBSD 6.4, NetBSD 5.0, OpenBSD 3.8, Minix 3.1.8, AIX 7.1, HP-UX 11.31, IRIX 6.5, OSF/1 5.1, Solaris 11 2011-11, Cygwin, mingw, MSVC 9, Interix 3.5, BeOS.

12.112.30 syscall

Gnulib module: —

Portability problems fixed by Gnulib:

Portability problems not fixed by Gnulib:

- This function is missing on some platforms: Minix 3.1.8, AIX 5.1, Cygwin, mingw, MSVC 9, BeOS.

12.112.31 ttyslot

Gnulib module: —

Portability problems fixed by Gnulib:

Portability problems not fixed by Gnulib:

- This function is missing on some platforms: mingw, MSVC 9, BeOS.

12.112.32 vhangup

Gnulib module: —

Portability problems fixed by Gnulib:

Portability problems not fixed by Gnulib:

- This function is missing on some platforms: Mac OS X 10.5, FreeBSD 6.0, NetBSD 5.0, OpenBSD 3.8, Minix 3.1.8, AIX 5.1, OSF/1 5.1, mingw, MSVC 9, Interix 3.5, BeOS.

12.113 Glibc <utmp.h>

12.113.1 endutent

Gnulib module: —

Portability problems fixed by Gnulib:

Portability problems not fixed by Gnulib:

- This function is missing on some platforms: Mac OS X 10.5, FreeBSD 6.0, OpenBSD 3.8, Minix 3.1.8, mingw, MSVC 9, Interix 3.5, BeOS.

12.113.2 getutent

Gnulib module: —

Portability problems fixed by Gnulib:

Portability problems not fixed by Gnulib:

- This function is missing on some platforms: Mac OS X 10.5, FreeBSD 6.0, OpenBSD 3.8, Minix 3.1.8, mingw, MSVC 9, Interix 3.5, BeOS.

12.113.3 getutent_r

Gnulib module: —

Portability problems fixed by Gnulib:

Portability problems not fixed by Gnulib:

- This function is missing on some platforms: Mac OS X 10.5, FreeBSD 6.0, NetBSD 5.0, OpenBSD 3.8, Minix 3.1.8, HP-UX 11, IRIX 6.5, Solaris 11 2011-11, Cygwin, mingw, MSVC 9, Interix 3.5, BeOS.

12.113.4 getutid

Gnulib module: —

Portability problems fixed by Gnulib:

Portability problems not fixed by Gnulib:

- This function is missing on some platforms: Mac OS X 10.5, FreeBSD 6.0, NetBSD 5.0, OpenBSD 3.8, Minix 3.1.8, mingw, MSVC 9, Interix 3.5, BeOS.

12.113.5 getutid_r

Gnulib module: —

Portability problems fixed by Gnulib:

Portability problems not fixed by Gnulib:

- This function is missing on some platforms: Mac OS X 10.5, FreeBSD 6.0, NetBSD 5.0, OpenBSD 3.8, Minix 3.1.8, HP-UX 11, IRIX 6.5, Solaris 11 2011-11, Cygwin, mingw, MSVC 9, Interix 3.5, BeOS.

12.113.6 getutline

Gnulib module: —

Portability problems fixed by Gnulib:

Portability problems not fixed by Gnulib:

- This function is missing on some platforms: Mac OS X 10.5, FreeBSD 6.0, NetBSD 5.0, OpenBSD 3.8, Minix 3.1.8, mingw, MSVC 9, Interix 3.5, BeOS.

12.113.7 getutline_r

Gnulib module: —

Portability problems fixed by Gnulib:

Portability problems not fixed by Gnulib:

- This function is missing on some platforms: Mac OS X 10.5, FreeBSD 6.0, NetBSD 5.0, OpenBSD 3.8, Minix 3.1.8, HP-UX 11, IRIX 6.5, Solaris 11 2011-11, Cygwin, mingw, MSVC 9, Interix 3.5, BeOS.

12.113.8 pututline

Gnulib module: —

Portability problems fixed by Gnulib:

Portability problems not fixed by Gnulib:

- This function is missing on some platforms: Mac OS X 10.5, FreeBSD 6.0, NetBSD 5.0, OpenBSD 3.8, Minix 3.1.8, mingw, MSVC 9, Interix 3.5, BeOS.

12.113.9 setutent

Gnulib module: —

Portability problems fixed by Gnulib:

Portability problems not fixed by Gnulib:

- This function is missing on some platforms: Mac OS X 10.5, FreeBSD 6.0, OpenBSD 3.8, Minix 3.1.8, mingw, MSVC 9, Interix 3.5, BeOS.

12.113.10 updwtmp

Gnulib module: —

Portability problems fixed by Gnulib:

Portability problems not fixed by Gnulib:

- This function is missing on some platforms: Mac OS X 10.5, FreeBSD 6.0, NetBSD 5.0, OpenBSD 3.8, Minix 3.1.8, AIX 4.3.2, HP-UX 11, OSF/1 5.1, mingw, MSVC 9, Interix 3.5, BeOS.

12.113.11 `utmpname`

Gnulib module: —

Portability problems fixed by Gnulib:

Portability problems not fixed by Gnulib:

- This function is missing on some platforms: Mac OS X 10.5, FreeBSD 6.0, OpenBSD 3.8, Minix 3.1.8, mingw, MSVC 9, Interix 3.5, BeOS.

12.113.12 `login`

Gnulib module: —

Portability problems fixed by Gnulib:

Portability problems not fixed by Gnulib:

- This function is missing on many non-glibc platforms: FreeBSD 6.0, NetBSD 5.0, OpenBSD 3.8, Minix 3.1.8, AIX 7.1, HP-UX 11.31, IRIX 6.5, Solaris 11 2011-11, mingw, MSVC 9, BeOS.

12.113.13 `login_tty`

Gnulib module: login_tty

Portability problems fixed by Gnulib:

- This function is missing on some platforms: Minix 3.1.8, AIX 5.1, HP-UX 11, IRIX 6.5, Solaris 11 2011-11.
- This function requires linking with `-lutil` on some platforms: glibc 2.3.6, FreeBSD 6.0, NetBSD 5.0, OpenBSD 3.8. It is available without link options on other platforms: Mac OS X 10.5, OSF/1 5.1, Cygwin, Interix 3.5.

Portability problems not fixed by Gnulib:

- This function is missing on some platforms: mingw, MSVC 9.
- This function is declared in `<utmp.h>` on glibc, Cygwin, in `<util.h>` on Mac OS X 10.5, NetBSD 5.0, OpenBSD 3.8, in `<libutil.h>` on FreeBSD 6.0, Haiku, and not declared at all on OSF/1 5.1, Interix 3.5. Also note that `<sys/types.h>` is a prerequisite of `<utmp.h>` on FreeBSD 8.0, OpenBSD 4.6 and of `<libutil.h>` on FreeBSD 8.0.

12.114 Glibc Extensions to `<utmpx.h>`

12.114.1 `getutmp`

Gnulib module: —

Portability problems fixed by Gnulib:

Portability problems not fixed by Gnulib:

- This function is missing on some platforms: Mac OS X 10.4, FreeBSD 6.0, OpenBSD 3.8, Minix 3.1.8, AIX 5.1, HP-UX 11, OSF/1 5.1, Cygwin, mingw, MSVC 9, Interix 3.5, BeOS.

12.114.2 `getutmpx`

Gnulib module: —

Portability problems fixed by Gnulib:

Portability problems not fixed by Gnulib:

- This function is missing on some platforms: Mac OS X 10.4, FreeBSD 6.0, OpenBSD 3.8, Minix 3.1.8, AIX 5.1, HP-UX 11, OSF/1 5.1, Cygwin, mingw, MSVC 9, Interix 3.5, BeOS.

12.114.3 `updwtmpx`

Gnulib module: —

Portability problems fixed by Gnulib:

Portability problems not fixed by Gnulib:

- This function is missing on some platforms: Mac OS X 10.5, FreeBSD 6.0, OpenBSD 3.8, Minix 3.1.8, AIX 5.1, HP-UX 11, OSF/1 5.1, Cygwin 1.5.x, mingw, MSVC 9, Interix 3.5, BeOS.

12.114.4 `utmpxname`

Gnulib module: —

Portability problems fixed by Gnulib:

Portability problems not fixed by Gnulib:

- This function is missing on some platforms: Mac OS X 10.4, FreeBSD 6.0, OpenBSD 3.8, Minix 3.1.8, AIX 5.1, HP-UX 11, OSF/1 5.1, mingw, MSVC 9, Interix 3.5, BeOS.

12.115 Glibc Extensions to `<wchar.h>`

12.115.1 `fgetwc_unlocked`

Gnulib module: —

Portability problems fixed by Gnulib:

Portability problems not fixed by Gnulib:

- This function is missing on all non-glibc platforms: Mac OS X 10.5, FreeBSD 6.0, NetBSD 5.0, OpenBSD 3.8, Minix 3.1.8, AIX 5.1, HP-UX 11, IRIX 6.5, OSF/1 5.1, Solaris 11 2011-11, Cygwin, mingw, MSVC 9, Interix 3.5, BeOS.
- On AIX and Windows platforms, `wchar_t` is a 16-bit type and therefore cannot accommodate all Unicode characters.

12.115.2 `fgetws_unlocked`

Gnulib module: —

Portability problems fixed by Gnulib:

Portability problems not fixed by Gnulib:

- This function is missing on all non-glibc platforms: Mac OS X 10.5, FreeBSD 6.0, NetBSD 5.0, OpenBSD 3.8, Minix 3.1.8, AIX 5.1, HP-UX 11, IRIX 6.5, OSF/1 5.1, Solaris 11 2011-11, Cygwin, mingw, MSVC 9, Interix 3.5, BeOS.

- On AIX and Windows platforms, `wchar_t` is a 16-bit type and therefore cannot accommodate all Unicode characters.

12.115.3 `fputwc_unlocked`

Gnulib module: —

Portability problems fixed by Gnulib:

Portability problems not fixed by Gnulib:

- This function is missing on all non-glibc platforms: Mac OS X 10.5, FreeBSD 6.0, NetBSD 5.0, OpenBSD 3.8, Minix 3.1.8, AIX 5.1, HP-UX 11, IRIX 6.5, OSF/1 5.1, Solaris 11 2011-11, Cygwin, mingw, MSVC 9, Interix 3.5, BeOS.
- On AIX and Windows platforms, `wchar_t` is a 16-bit type and therefore cannot accommodate all Unicode characters.

12.115.4 `fputws_unlocked`

Gnulib module: —

Portability problems fixed by Gnulib:

Portability problems not fixed by Gnulib:

- This function is missing on all non-glibc platforms: Mac OS X 10.5, FreeBSD 6.0, NetBSD 5.0, OpenBSD 3.8, Minix 3.1.8, AIX 5.1, HP-UX 11, IRIX 6.5, OSF/1 5.1, Solaris 11 2011-11, Cygwin, mingw, MSVC 9, Interix 3.5, BeOS.
- On AIX and Windows platforms, `wchar_t` is a 16-bit type and therefore cannot accommodate all Unicode characters.

12.115.5 `getwc_unlocked`

Gnulib module: —

Portability problems fixed by Gnulib:

Portability problems not fixed by Gnulib:

- This function is missing on some platforms: Mac OS X 10.5, FreeBSD 6.0, NetBSD 5.0, OpenBSD 3.8, Minix 3.1.8, AIX 5.1, HP-UX 11, IRIX 6.5, Solaris 11 2011-11, Cygwin, mingw, MSVC 9, Interix 3.5, BeOS.
- On AIX and Windows platforms, `wchar_t` is a 16-bit type and therefore cannot accommodate all Unicode characters.

12.115.6 `getwchar_unlocked`

Gnulib module: —

Portability problems fixed by Gnulib:

Portability problems not fixed by Gnulib:

- This function is missing on all non-glibc platforms: Mac OS X 10.5, FreeBSD 6.0, NetBSD 5.0, OpenBSD 3.8, Minix 3.1.8, AIX 5.1, HP-UX 11, IRIX 6.5, OSF/1 5.1, Solaris 11 2011-11, Cygwin, mingw, MSVC 9, Interix 3.5, BeOS.
- On AIX and Windows platforms, `wchar_t` is a 16-bit type and therefore cannot accommodate all Unicode characters.

12.115.7 putwc_unlocked

Gnulib module: —

Portability problems fixed by Gnulib:

Portability problems not fixed by Gnulib:

- This function is missing on some platforms: Mac OS X 10.5, FreeBSD 6.0, NetBSD 5.0, OpenBSD 3.8, Minix 3.1.8, AIX 5.1, HP-UX 11, IRIX 6.5, Solaris 11 2011-11, Cygwin, mingw, MSVC 9, Interix 3.5, BeOS.
- On AIX and Windows platforms, wchar_t is a 16-bit type and therefore cannot accommodate all Unicode characters.

12.115.8 putwchar_unlocked

Gnulib module: —

Portability problems fixed by Gnulib:

Portability problems not fixed by Gnulib:

- This function is missing on all non-glibc platforms: Mac OS X 10.5, FreeBSD 6.0, NetBSD 5.0, OpenBSD 3.8, Minix 3.1.8, AIX 5.1, HP-UX 11, IRIX 6.5, OSF/1 5.1, Solaris 11 2011-11, Cygwin, mingw, MSVC 9, Interix 3.5, BeOS.
- On AIX and Windows platforms, wchar_t is a 16-bit type and therefore cannot accommodate all Unicode characters.

12.115.9 wcschrnul

Gnulib module: —

Portability problems fixed by Gnulib:

Portability problems not fixed by Gnulib:

- This function is missing on all non-glibc platforms: Mac OS X 10.5, FreeBSD 6.0, NetBSD 5.0, OpenBSD 3.8, Minix 3.1.8, AIX 5.1, HP-UX 11, IRIX 6.5, OSF/1 5.1, Solaris 11 2011-11, Cygwin, mingw, MSVC 9, Interix 3.5, BeOS.
- On AIX and Windows platforms, wchar_t is a 16-bit type and therefore cannot accommodate all Unicode characters.

12.115.10 wcsftime_l

Gnulib module: —

Portability problems fixed by Gnulib:

Portability problems not fixed by Gnulib:

- This function is missing on many platforms: Mac OS X 10.3, FreeBSD 6.0, NetBSD 5.0, OpenBSD 3.8, Minix 3.1.8, AIX 5.1, HP-UX 11, IRIX 6.5, OSF/1 5.1, Solaris 11 2011-11, Cygwin, mingw, MSVC 9, Interix 3.5, BeOS.
- On AIX and Windows platforms, wchar_t is a 16-bit type and therefore cannot accommodate all Unicode characters.

12.115.11 `wcstod_l`

Gnulib module: —

Portability problems fixed by Gnulib:

Portability problems not fixed by Gnulib:

- This function is missing on many platforms: Mac OS X 10.3, FreeBSD 6.0, NetBSD 5.0, OpenBSD 3.8, Minix 3.1.8, AIX 5.1, HP-UX 11, IRIX 6.5, OSF/1 5.1, Solaris 11 2011-11, Cygwin, mingw, MSVC 9, Interix 3.5, BeOS.
- On AIX and Windows platforms, `wchar_t` is a 16-bit type and therefore cannot accommodate all Unicode characters.

12.115.12 `wcstof_l`

Gnulib module: —

Portability problems fixed by Gnulib:

Portability problems not fixed by Gnulib:

- This function is missing on many platforms: Mac OS X 10.3, FreeBSD 6.0, NetBSD 5.0, OpenBSD 3.8, Minix 3.1.8, AIX 5.1, HP-UX 11, IRIX 6.5, OSF/1 5.1, Solaris 11 2011-11, Cygwin, mingw, MSVC 9, Interix 3.5, BeOS.
- On AIX and Windows platforms, `wchar_t` is a 16-bit type and therefore cannot accommodate all Unicode characters.

12.115.13 `wcstol_l`

Gnulib module: —

Portability problems fixed by Gnulib:

Portability problems not fixed by Gnulib:

- This function is missing on many platforms: Mac OS X 10.3, FreeBSD 6.0, NetBSD 5.0, OpenBSD 3.8, Minix 3.1.8, AIX 5.1, HP-UX 11, IRIX 6.5, OSF/1 5.1, Solaris 11 2011-11, Cygwin, mingw, MSVC 9, Interix 3.5, BeOS.
- On AIX and Windows platforms, `wchar_t` is a 16-bit type and therefore cannot accommodate all Unicode characters.

12.115.14 `wcstold_l`

Gnulib module: —

Portability problems fixed by Gnulib:

Portability problems not fixed by Gnulib:

- This function is missing on many platforms: Mac OS X 10.3, FreeBSD 6.0, NetBSD 5.0, OpenBSD 3.8, Minix 3.1.8, AIX 5.1, HP-UX 11, IRIX 6.5, OSF/1 5.1, Solaris 11 2011-11, Cygwin, mingw, MSVC 9, Interix 3.5, BeOS.
- On AIX and Windows platforms, `wchar_t` is a 16-bit type and therefore cannot accommodate all Unicode characters.

12.115.15 wcstoll_l

Gnulib module: —

Portability problems fixed by Gnulib:

Portability problems not fixed by Gnulib:

- This function is missing on many platforms: Mac OS X 10.3, FreeBSD 6.0, NetBSD 5.0, OpenBSD 3.8, Minix 3.1.8, AIX 5.1, HP-UX 11, IRIX 6.5, OSF/1 5.1, Solaris 11 2011-11, Cygwin, mingw, MSVC 9, Interix 3.5, BeOS.

- On AIX and Windows platforms, wchar_t is a 16-bit type and therefore cannot accommodate all Unicode characters.

12.115.16 wcstoq

Gnulib module: —

Portability problems fixed by Gnulib:

Portability problems not fixed by Gnulib:

- This function is missing on all non-glibc platforms: Mac OS X 10.5, FreeBSD 6.0, NetBSD 5.0, OpenBSD 3.8, Minix 3.1.8, AIX 5.1, HP-UX 11, IRIX 6.5, OSF/1 5.1, Solaris 11 2011-11, Cygwin, mingw, MSVC 9, Interix 3.5, BeOS.

- On AIX and Windows platforms, wchar_t is a 16-bit type and therefore cannot accommodate all Unicode characters.

12.115.17 wcstoul_l

Gnulib module: —

Portability problems fixed by Gnulib:

Portability problems not fixed by Gnulib:

- This function is missing on many platforms: Mac OS X 10.3, FreeBSD 6.0, NetBSD 5.0, OpenBSD 3.8, Minix 3.1.8, AIX 5.1, HP-UX 11, IRIX 6.5, OSF/1 5.1, Solaris 11 2011-11, Cygwin, mingw, MSVC 9, Interix 3.5, BeOS.

- On AIX and Windows platforms, wchar_t is a 16-bit type and therefore cannot accommodate all Unicode characters.

12.115.18 wcstoull_l

Gnulib module: —

Portability problems fixed by Gnulib:

Portability problems not fixed by Gnulib:

- This function is missing on many platforms: Mac OS X 10.3, FreeBSD 6.0, NetBSD 5.0, OpenBSD 3.8, Minix 3.1.8, AIX 5.1, HP-UX 11, IRIX 6.5, OSF/1 5.1, Solaris 11 2011-11, Cygwin, mingw, MSVC 9, Interix 3.5, BeOS.

- On AIX and Windows platforms, wchar_t is a 16-bit type and therefore cannot accommodate all Unicode characters.

12.115.19 `wcstouq`

Gnulib module: —

Portability problems fixed by Gnulib:

Portability problems not fixed by Gnulib:

- This function is missing on all non-glibc platforms: Mac OS X 10.5, FreeBSD 6.0, NetBSD 5.0, OpenBSD 3.8, Minix 3.1.8, AIX 5.1, HP-UX 11, IRIX 6.5, OSF/1 5.1, Solaris 11 2011-11, Cygwin, mingw, MSVC 9, Interix 3.5, BeOS.

- On AIX and Windows platforms, `wchar_t` is a 16-bit type and therefore cannot accommodate all Unicode characters.

12.115.20 `wmempcpy`

Gnulib module: —

Portability problems fixed by Gnulib:

Portability problems not fixed by Gnulib:

- This function is missing on all non-glibc platforms: Mac OS X 10.5, FreeBSD 6.0, NetBSD 5.0, OpenBSD 3.8, Minix 3.1.8, AIX 5.1, HP-UX 11, IRIX 6.5, OSF/1 5.1, Solaris 11 2011-11, Cygwin, mingw, MSVC 9, Interix 3.5, BeOS.

- On AIX and Windows platforms, `wchar_t` is a 16-bit type and therefore cannot accommodate all Unicode characters.

13 Particular Modules

13.1 alloca

The alloca module provides for a function `alloca` which allocates memory on the stack, where the system allows it. A memory block allocated with `alloca` exists only until the function that calls `alloca` returns or exits abruptly.

There are a few systems where this is not possible: HP-UX systems, and some other platforms when the C++ compiler is used. On these platforms the alloca module provides a `malloc` based emulation. This emulation will not free a memory block immediately when the calling function returns, but rather will wait until the next `alloca` call from a function with the same or a shorter stack length. Thus, in some cases, a few memory blocks will be kept although they are not needed any more.

The user can `#include <alloca.h>` and use `alloca` on all platforms. Note that the `#include <alloca.h>` must be the first one after the autoconf-generated `config.h`, for AIX 3 compatibility. Thanks to IBM for this nice restriction!

Note that GCC 3.1 and 3.2 can *inline* functions that call `alloca`. When this happens, the memory blocks allocated with `alloca` will not be freed until *the end of the calling function*. If this calling function runs a loop calling the function that uses `alloca`, the program easily gets a stack overflow and crashes. To protect against this compiler behaviour, you can mark the function that uses `alloca` with the following attribute:

```
#ifdef __GNUC__
__attribute__ ((__noinline__))
#endif
```

An alternative to this module is the 'alloca-opt' module.

13.2 alloca-opt

The alloca-opt module provides for a function `alloca` which allocates memory on the stack, where the system allows it. A memory block allocated with `alloca` exists only until the function that calls `alloca` returns or exits abruptly.

There are a few systems where this is not possible: HP-UX systems, and some other platforms when the C++ compiler is used. On these platforms the alloca-opt module provides no replacement, just a preprocessor macro HAVE_ALLOCA.

The user can `#include <alloca.h>` on all platforms, and use `alloca` on those platforms where the preprocessor macro HAVE_ALLOCA evaluates to true. If HAVE_ALLOCA is false, the code should use a heap-based memory allocation based on `malloc` or (in C++) `new`. Note that the `#include <alloca.h>` must be the first one after the autoconf-generated `config.h`, for AIX 3 compatibility. Thanks to IBM for this nice restriction!

Note that GCC 3.1 and 3.2 can *inline* functions that call `alloca`. When this happens, the memory blocks allocated with `alloca` will not be freed until *the end of the calling function*. If this calling function runs a loop calling the function that uses `alloca`, the program easily gets a stack overflow and crashes. To protect against this compiler behaviour, you can mark the function that uses `alloca` with the following attribute:

```
#ifdef __GNUC__
__attribute__ ((__noinline__))
#endif
```

13.3 Safe Allocation Macros

The standard C library malloc/realloc/calloc/free APIs are prone to a number of common coding errors. The `safe-alloc` module provides macros that make it easier to avoid many of them. It still uses the standard C allocation functions behind the scenes.

Some of the memory allocation mistakes that are commonly made are

- passing the incorrect number of bytes to `malloc`, especially when allocating an array,
- fail to check the return value of `malloc` and `realloc` for errors,
- forget to fully initialize memory just allocated with `malloc`,
- duplicate calls to `free` by forgetting to set the pointer variable to `NULL`,
- leaking memory in calls to `realloc` when that call fails.

The `safe-alloc` module addresses these problems in the following way:

- It defines macros that wrap around the standard C allocation functions. That makes it possible to use the compiler's knowledge of the size of objects for allocation; it also allows setting pointers passed in as arguments when appropriate.
- It uses return values only for a success/failure error condition flag, and annotates them with GCC's `__warn_unused_result__` attribute.
- It uses `calloc` instead of `malloc`.

int *ALLOC* (*ptr*)   [Macro]
> Allocate `sizeof(*ptr)` bytes of memory and store the address of allocated memory in `ptr`. Fill the newly allocated memory with zeros.
>
> Returns −1 on failure, 0 on success.

int *ALLOC_N* (*ptr, count*)   [Macro]
> Allocate an array of `count` elements, each `sizeof(*ptr)` bytes long, and store the address of allocated memory in `ptr`. Fill the newly allocated memory with zeros.
>
> Returns −1 on failure, 0 on success.

int *ALLOC_N_UNINITIALIZED* (*ptr, count*)   [Macro]
> Allocate an array of `count` elements, each `sizeof(*ptr)` bytes long, and store the address of allocated memory in `ptr`. The allocated memory is not initialized.
>
> Returns −1 on failure, 0 on success.

int *REALLOC_N* (*ptr, count*)   [Macro]
> Reallocate the memory pointed to by `ptr` to be big enough to hold at least `count` elements, each `sizeof(*ptr)` bytes long, and store the address of allocated memory in `ptr`. If reallocation fails, the `ptr` variable is not modified.
>
> Returns −1 on failure, 0 on success.

void *FREE* (*ptr*)   [Macro]
> Free the memory stored in `ptr` and set `ptr` to `NULL`.

13.4 Compile-time Assertions

This module provides a header file `verify.h` that defines macros related to compile-time verification.

Two of these macros are `verify (V)` and `verify_expr (V, EXPR)`. Both accept an integer constant expression argument V and verify that it is nonzero. If not, a compile-time error results.

These two macros implement compile-time tests, as opposed to the standard `assert` macro which supports only runtime tests. Since the tests occur at compile-time, they are more reliable, and they require no runtime overhead.

`verify (V);` is a declaration; it can occur outside of functions. In contrast, `verify_expr (V, EXPR)` is an expression that returns the value of $EXPR$; it can be used in macros that expand to expressions. If $EXPR$ is an integer constant expression, then `verify_expr (V, EXPR)` is also an integer constant expression. Although $EXPR$ and `verify_expr (V, EXPR)` are guaranteed to have the same side effects and value and type (after integer promotion), they need not have the same type if $EXPR$'s type is an integer that is narrower than `int` or `unsigned int`.

V should be an integer constant expression in the sense of the C standard. Its leaf operands should be integer, enumeration, or character constants; or `sizeof` expressions that return constants; or floating constants that are the immediate operands of casts. Outside a `sizeof` subexpression, V should not contain any assignments, function calls, comma operators, casts to non-integer types, or subexpressions whose values are outside the representable ranges for their types. If V is not an integer constant expression, then a compiler might reject a usage like '`verify (V);`' even when V is nonzero.

Although the standard `assert` macro is a runtime test, C11 specifies a builtin `_Static_assert (V, STRING-LITERAL)`, its `assert.h` header has a similar macro named `static_assert`, and C++11 has a similar `static_assert` builtin. These builtins and macros differ from `verify` in two major ways. First, they can also be used within a `struct` or `union` specifier, in place of an ordinary member declaration. Second, they require the programmer to specify a compile-time diagnostic as a string literal.

The `verify.h` header defines one more macro, `assume (E)`, which expands to an expression of type `void` that causes the compiler to assume that E yields a nonzero value. E should be a scalar expression, and should not have side effects; it may or may not be evaluated. The behavior is undefined if E would yield zero. The main use of `assume` is optimization, as the compiler may be able to generate better code if it assumes E. For best results, E should be simple enough that a compiler can determine that it has no side effects: if E calls an external function or accesses volatile storage the compiler may not be able to optimize E away and `assume (E)` may therefore slow down the program.

Here are some example uses of these macros.

```
#include <verify.h>

#include <limits.h>
#include <time.h>

/* Verify that time_t is an integer type.  */
verify ((time_t) 1.5 == 1);
```

```
/* Verify that time_t is no smaller than int.  */
verify (sizeof (int) <= sizeof (time_t));

/* Verify that time_t is signed.  */
verify ((time_t) -1 < 0);

/* Verify that time_t uses two's complement representation.  */
verify (~ (time_t) -1 == 0);

/* Return the maximum value of the integer type T,
   verifying that T is an unsigned integer type.
   The cast to (T) is outside the call to verify_expr
   so that the result is of type T
   even when T is narrower than unsigned int.  */
#define MAX_UNSIGNED_VAL(t) \
  ((T) verify_expr (0 < (T) -1, -1))

/* Return T divided by CHAR_MAX + 1, where behavior is
   undefined if T < 0.  In the common case where CHAR_MAX
   is 127 the compiler can therefore implement the division
   by shifting T right 7 bits, an optimization that would
   not be valid if T were negative.  */
time_t
time_index (time_t t)
{
  assume (0 <= t);
  return t / (CHAR_MAX + 1);
}
```

13.5 Integer Properties

The intprops module consists of an include file <intprops.h> that defines several macros useful for testing properties of integer types.

Integer overflow is a common source of problems in programs written in C and other languages. In some cases, such as signed integer arithmetic in C programs, the resulting behavior is undefined, and practical platforms do not always behave as if integers wrap around reliably. In other cases, such as unsigned integer arithmetic in C, the resulting behavior is well-defined, but programs may still misbehave badly after overflow occurs.

Many techniques have been proposed to attack these problems. These include precondition testing, wraparound behavior where signed integer arithmetic is guaranteed to be modular, saturation semantics where overflow reliably yields an extreme value, undefined behavior sanitizers where overflow is guaranteed to trap, and various static analysis techniques.

Gnulib supports wraparound arithmetic and precondition testing, as these are relatively easy to support portably and efficiently. There are two families of precondition tests: the first, for integer types, is easier to use, while the second, for integer ranges, has a simple and straightforward portable implementation.

13.5.1 Arithmetic Type Properties

TYPE_IS_INTEGER (t) is an arithmetic constant expression that is 1 if the arithmetic type t is an integer type. _Bool counts as an integer type.

TYPE_SIGNED (t) is an arithmetic constant expression that is 1 if the real type t is a signed integer type or a floating type. If t is an integer type, TYPE_SIGNED (t) is an integer constant expression.

EXPR_SIGNED (e) is 1 if the real expression e has a signed integer type or a floating type. If e is an integer constant expression or an arithmetic constant expression, EXPR_SIGNED (e) is likewise. Although e is evaluated, if e is free of side effects then EXPR_SIGNED (e) is typically optimized to a constant.

Example usage:

```
#include <intprops.h>
#include <time.h>

enum
{
  time_t_is_signed_integer =
    TYPE_IS_INTEGER (time_t) && TYPE_SIGNED (time_t)
};

int
CLOCKS_PER_SEC_is_signed (void)
{
  return EXPR_SIGNED (CLOCKS_PER_SEC);
}
```

13.5.2 Integer Bounds

INT_BUFSIZE_BOUND (t) is an integer constant expression that is a bound on the size of the string representing an integer type or expression t in decimal notation, including the terminating null character and any leading - character. For example, if INT_STRLEN_BOUND (int) is 12, any value of type int can be represented in 12 bytes or less, including the terminating null. The bound is not necessarily tight.

Example usage:

```
#include <intprops.h>
#include <stdio.h>
int
int_strlen (int i)
{
  char buf[INT_BUFSIZE_BOUND (int)];
  return sprintf (buf, "%d", i);
```

```
}
```

`INT_STRLEN_BOUND (t)` is an integer constant expression that is a bound on the length of the string representing an integer type or expression t in decimal notation, including any leading - character. This is one less than `INT_BUFSIZE_BOUND (t)`.

`TYPE_MINIMUM (t)` and `TYPE_MAXIMUM (t)` are integer constant expressions equal to the minimum and maximum values of the integer type t. These expressions are of the type t (or more precisely, the type t after integer promotions).

Example usage:

```
#include <stdint.h>
#include <sys/types.h>
#include <intprops.h>
int
in_off_t_range (intmax_t a)
{
  return TYPE_MINIMUM (off_t) <= a && a <= TYPE_MAXIMUM (off_t);
}
```

13.5.3 Wraparound Arithmetic with Signed Integers

Signed integer arithmetic has undefined behavior on overflow in C. Although almost all modern computers use two's complement signed arithmetic that is well-defined to wrap around, C compilers routinely optimize assuming that signed integer overflow cannot occur, which means that a C program cannot easily get at the underlying machine arithmetic. For example, on a typical machine with 32-bit two's complement `int` the expression `INT_MAX + 1` does not necessarily yield `INT_MIN`, because the compiler may do calculations with a 64-bit register, or may generate code that traps on signed integer overflow.

The following macros work around this problem by storing the wraparound value, i.e., the low-order bits of the correct answer, and by returning an overflow indication. For example, if `i` is of type `int`, `INT_ADD_WRAPV (INT_MAX, 1, &i)` sets `i` to `INT_MIN` and returns 1 on a two's complement machine. On newer platforms, these macros are typically more efficient than the overflow-checking macros. See Section 13.5.4 [Integer Type Overflow], page 616.

Example usage:

```
#include <intprops.h>
#include <stdio.h>

/* Print the low order bits of A * B,
   reporting whether overflow occurred.  */
void
print_product (long int a, long int b)
{
  long int r;
  int overflow = INT_MULTIPLY_WRAPV (a, b, &r);
  printf ("result is %ld (%s)\n", r,
          (overflow
            ? "after overflow"
            : "no overflow"));
```

```
}
```
These macros have the following restrictions:

- Their first two arguments must be integer expressions.

- Their last argument must be a non-null pointer to a signed integer. To calculate a wraparound unsigned integer you can use ordinary C arithmetic; to tell whether it overflowed, you can use the overflow-checking macros.

- They may evaluate their arguments zero or multiple times, so the arguments should not have side effects.

- They are not necessarily constant expressions, even if all their arguments are constant expressions.

INT_ADD_WRAPV (a, b, r)

> Store the low-order bits of the sum of a and b into *r. Return true if overflow occurred, false if the low-order bits are the mathematically-correct sum. See above for restrictions.

INT_SUBTRACT_WRAPV (a, b, r)

> Store the low-order bits of the difference between a and b into *r. Return true if overflow occurred, false if the low-order bits are the mathematically-correct difference. See above for restrictions.

INT_MULTIPLY_WRAPV (a, b, r)

> Store the low-order bits of the product of a and b into *r. Return true if overflow occurred, false if the low-order bits are the mathematically-correct product. See above for restrictions.

13.5.4 Integer Type Overflow

Although unsigned integer arithmetic wraps around modulo a power of two, signed integer arithmetic has undefined behavior on overflow in C. Almost all modern computers use two's complement signed arithmetic that is well-defined to wrap around, but C compilers routinely optimize based on the assumption that signed integer overflow cannot occur, which means that a C program cannot easily get at the underlying machine behavior. For example, the signed integer expression (a + b < b) != (a < 0) is not a reliable test for whether a + b overflows, because a compiler can assume that signed overflow cannot occur and treat the entire expression as if it were false.

These macros yield 1 if the corresponding C operators might not yield numerically correct answers due to arithmetic overflow of an integer type. They work correctly on all known practical hosts, and do not rely on undefined behavior due to signed arithmetic overflow. They are integer constant expressions if their arguments are. They are typically easier to use than the integer range overflow macros (see Section 13.5.5 [Integer Range Overflow], page 618), and they support more operations and evaluation contexts than the wraparound macros (see Section 13.5.3 [Wraparound Arithmetic], page 615).

Example usage:

```
#include <intprops.h>
#include <limits.h>
#include <stdio.h>
```

```
/* Print A * B if in range, an overflow
   indicator otherwise.  */
void
print_product (long int a, long int b)
{
  if (INT_MULTIPLY_OVERFLOW (a, b))
    printf ("multiply would overflow");
  else
    printf ("product is %ld", a * b);
}


/* Does the product of two ints always fit
   in a long int?  */
enum {
  INT_PRODUCTS_FIT_IN_LONG
    = ! (INT_MULTIPLY_OVERFLOW
          ((long int) INT_MIN, INT_MIN))
};
```

These macros have the following restrictions:

- Their arguments must be integer expressions.

- They may evaluate their arguments zero or multiple times, so the arguments should not have side effects.

These macros are tuned for their last argument being a constant.

INT_ADD_OVERFLOW (a, b)

> Yield 1 if a + b would overflow. See above for restrictions.

INT_SUBTRACT_OVERFLOW (a, b)

> Yield 1 if a - b would overflow. See above for restrictions.

INT_NEGATE_OVERFLOW (a)

> Yields 1 if -a would overflow. See above for restrictions.

INT_MULTIPLY_OVERFLOW (a, b)

> Yield 1 if a * b would overflow. See above for restrictions.

INT_DIVIDE_OVERFLOW (a, b)

> Yields 1 if a / b would overflow. See above for restrictions. Division overflow can happen on two's complement hosts when dividing the most negative integer by -1. This macro does not check for division by zero.

INT_REMAINDER_OVERFLOW (a, b)

> Yield 1 if a % b would overflow. See above for restrictions. Remainder overflow can happen on two's complement hosts when dividing the most negative integer by -1; although the mathematical result is always 0, in practice some implementations trap, so this counts as an overflow. This macro does not check for division by zero.

INT_LEFT_SHIFT_OVERFLOW (a, b)

> Yield 1 if a << b would overflow. See above for restrictions. The C standard says that behavior is undefined for shifts unless $0 \leq b < w$ where w is a's word

width, and that when *a* is negative then *a* << *b* has undefined behavior, but this macro does not check these other restrictions.

13.5.5 Integer Range Overflow

These macros yield 1 if the corresponding C operators might not yield numerically correct answers due to arithmetic overflow. They do not rely on undefined or implementation-defined behavior. They are integer constant expressions if their arguments are. Their implementations are simple and straightforward, but they are typically harder to use than the integer type overflow macros. See Section 13.5.4 [Integer Type Overflow], page 616.

Although the implementation of these macros is similar to that suggested in Seacord R, The CERT C Secure Coding Standard (2009, revised 2011), in its two sections "INT30-C. Ensure that unsigned integer operations do not wrap" and "INT32-C. Ensure that operations on signed integers do not result in overflow", Gnulib's implementation was derived independently of CERT's suggestions.

Example usage:

```
#include <intprops.h>
#include <limits.h>
#include <stdio.h>

void
print_product (long int a, long int b)
{
  if (INT_MULTIPLY_RANGE_OVERFLOW (a, b, LONG_MIN, LONG_MAX))
    printf ("multiply would overflow");
  else
    printf ("product is %ld", a * b);
}

/* Does the product of two ints always fit
   in a long int?  */
enum {
  INT_PRODUCTS_FIT_IN_LONG
    = ! (INT_MULTIPLY_RANGE_OVERFLOW
          ((long int) INT_MIN, (long int) INT_MIN,
           LONG_MIN, LONG_MAX))
};
```

These macros have the following restrictions:

- Their arguments must be integer expressions.

- They may evaluate their arguments zero or multiple times, so the arguments should not have side effects.

- The arithmetic arguments (including the *min* and *max* arguments) must be of the same integer type after the usual arithmetic conversions, and the type must have minimum value *min* and maximum *max*. Unsigned values should use a zero *min* of the proper type, for example, (**unsigned int**) 0.

These macros are tuned for constant *min* and *max*. For commutative operations such as **a + b**, they are also tuned for constant *b*.

INT_ADD_RANGE_OVERFLOW (a, b, min, max)

>Yield 1 if **a + b** would overflow in [*min,max*] integer arithmetic. See above for restrictions.

INT_SUBTRACT_RANGE_OVERFLOW (a, b, min, max)

>Yield 1 if **a - b** would overflow in [*min,max*] integer arithmetic. See above for restrictions.

INT_NEGATE_RANGE_OVERFLOW (a, min, max)

>Yield 1 if **-a** would overflow in [*min,max*] integer arithmetic. See above for restrictions.

INT_MULTIPLY_RANGE_OVERFLOW (a, b, min, max)

>Yield 1 if **a * b** would overflow in [*min,max*] integer arithmetic. See above for restrictions.

INT_DIVIDE_RANGE_OVERFLOW (a, b, min, max)

>Yield 1 if **a / b** would overflow in [*min,max*] integer arithmetic. See above for restrictions. Division overflow can happen on two's complement hosts when dividing the most negative integer by -1. This macro does not check for division by zero.

INT_REMAINDER_RANGE_OVERFLOW (a, b, min, max)

>Yield 1 if **a % b** would overflow in [*min,max*] integer arithmetic. See above for restrictions. Remainder overflow can happen on two's complement hosts when dividing the most negative integer by -1; although the mathematical result is always 0, in practice some implementations trap, so this counts as an overflow. This macro does not check for division by zero.

INT_LEFT_SHIFT_RANGE_OVERFLOW (a, b, min, max)

>Yield 1 if **a << b** would overflow in [*min,max*] integer arithmetic. See above for restrictions. Here, *min* and *max* are for *a* only, and *b* need not be of the same type as the other arguments. The C standard says that behavior is undefined for shifts unless $0 \leq b < w$ where *w* is *a*'s word width, and that when *a* is negative then **a << b** has undefined behavior, but this macro does not check these other restrictions.

13.6 Extern inline functions

The `extern-inline` module supports the use of C99-style `extern inline` functions so that the code still runs on pre-C99 compilers.

C code ordinarily should not use `inline`. Typically it is better to let the compiler figure out whether to inline, as compilers are pretty good about optimization nowadays. In this sense, `inline` is like `register`, another keyword that is typically no longer needed.

Functions defined (not merely declared) in headers are an exception, as avoiding `inline` would commonly cause problems for these functions. Suppose `aaa.h` defines the function `aaa_fun`, and `aaa.c`, `bbb.c` and `ccc.c` all include `aaa.h`. If code is intended to portable to pre-C99 compilers, `aaa_fun` cannot be declared with the C99 `inline` keyword. This problem cannot be worked around by making `aaa_fun` an ordinary function, as it would be defined three times with external linkage and the definitions would clash. Although `aaa_fun` could be a static function, with separate compilation if `aaa_fun` is not inlined its code will appear in the executable three times.

To avoid this code bloat, `aaa.h` can do this:

```
/* aaa.h */
/* #include any other headers here */
#ifndef _GL_INLINE_HEADER_BEGIN
 #error "Please include config.h first."
#endif
_GL_INLINE_HEADER_BEGIN
#ifndef AAA_INLINE
# define AAA_INLINE _GL_INLINE
#endif
...
AAA_INLINE int
aaa_fun (int i)
{
  return i + 1;
}
...
_GL_INLINE_HEADER_END
```

and `aaa.c` can do this:

```
/* aaa.c */
#include <config.h>
#define AAA_INLINE _GL_EXTERN_INLINE
#include <aaa.h>
```

whereas `bbb.c` and `ccc.c` can include `aaa.h` in the usual way. C99 compilers expand `AAA_INLINE` to C99-style `inline` usage, where `aaa_fun` is declared `extern inline` in `aaa.c` and plain `inline` in other modules. Pre-C99 compilers that are compatible with GCC use GCC-specific syntax to accomplish the same ends. Other pre-C99 compilers use `static inline` so they suffer from code bloat, but they are not mainline platforms and will die out eventually.

`_GL_INLINE` is a portable alternative to C99 plain `inline`.

`_GL_EXTERN_INLINE` is a portable alternative to C99 `extern inline`.

Invoke `_GL_INLINE_HEADER_BEGIN` before all uses of `_GL_INLINE` in an include file. This suppresses some bogus warnings in GCC versions before 5.1. If an include file includes other files, it is better to invoke this macro after including the other files.

Invoke `_GL_INLINE_HEADER_END` after all uses of `_GL_INLINE` in an include file.

13.7 Character and String Functions in C Locale

The functions in this section are similar to the generic string functions from the standard C library, except that

- They behave as if the locale was set to the "C" locale, even when the locale is different, and/or

- They are specially optimized for the case where all characters are plain ASCII characters.

13.7.1 c-ctype

The `c-ctype` module contains functions operating on single-byte characters, like the functions in `<ctype.h>`, that operate as if the locale encoding was ASCII. (The "C" locale on many systems has the locale encoding "ASCII".)

The functions are:

```
extern bool c_isascii (int c);

extern bool c_isalnum (int c);
extern bool c_isalpha (int c);
extern bool c_isblank (int c);
extern bool c_iscntrl (int c);
extern bool c_isdigit (int c);
extern bool c_islower (int c);
extern bool c_isgraph (int c);
extern bool c_isprint (int c);
extern bool c_ispunct (int c);
extern bool c_isspace (int c);
extern bool c_isupper (int c);
extern bool c_isxdigit (int c);

extern int c_tolower (int c);
extern int c_toupper (int c);
```

These functions assign properties only to ASCII characters.

The *c* argument can be a **char** or **unsigned char** value, whereas the corresponding functions in `<ctype.h>` take an argument that is actually an **unsigned char** value.

The `c_is*` functions return 'bool', where the corresponding functions in `<ctype.h>` return 'int' for historical reasons.

Note: The `<ctype.h>` functions support only unibyte locales.

13.7.2 c-strcase

The `c-strcase` module contains case-insensitive string comparison functions operating on single-byte character strings, like the functions in `<strings.h>`, that operate as if the locale encoding was ASCII. (The "C" locale on many systems has the locale encoding "ASCII".)

The functions are:

```
extern int c_strcasecmp (const char *s1, const char *s2);
extern int c_strncasecmp (const char *s1, const char *s2, size_t n);
```

For case conversion here, only ASCII characters are considered to be upper case or lower case.

Note: The functions strcasecmp, strncasecmp from `<strings.h>` support only unibyte locales; for multibyte locales, you need the functions mbscasecmp, mbsncasecmp, mbspcasecmp.

13.7.3 c-strcaseeq

The `c-strcaseeq` module contains an optimized case-insensitive string comparison function operating on single-byte character strings, that operate as if the locale encoding was ASCII. (The "C" locale on many systems has the locale encoding "ASCII".)

The functions is actually implemented as a macro:

```
extern int STRCASEEQ (const char *s1, const char *s2,
                      int s20, int s21, int s22, int s23, int s24, int s25,
                      int s26, int s27, int s28);
```

s2 should be a short literal ASCII string, and *s20*, *s21*, ... the individual characters of *s2*.

For case conversion here, only ASCII characters are considered to be upper case or lower case.

13.7.4 c-strcasestr

The `c-strcasestr` module contains a case-insensitive string search function operating on single-byte character strings, that operate as if the locale encoding was ASCII. (The "C" locale on many systems has the locale encoding "ASCII".)

The function is:

```
extern char *c_strcasestr (const char *haystack, const char *needle);
```

For case conversion here, only ASCII characters are considered to be upper case or lower case.

Note: The function `strcasestr` from `<string.h>` supports only unibyte locales; for multibyte locales, you need the function `mbscasestr`.

13.7.5 c-strstr

The `c-strstr` module contains a substring search function operating on single-byte character strings, that operate as if the locale encoding was ASCII. (The "C" locale on many systems has the locale encoding "ASCII".)

The function is:

```
extern char *c_strstr (const char *haystack, const char *needle);
```

Note: The function `strstr` from `<string.h>` supports only unibyte locales; for multibyte locales, you need the function `mbsstr`.

13.7.6 c-strtod

The `c-strtod` module contains a string to number ('double') conversion function operating on single-byte character strings, that operates as if the locale encoding was ASCII. (The "C" locale on many systems has the locale encoding "ASCII".)

The function is:

```
extern double c_strtod (const char *string, char **endp);
```

In particular, only a period '.' is accepted as decimal point, even when the current locale's notion of decimal point is a comma ',', and no characters outside the basic character set are accepted.

On platforms without `strtod_l`, this function is not safe for use in multi-threaded applications since it calls `setlocale`.

13.7.7 c-strtold

The `c-strtold` module contains a string to number ('`long double`') conversion function operating on single-byte character strings, that operates as if the locale encoding was ASCII. (The `"C"` locale on many systems has the locale encoding `"ASCII"`.)

The function is:

```
extern long double c_strtold (const char *string, char **endp);
```

In particular, only a period '.' is accepted as decimal point, even when the current locale's notion of decimal point is a comma ','.

13.8 Quoting

Gnulib provides '`quote`' and '`quotearg`' modules to help with quoting text, such as file names, in messages to the user. Here's an example of using '`quote`':

```
#include <quote.h>
  ...
   error (0, errno, _("cannot change owner of %s"), quote (fname));
```

This differs from

```
   error (0, errno, _("cannot change owner of '%s'"), fname);
```

in that `quote` escapes unusual characters in `fname`, e.g., ' ' and control characters like '`\n`'.

However, a caveat: `quote` reuses the storage that it returns. Hence if you need more than one thing quoted at the same time, you need to use `quote_n`.

Also, the quote module is not suited for multithreaded applications. In that case, you have to use `quotearg_alloc`, defined in the '`quotearg`' module, which is decidedly less convenient.

13.9 error and progname

The `error` function uses the `program_name` variable, but does not depend on the `progname` module. Why? Because `error` is released under the LGPL, whereas `progname` is GPL. RMS does not want additional baggage accompanying the `error` module, so an LGPL user must provide their own replacement `program_name`, and a GPL user should manually specify using the `progname` module.

Additionally, using the `progname` module is not something that can be done implicitly. It requires that every `main` function be modified to set `program_name` as one of its first actions.

13.10 gcd: greatest common divisor

The `gcd` function returns the greatest common divisor of two numbers a > 0 and b > 0. It is the caller's responsibility to ensure that the arguments are non-zero.

If you need a gcd function for an integer type larger than '`unsigned long`', you can include the `gcd.c` implementation file with parametrization. The parameters are:

- WORD_T Define this to the unsigned integer type that you need this function for.
- GCD Define this to the name of the function to be created.

The created function has the prototype

```
WORD_T GCD (WORD_T a, WORD_T b);
```

If you need the least common multiple of two numbers, it can be computed like this: `lcm(a,b) = (a / gcd(a,b)) * b` or `lcm(a,b) = a * (b / gcd(a,b))`. Avoid the formula `lcm(a,b) = (a * b) / gcd(a,b)` because—although mathematically correct—it can yield a wrong result, due to integer overflow.

In some applications it is useful to have a function taking the gcd of two signed numbers. In this case, the gcd function result is usually normalized to be non-negative (so that two gcd results can be compared in magnitude or compared against 1, etc.). Note that in this case the prototype of the function has to be

```
unsigned long gcd (long a, long b);
```

and not

```
long gcd (long a, long b);
```

because `gcd(LONG_MIN,LONG_MIN) = -LONG_MIN = LONG_MAX + 1` does not fit into a signed 'long'.

13.11 Searching for Libraries

The following macros check for the presence or location of certain C, C++, or Fortran library archive files.

Simple Library Tests

The macros `AC_CHECK_LIB`, `AC_SEARCH_LIBS` from GNU Autoconf check for the presence of certain C, C++, or Fortran library archive files. The libraries are looked up in the default linker path—a system dependent list of directories, that usually contains the `/usr/lib` directory—and those directories given by -L options in the `LDFLAGS` variable.

Locating Libraries

The following macros, defined in the Gnulib module `havelib`, search for the location of certain C, C++, or Fortran library archive files and make the found location available to the compilation process and to further Autoconf tests.

AC_LIB_LINKFLAGS(*name*, [*dependencies*])   [Macro]
Searches for lib<*name*> and the libraries corresponding to explicit and implicit dependencies. Sets and AC_SUBSTs the LIB<*NAME*> and LTLIB<*NAME*> variables (with <*NAME*> in upper case) and augments the CPPFLAGS variable by -I options.

This macro should be used when lib<*name*> is expected to be found.

AC_LIB_HAVE_LINKFLAGS(*name*, [*dependencies*], [*includes*],   [Macro]
  [*testcode*], [*missing-message*])
Searches for lib<*name*> and the libraries corresponding to explicit and implicit dependencies, together with the specified include files and the ability to compile and link the specified *testcode*. The *missing-message* defaults to no and may contain additional hints for the user. If found, it sets and AC_SUBSTs HAVE_LIB<*NAME*>=yes and the LIB<*NAME*> and LTLIB<*NAME*> variables (with <*NAME*> in upper case) and augments the CPPFLAGS variable by -I options, and #defines HAVE_LIB<*NAME*> to 1. Otherwise, it sets and AC_SUBSTs HAVE_LIB<*NAME*>=no and LIB<*NAME*> and LTLIB<*NAME*> to empty.

These macros assume that when a library is installed in *some_directory*/lib, its include files are installed in *some_directory*/include.

The complexities that AC_LIB_LINKFLAGS and AC_LIB_HAVE_LINKFLAGS deal with are the following:

- The library is not necessarily already in the search path (CPPFLAGS for the include file search path, LDFLAGS for the library search path). The macro provides a '--with-lib<*name*>' option. The user of the 'configure' script can use this option to indicate the location of the library and its include files. If not provided, the --prefix directory is searched as well.

- The library is not necessarily already in the run time library search path. To avoid the need for setting an environment variable like LD_LIBRARY_PATH, the macro adds the appropriate run time search path options to the LIB<*NAME*> variable. This works on most systems. It can also be inhibited: The user of 'configure' can use the --disable-rpath option to force an installation that doesn't contain hardcoded library search paths but instead may require the use of an environment variable like LD_LIBRARY_PATH.

The macros also set a variable LTLIB<*NAME*>, that should be used when linking with libtool. Both LTLIB<*NAME*> and LIB<*NAME*> contain essentially the same option, but where LIB<*NAME*> contains platform dependent flags like '-Wl,-rpath', LTLIB<*NAME*> contains platform independent flags like '-R'.

Example of using AC_LIB_LINKFLAGS

Suppose you want to use libz, the compression library.

1. In configure.ac you add the line

   ```
   AC_CONFIG_AUX_DIR([build-aux])
   AC_LIB_LINKFLAGS([z])
   ```

   Note that since the AC_LIB_LINKFLAGS invocation modifies the CPPFLAGS, it should precede all tests that check for header files, declarations, structures or types.

2. To the package's build-aux directory you add the file config.rpath, also part of the Gnulib havelib module. (gnulib-tool will usually do this for you automatically.)

3. In Makefile.in you add @LIBZ@ to the link command line of your program. Or, if you are using Automake, you add $(LIBZ) to the LDADD variable that corresponds to your program.

Dependencies

The dependencies list is a space separated list of library names that lib*name* is known to depend upon. Example: If libfooy depends on libfoox, and libfooz depends on libfoox and libfooy, you can write:

```
AC_LIB_LINKFLAGS([foox])
AC_LIB_LINKFLAGS([fooy], [foox])
AC_LIB_LINKFLAGS([fooz], [foox fooy])
```

Explicit dependencies are necessary if you cannot assume that a .la file, created by libtool, is installed. If you can assume that libfooy.la is installed by libtool (and has not been omitted by the package distributor!), you can omit the explicit dependency and just write

```
AC_LIB_LINKFLAGS([fooy])
```
This way, you don't need to know in advance which libraries the needed library depends upon.

Static vs. shared

The macros find the libraries regardless whether they are installed as shared or static libraries.

CPPFLAGS vs. LDFLAGS

The macros determine the directories that should be added to the compiler preprocessor's search path and to the linker's search path. For the compiler preprocessor, -I options with the necessary directories are added to the CPPFLAGS variable, for use by the whole package. For the linker, appropriate options are added to the LIB<NAME> and LTLIB<NAME> variables, for use during linking by those programs and libraries that need the dependency on lib<name>. You need to use the value of LIB<NAME> or LTLIB<NAME> in the Makefiles. LTLIB<NAME> is for use with libtool, whereas LIB<NAME> is for when libtool is not involved in linking.

The macros do not check whether the include files and the library found match. If you want to verify this at configure time, one technique is to have a version number in the include files and a version number in the library, like this:

```
#define LIBNAME_VERSION 10203
extern int libname_version; /* initialized to LIBNAME_VERSION */
```
and use a test like

```
AC_TRY_RUN([int main () { return libname_version != LIBNAME_VERSION; }])
```

Bi-arch systems

A bi-arch system is one where

- the processor has a 32-bit execution mode and a 64-bit execution mode (for example, x86_64, ia64, sparc64, powerpc64), and
- 32-bit mode libraries and executables and 64-bit mode libraries are both installed, and
- 32-bit mode libraries and object files cannot be mixed with 64-bit mode ones.

On several types of such systems, for historical reasons, the 32-bit libraries are installed in *prefix*/lib, whereas the 64-bit libraries are installed in

- *prefix*/lib64 on many glibc systems,
- *prefix*/lib/64 on Solaris systems.

On such systems, in 64-bit mode, configure will search for the libraries in *prefix*/lib64 or *prefix*/lib/64, respectively, not in *prefix*/lib. A user can adhere to these system-wide conventions by using the '--libdir' option when installing packages. When a user has already installed packages in 64-bit mode using the GNU default '--libdir=*prefix*/lib', he can make this directory adhere to the system-wide convention by placing a symbolic link:

On glibc systems:

```
ln -s lib prefix/lib64
```

On Solaris systems:

```
ln -s . prefix/lib/64
```

13.12 Controlling the Exported Symbols of Shared Libraries

The `lib-symbol-visibility` module allows precise control of the symbols exported by a shared library. This is useful because

- It prevents abuse of undocumented APIs of your library. Symbols that are not exported from the library cannot be used. This eliminates the problem that when the maintainer of the library changes internals of the library, maintainers of other projects cry "breakage". Instead, these maintainers are forced to negotiate the desired API from the maintainer of the library.

- It reduces the risk of symbol collision between your library and other libraries. For example, the symbol 'readline' is defined in several libraries, most of which don't have the same semantics and the same calling convention as the GNU readline library.

- It reduces the startup time of programs linked to the library. This is because the dynamic loader has less symbols to process.

- It allows the compiler to generate better code. Within a shared library, a call to a function that is a global symbol costs a "call" instruction to a code location in the so-called PLT (procedure linkage table) which contains a "jump" instruction to the actual function's code. (This is needed so that the function can be overridden, for example by a function with the same name in the executable or in a shared library interposed with `LD_PRELOAD`.) Whereas a call to a function for which the compiler can assume that it is in the same shared library is just a direct "call" instructions. Similarly for variables: A reference to a global variable fetches a pointer in the so-called GOT (global offset table); this is a pointer to the variable's memory. So the code to access it is two memory load instructions. Whereas for a variable which is known to reside in the same shared library, it is just a direct memory access: one memory load instruction.

There are traditionally three ways to specify the exported symbols of a shared library.

- The programmer specifies the list of symbols to be exported when the shared library is created. Usually a command-line option is passed to the linker, with the name of a file containing the symbols.

  The upside of this approach is flexibility: it allows the same code to be used in different libraries with different export lists. The downsides are: 1. it's a lot of maintenance overhead when the symbol list is platform dependent, 2. it doesn't work well with C++, due to name mangling.

- The programmer specifies a "hidden" attribute for every variable and function that shall not be exported.

  The drawbacks of this approach are: Symbols are still exported from the library by default. It's a lot of maintenance work to mark every non- exported variable and function. But usually the exported API is quite small, compared to the internal API of the library. And it's the wrong paradigm: It doesn't force thinking when introducing new exported API.

- The programmer specifies a "hidden" attribute for all files that make up the shared library, and an "exported" attribute for those symbols in these files that shall be exported.

  This is perfect: It burdens the maintainer only for exported API, not for library-internal API. And it keeps the annotations in the source code.

GNU libtool's -export-symbols option implements the first approach.

This gnulib module implements the third approach. For this it relies on GNU GCC 4.0 or newer, namely on its '-fvisibility=hidden' command-line option and the "visibility" attribute. (The "visibility" attribute was already supported in GCC 3.4, but without the command line option, introduced in GCC 4.0, the third approach could not be used.)

More explanations on this subject can be found in http://gcc.gnu.org/wiki/Visibility, which contains more details on the GCC features and additional advice for C++ libraries, and in Ulrich Drepper's paper http://people.redhat.com/drepper/dsohowto.pdf, which also explains other tricks for reducing the startup time impact of shared libraries.

The gnulib autoconf macro gl_VISIBILITY tests for GCC 4.0 or newer. It defines a Makefile variable @CFLAG_VISIBILITY@ containing '-fvisibility=hidden' or nothing. It also defines as a C macro and as a substituted variable: @HAVE_VISIBILITY@. Its value is 1 when symbol visibility control is supported, and 0 otherwise.

To use this module in a library, say libfoo, you will do these steps:

1. Add @CFLAG_VISIBILITY@ or (in a Makefile.am) $(CFLAG_VISIBILITY) to the CFLAGS for the compilation of the sources that make up the library.

2. Add a C macro definition, say '-DBUILDING_LIBFOO', to the CPPFLAGS for the compilation of the sources that make up the library.

3. Define a macro specific to your library like this.

   ```
   #if BUILDING_LIBFOO && HAVE_VISIBILITY
   #define LIBFOO_DLL_EXPORTED __attribute__((__visibility__("default")))
   #else
   #define LIBFOO_DLL_EXPORTED
   #endif
   ```

   This macro should be enabled in all public header files of your library.

4. Annotate all variable, function and class declarations in all public header files of your library with 'LIBFOO_DLL_EXPORTED'. This annotation can occur at different locations: between the 'extern' and the type or return type, or just before the entity being declared, or after the entire declarator. My preference is to put it right after 'extern', so that the declarations in the header files remain halfway readable.

Note that the precise control of the exported symbols will not work with other compilers than GCC >= 4.0, and will not work on systems where the assembler or linker lack the support of "hidden" visibility. Therefore, it's good if, in order to reduce the risk of collisions with symbols in other libraries, you continue to use a prefix specific to your library for all non-static variables and functions and for all C++ classes in your library.

Note about other compilers: MSVC support can be added easily, by extending the definition of the macro mentioned above, to something like this:

```
#if BUILDING_LIBFOO && HAVE_VISIBILITY
#define LIBFOO_DLL_EXPORTED __attribute__((__visibility__("default")))
#elif BUILDING_LIBFOO && defined _MSC_VER
#define LIBFOO_DLL_EXPORTED __declspec(dllexport)
#elif defined _MSC_VER
#define LIBFOO_DLL_EXPORTED __declspec(dllimport)
#else
#define LIBFOO_DLL_EXPORTED
#endif
```

13.13 LD Version Scripts

The `lib-symbol-versions` module can be used to add shared library versioning support. Currently, only GNU LD and the Solaris linker supports this.

Version scripts provides information that can be used by GNU/Linux distribution packaging tools. For example, Debian has a tool `dpkg-shlibdeps` that can determine the minimal required version of each dependency (by looking at the symbol list) and stuff the information into the Debian specific packaging files.

For more information and other uses of version scripts, see Ulrich Drepper's paper `http://people.redhat.com/drepper/dsohowto.pdf`

You use the module by importing it to your library, and then add the following lines to the `Makefile.am` that builds the library:

```
if HAVE_LD_VERSION_SCRIPT
libfoo_la_LDFLAGS += -Wl,--version-script=$(srcdir)/libfoo.map
endif
```

The version script file format is documented in the GNU LD manual, but a small example would be:

```
LIBFOO_1.0 {
  global:
    libfoo_init; libfoo_doit; libfoo_done;

  local:
    *;
};
```

If you target platforms that do not support linker scripts (i.e., all platforms that doesn't use GNU LD) you may want to consider a more portable but less powerful alternative: libtool `-export-symbols`. It will hide internal symbols from your library, but will not add ELF versioning symbols. Your usage would then be something like:

```
if HAVE_LD_VERSION_SCRIPT
libfoo_la_LDFLAGS += -Wl,--version-script=$(srcdir)/libfoo.map
else
libfoo_la_LDFLAGS += -export-symbols $(srcdir)/libfoo.sym
endif
```

See the Libtool manual for the file syntax, but a small example would be:

```
libfoo_init
libfoo_doit
libfoo_done
```

To avoid the need for a `*.sym` file if your symbols are easily expressed using a regular expression, you may use `-export-symbols-regex`:

```
if HAVE_LD_VERSION_SCRIPT
libfoo_la_LDFLAGS += -Wl,--version-script=$(srcdir)/libfoo.map
else
libfoo_la_LDFLAGS += -export-symbols-regex '^libfoo_.*'
endif
```

For more discussions about symbol visibility, rather than shared library versioning, see the **visibility** module (see Section 13.12 [Exported Symbols of Shared Libraries], page 627).

13.14 Visual Studio Compatibility

The `lib-msvc-compat` module detects whether the linker supports `--output-def` when building a library. That parameter is used to generate a DEF file for a shared library (DLL). DEF files are useful for developers that use Visual Studio to develop programs that links to your library. See the GNU LD manual for more information.

There are other ways to create a DEF file, but we believe they are all sub-optimal to using `--output-def` during the build process. The variants we have considered include:

- Use DUMPBIN /EXPORTS. This is explained in http://support.microsoft.com/kb/131313/en-us. The tool does not generate DEF files directly, so its output needs to be post processed manually:

      $ { echo EXPORTS; \
          dumpbin /EXPORTS libfoo-0.dll | tail -n+20 | awk '{ print $4 }'; \
        } > libfoo-0.def
      $ lib /def:libfoo-0.def

- Use IMPDEF. There is a tool called IMPDEF (http://sei.pku.edu.cn/~caodg/course/c/reference/win32/tools/dlltool.html) that can generate DEF files. However, it is not part of a standard Visual Studio installation. Further, it is documented as being an unreliable process.

- Use DLLTOOL. The dlltool is part of the MinGW suite, and thus not part of a standard Visual Studio installation. The documentation for the IMPDEF tool claims that DLLTOOL is the wrong tool for this job. Finally, DLLTOOL does not generate DEF files directly, so it requires post-processing of the output.

If you are using libtool to build your shared library, here is how to use this module. Import `lib-msvc-compat` to your project, and then add the following lines to the `Makefile.am` that builds the library:

```
if HAVE_LD_OUTPUT_DEF
libfoo_la_LDFLAGS += -Wl,--output-def,libfoo-$(DLL_VERSION).def
defexecdir = $(bindir)
defexec_DATA = libfoo-$(DLL_VERSION).def
DISTCLEANFILES += $(defexec_DATA)
endif
```

The `DLL_VERSION` variable needs to be defined. It should be the shared library version number used in the DLL filename. For Windows targets you compute this value from the values you pass to Libtool's `-version-info`. Assuming you have variables `LT_CURRENT` and `LT_AGE` defined for the `CURRENT` and `AGE` libtool version integers, you compute `DLL_VERSION` as follows:

```
DLL_VERSION=`expr ${LT_CURRENT} - ${LT_AGE}`
AC_SUBST(DLL_VERSION)
```

13.15 Supporting Relocation

It has been a pain for many users of GNU packages for a long time that packages are not relocatable. It means a user cannot copy a program, installed by another user on the same machine, to his home directory, and have it work correctly (including i18n). So many users need to go through `configure; make; make install` with all its dependencies, options, and hurdles.

Red Hat, Debian, and other binary distributions solve the "ease of installation" problem, but they hardwire path names, usually to /usr or /usr/local. This means that users need root privileges to install a binary package, and prevents installing two different versions of the same binary package.

A relocatable program can be moved or copied to a different location on the file system. It is possible to make symlinks to the installed and moved programs, and invoke them through the symlink. It is possible to do the same thing with a hard link *only* if the hard link file is in the same directory as the real program.

The relocatable-prog module aims to ease the process of making a GNU program relocatable. It helps overcome two obstacles. First, it aids with relocating the hard-coded references to absolute file names that GNU programs often contain. These references must be fixed up at runtime if a program is to be successfully relocated. The relocatable-prog module provides a function relocate that does this job.

Second, the loader must be able to find shared libraries linked to relocatable executables or referenced by other shared libraries linked to relocatable executables. The relocatable-prog module helps out here in a platform-specific way:

- On GNU/Linux, it adds a linker option (-rpath) that causes the dynamic linker to search for libraries in a directory relative to the location of the invoked executable.

- On other Unix systems, it installs a wrapper executable. The wrapper sets the environment variable that controls shared library searching (usually LD_LIBRARY_PATH) and then invokes the real executable.

  This approach does not always work. On OpenBSD and OpenServer, prereleases of Libtool 1.5 put absolute file names of libraries in executables, which prevents searching any other locations.

- On Windows, the executable's own directory is searched for libraries, so installing shared libraries into the executable's directory is sufficient.

You can make your program relocatable by following these steps:

1. Import the relocatable-prog module.

2. In every program, add to main as the first statement (even before setting the locale or doing anything related to libintl):

       set_program_name (argv[0]);

   The prototype for this function is in progname.h.

3. Everywhere where you use a constant pathname from installation-time, wrap it in relocate so it gets translated to the run-time situation. Example:

       bindtextdomain (PACKAGE, LOCALEDIR);

   becomes:

       bindtextdomain (PACKAGE, relocate (LOCALEDIR));

   The prototype for this function is in relocatable.h.

4. The set_program_name function can also configure some additional libraries to relocate files that they access, by defining corresponding C preprocessor symbols to 1. The libraries for which this is supported and the corresponding preprocessor symbols are:

   libcharset   DEPENDS_ON_LIBCHARSET

libiconv DEPENDS_ON_LIBICONV

libintl DEPENDS_ON_LIBINTL

Defining the symbol for a library makes every program in the package depend on that library, whether the program really uses the library or not, so this feature should be used with some caution.

5. If your package installs shell scripts, also import the `relocatable-script` module. Then, near the beginning of each shell script that your package installs, add the following:

```
@relocatable_sh@
if test "@RELOCATABLE@" = yes; then
  exec_prefix="@exec_prefix@"
  bindir="@bindir@"
  orig_installdir="$bindir" # see Makefile.am's *_SCRIPTS variables
  func_find_curr_installdir # determine curr_installdir
  func_find_prefixes
  relocate () {
    echo "$1/" \
    | sed -e "s%^${orig_installprefix}/%${curr_installprefix}/%" \
    | sed -e 's,/$,,'
  }
else
  relocate () {
    echo "$1"
  }
fi

# Get some relocated directory names.
sysconfdir=`relocate "@sysconfdir@"`
some_datadir=`relocate "@datadir@/something"`
```

You must adapt the definition of `orig_installdir`, depending on where the script gets installed. Also, at the end, instead of `sysconfdir` and `some_datadir`, transform those variables that you need.

6. If your package installs Perl scripts, also import the `relocatable-perl` module. Then, near the beginning of each Perl script that your package installs, add the following:

```
@relocatable_pl@
if ("@RELOCATABLE@" eq "yes") {
  my $exec_prefix = "@exec_prefix@";
  my $orig_installdir = "@bindir@"; # see Makefile.am's *_SCRIPTS variables
  my ($orig_installprefix, $curr_installprefix) = find_prefixes($orig_installdir,
  sub relocate { # the subroutine is defined whether or not the enclosing block is
    my ($dir) = @_;
    if ("@RELOCATABLE@" eq "yes") {
      $dir =~ s%^$orig_installprefix/%$curr_installprefix/%;
      $dir =~ s,/$,,;
    }
```

```
      return $dir;
    }
  }

  # Get some relocated directory names.
  $sysconfdir = relocate("@sysconfdir@");
  $some_datadir = relocate(@datadir@/something");
```

You must adapt the definition of $orig_installdir, depending on where the script gets installed. Also, at the end, instead of sysconfdir and some_datadir, transform those variables that you need.

7. In your Makefile.am, for every program foo that gets installed in, say, $(bindir), you add:

```
foo_CPPFLAGS = -DINSTALLDIR=\"$(bindir)\"
if RELOCATABLE_VIA_LD
foo_LDFLAGS = '$(RELOCATABLE_LDFLAGS) $(bindir)'
endif
```

8. You may also need to add a couple of variable assignments to your configure.ac.

If your package (or any package you rely on, e.g. gettext-runtime) will be relocated together with a set of installed shared libraries, then set *RELOCATABLE_LIBRARY_PATH* to a colon-separated list of those libraries' directories, e.g.

```
RELOCATABLE_LIBRARY_PATH='$(libdir)'
```

If your config.h is not in $(top_builddir), then set *RELOCATABLE_CONFIG_H_DIR* to its directory, e.g.

```
RELOCATABLE_CONFIG_H_DIR='$(top_builddir)/src'
```

13.16 func

The func module makes sure that you can use the predefined identifier __func__ as defined by C99 in your code.

A small example is:

```
#include <config.h>
#include <stdio.h> /* for printf */

int main (void)
{
    printf ("%s: hello world\n", __func__);
}
```

Note that sizeof cannot be applied to __func__: On SunPRO C compiler, sizeof __func__ evaluates to 0.

13.17 configmake

The configmake module builds a C include file named configmake.h containing the usual installation directory values; for example, those specified by --prefix or --libdir to configure. Each variable is given a #define with an all-uppercase macro name, such as `PREFIX` and `LIBDIR`. (Automake cannot create this file directly because the user might override directory values at `make` time.)

Specifically, the module retrieves values of the variables through `configure` followed by `make`, not directly through `configure`, so that a user who sets some of these variables consistently on the `make` command line gets correct results.

One advantage of this approach, compared to the classical approach of adding `-DLIBDIR=\"$(libdir)\"` etc. to `AM_CPPFLAGS`, is that it protects against the use of undefined variables. That is, if, say, `$(libdir)` is not set in the Makefile, `LIBDIR` is not defined by this module, and code using `LIBDIR` gives a compilation error.

Another advantage is that `make` output is shorter.

For the complete list of variables which are `#define`d this way, see the file `gnulib/modules/configmake`, or inspect your resulting gnulib Makefile.

13.18 warnings

The `warnings` module allows to regularly build a package with more GCC warnings than the default warnings emitted by GCC.

It provides the following functionality:

- You can select some warning options, such as '`-Wall`', to be enabled whenever building with a GCC version that supports these options. The user can choose to override these warning options by providing the opposite options in the `CFLAGS` variable at configuration time.

- You can make these warnings apply to selected directories only. In projects where subprojects are maintained by different people, or where parts of the source code are imported from external sources (for example from gnulib), it is useful to apply different warning options to different directories.

- It lets you use '`-Werror`' at '`make distcheck`' time, to verify that on the maintainer's system, no warnings remain. (Note that use of '`-Werror`' in `CFLAGS` does not work in general, because it may break autoconfiguration.)

- Similarly, it lets you use '`-Werror`' when the builder runs `configure` with an option such as `--enable-gcc-warnings`.

To use this module, you need the following:

1. In `configure.ac`, use for example
   ```
   gl_WARN_ADD([-Wall], [WARN_CFLAGS])
   gl_WARN_ADD([-Wpointer-arith], [WARN_CFLAGS])
   ```

2. In the directories which shall use `WARN_CFLAGS`, use it in the definition of `AM_CFLAGS`, like this:
   ```
   AM_CFLAGS = $(WARN_CFLAGS)
   ```

   Note that the `AM_CFLAGS` is used in combination with `CFLAGS` and before `CFLAGS` in build rules emitted by Automake. This allows the user to provide `CFLAGS` that override the `WARN_CFLAGS`.

'`gl_WARN_ADD([-Werror])`' is intended for developers, and should be avoided in contexts where it would affect ordinary installation builds. The warnings emitted by GCC depend, to some extent, on the contents of the system header files, on the size and signedness of built-in types, etc. Use of '-Werror' would cause frustration to all users on platforms that the maintainer has not tested before the release. It is better if '-Werror' is off by default, and is enabled only by developers. For example, '-Werror' could affect 'make distcheck' or 'configure --enable-gcc-warnings' as mentioned above.

13.19 manywarnings

The manywarnings module allows you to enable as many GCC warnings as possible for your package. The purpose is to protect against introducing new code that triggers warnings that weren't already triggered by the existing code base.

An example use of the module is as follows:

```
gl_MANYWARN_ALL_GCC([warnings])
# Set up the list of the pointless, undesired warnings.
nw=
nw="$nw -Wsystem-headers"       # Don't let system headers trigger warnings
nw="$nw -Wundef"                # All compiler preprocessors support #if UNDEF
nw="$nw -Wtraditional"          # All compilers nowadays support ANSI C
nw="$nw -Wconversion"           # These warnings usually don't point to mistakes.
nw="$nw -Wsign-conversion"      # Likewise.
# Enable all GCC warnings not in this list.
gl_MANYWARN_COMPLEMENT([warnings], [$warnings], [$nw])
for w in $warnings; do
  gl_WARN_ADD([$w])
done
```

This module is meant to be used by developers who are not very experienced regarding the various GCC warning options. In the beginning you will set the list of undesired warnings ('nw' in the example above) to empty, and compile the package with all possible warnings enabled. The GCC option -fdiagnostics-show-option, available in GCC 4.1 or newer, helps understanding which warnings originated from which option. Then you will go through the list of warnings. You will likely deactivate warnings that occur often and don't point to mistakes in the code, by adding them to the 'nw' variable, then reconfiguring and recompiling. When warnings point to real mistakes and bugs in the code, you will of course not disable them.

There are also many GCC warning options which usually don't point to mistakes in the code; these warnings enforce a certain programming style. It is a project management decision whether you want your code to follow any of these styles. Note that some of these programming styles are conflicting. You cannot have them all; you have to choose among them.

When a new version of GCC is released, you can add the new warning options that it introduces into the gl_MANYWARN_ALL_GCC macro (and submit your modification to the Gnulib maintainers :-)), and enjoy the benefits of the new warnings, while adding the undesired ones to the 'nw' variable.

13.20 Running self-tests under valgrind

For projects written in C or similar languages, running the self-tests under Valgrind can reveal hard to find memory issues. The valgrind-tests module searches for Valgrind and declares the VALGRIND automake variable for use with automake's TESTS_ENVIRONMENT.

After importing the `valgrind-tests` module to your project, you use it by adding the following to the `Makefile.am` that runs the self-tests:

```
TESTS_ENVIRONMENT = $(VALGRIND)
```

This will run all self-checks under valgrind. This can be wasteful if you have many shell scripts or other non-binaries. Using the Automake parallel-tests feature, this can be avoided by using the following instead:

```
AUTOMAKE_OPTIONS = parallel-tests
TEST_EXTENSIONS = .pl .sh
LOG_COMPILER = $(VALGRIND)
```

Then valgrind will only be used for the non-.sh and non-.pl tests. However, this means that binaries invoked through scripts will not be invoked under valgrind, which could be solved by adding the following:

```
TESTS_ENVIRONMENT = VALGRIND='$(VALGRIND)'
```

And then modify the shell scripts to invoke the binary prefixed with `$VALGRIND`.

13.21 stat-size

The `stat-size` module provides a small number of macros intended for interpreting the file size information in an instance of `struct stat`.

On POSIX systems, the `st_blocks` member of `struct stat` contains the number of disk blocks occupied by a file. The `ST_NBLOCKS` macro is used to estimate this quantity on systems which don't actually have `st_blocks`. Each of these blocks contains `ST_NBLOCKSIZE` bytes.

The value of `ST_NBLOCKSIZE` is often quite small, small enough that performing I/O in chunks that size would be inefficient. `ST_BLKSIZE` is the I/O block size recommended for I/O to this file. This is not guaranteed to give optimum performance, but it should be reasonably efficient.

14 Regular expressions

14.1 Overview

A *regular expression* (or *regexp*, or *pattern*) is a text string that describes some (mathematical) set of strings. A regexp *r* *matches* a string *s* if *s* is in the set of strings described by *r*.

Using the Regex library, you can:

- see if a string matches a specified pattern as a whole, and

- search within a string for a substring matching a specified pattern.

Some regular expressions match only one string, i.e., the set they describe has only one member. For example, the regular expression 'foo' matches the string 'foo' and no others. Other regular expressions match more than one string, i.e., the set they describe has more than one member. For example, the regular expression 'f*' matches the set of strings made up of any number (including zero) of 'f's. As you can see, some characters in regular expressions match themselves (such as 'f') and some don't (such as '*'); the ones that don't match themselves instead let you specify patterns that describe many different strings.

To either match or search for a regular expression with the Regex library functions, you must first compile it with a Regex pattern compiling function. A *compiled pattern* is a regular expression converted to the internal format used by the library functions. Once you've compiled a pattern, you can use it for matching or searching any number of times.

The Regex library is used by including **regex.h**. Regex provides three groups of functions with which you can operate on regular expressions. One group—the GNU group—is more powerful but not completely compatible with the other two, namely the POSIX and Berkeley Unix groups; its interface was designed specifically for GNU.

We wrote this chapter with programmers in mind, not users of programs—such as Emacs—that use Regex. We describe the Regex library in its entirety, not how to write regular expressions that a particular program understands.

14.2 Regular Expression Syntax

Characters are things you can type. *Operators* are things in a regular expression that match one or more characters. You compose regular expressions from operators, which in turn you specify using one or more characters.

Most characters represent what we call the match-self operator, i.e., they match themselves; we call these characters *ordinary*. Other characters represent either all or parts of fancier operators; e.g., '.' represents what we call the match-any-character operator (which, no surprise, matches (almost) any character); we call these characters *special*. Two different things determine what characters represent what operators:

1. the regular expression syntax your program has told the Regex library to recognize, and

2. the context of the character in the regular expression.

In the following sections, we describe these things in more detail.

14.2.1 Syntax Bits

In any particular syntax for regular expressions, some characters are always special, others are sometimes special, and others are never special. The particular syntax that Regex recognizes for a given regular expression depends on the current syntax (as set by `re_set_syntax`) when the pattern buffer of that regular expression was compiled.

You get a pattern buffer by compiling a regular expression. See Section 14.7.1.1 [GNU Pattern Buffers], page 653, for more information on pattern buffers. See Section 14.7.1.2 [GNU Regular Expression Compiling], page 653, and Section 14.7.2.1 [BSD Regular Expression Compiling], page 660, for more information on compiling.

Regex considers the current syntax to be a collection of bits; we refer to these bits as *syntax bits*. In most cases, they affect what characters represent what operators. We describe the meanings of the operators to which we refer in Section 14.3 [Common Operators], page 643, Section 14.4 [GNU Operators], page 650, and Section 14.5 [GNU Emacs Operators], page 651.

For reference, here is the complete list of syntax bits, in alphabetical order:

RE_BACKSLASH_ESCAPE_IN_LISTS

> If this bit is set, then '\' inside a list (see Section 14.3.6 [List Operators], page 646 quotes (makes ordinary, if it's special) the following character; if this bit isn't set, then '\' is an ordinary character inside lists. (See Section 14.2.4 [The Backslash Character], page 642, for what '\' does outside of lists.)

RE_BK_PLUS_QM

> If this bit is set, then '\+' represents the match-one-or-more operator and '\?' represents the match-zero-or-more operator; if this bit isn't set, then '+' represents the match-one-or-more operator and '?' represents the match-zero-or-one operator. This bit is irrelevant if RE_LIMITED_OPS is set.

RE_CHAR_CLASSES

> If this bit is set, then you can use character classes in lists; if this bit isn't set, then you can't.

RE_CONTEXT_INDEP_ANCHORS

> If this bit is set, then '^' and '$' are special anywhere outside a list; if this bit isn't set, then these characters are special only in certain contexts. See Section 14.3.9.1 [Match-beginning-of-line Operator], page 650, and Section 14.3.9.2 [Match-end-of-line Operator], page 650.

RE_CONTEXT_INDEP_OPS

> If this bit is set, then certain characters are special anywhere outside a list; if this bit isn't set, then those characters are special only in some contexts and are ordinary elsewhere. Specifically, if this bit isn't set then '*', and (if the syntax bit RE_LIMITED_OPS isn't set) '+' and '?' (or '\+' and '\?', depending on the syntax bit RE_BK_PLUS_QM) represent repetition operators only if they're not first in a regular expression or just after an open-group or alternation operator. The same holds for '{' (or '\{', depending on the syntax bit RE_NO_BK_BRACES) if it is the beginning of a valid interval and the syntax bit RE_INTERVALS is set.

RE_CONTEXT_INVALID_DUP

> If this bit is set, then an open-interval operator cannot occur at the start of a regular expression, or immediately after an alternation, open-group or close-interval operator.

RE_CONTEXT_INVALID_OPS

> If this bit is set, then repetition and alternation operators can't be in certain positions within a regular expression. Specifically, the regular expression is invalid if it has:
>
> - a repetition operator first in the regular expression or just after a match-beginning-of-line, open-group, or alternation operator; or
>
> - an alternation operator first or last in the regular expression, just before a match-end-of-line operator, or just after an alternation or open-group operator.
>
> If this bit isn't set, then you can put the characters representing the repetition and alternation characters anywhere in a regular expression. Whether or not they will in fact be operators in certain positions depends on other syntax bits.

RE_DEBUG   If this bit is set, and the regex library was compiled with -DDEBUG, then internal debugging is turned on; if unset, then it is turned off.

RE_DOT_NEWLINE

> If this bit is set, then the match-any-character operator matches a newline; if this bit isn't set, then it doesn't.

RE_DOT_NOT_NULL

> If this bit is set, then the match-any-character operator doesn't match a null character; if this bit isn't set, then it does.

RE_HAT_LISTS_NOT_NEWLINE

> If this bit is set, nonmatching lists '[^...]' do not match newline; if not set, they do.

RE_ICASE   If this bit is set, then ignore case when matching; otherwise, case is significant.

RE_INTERVALS

> If this bit is set, then Regex recognizes interval operators; if this bit isn't set, then it doesn't.

RE_INVALID_INTERVAL_ORD

> If this bit is set, a syntactically invalid interval is treated as a string of ordinary characters. For example, the extended regular expression 'a{1' is treated as 'a\{1'.

RE_LIMITED_OPS

> If this bit is set, then Regex doesn't recognize the match-one-or-more, match-zero-or-one or alternation operators; if this bit isn't set, then it does.

RE_NEWLINE_ALT

> If this bit is set, then newline represents the alternation operator; if this bit isn't set, then newline is ordinary.

RE_NO_BK_BRACES

>If this bit is set, then '{' represents the open-interval operator and '}' represents the close-interval operator; if this bit isn't set, then '\{' represents the open-interval operator and '\}' represents the close-interval operator. This bit is relevant only if RE_INTERVALS is set.

RE_NO_BK_PARENS

>If this bit is set, then '(' represents the open-group operator and ')' represents the close-group operator; if this bit isn't set, then '\(' represents the open-group operator and '\)' represents the close-group operator.

RE_NO_BK_REFS

>If this bit is set, then Regex doesn't recognize '\'*digit* as the back reference operator; if this bit isn't set, then it does.

RE_NO_BK_VBAR

>If this bit is set, then '|' represents the alternation operator; if this bit isn't set, then '\|' represents the alternation operator. This bit is irrelevant if RE_LIMITED_OPS is set.

RE_NO_EMPTY_RANGES

>If this bit is set, then a regular expression with a range whose ending point collates lower than its starting point is invalid; if this bit isn't set, then Regex considers such a range to be empty.

RE_NO_GNU_OPS

>If this bit is set, GNU regex operators are not recognized; otherwise, they are.

RE_NO_POSIX_BACKTRACKING

>If this bit is set, succeed as soon as we match the whole pattern, without further backtracking. This means that a match may not be the leftmost longest; see Section 14.6 [What Gets Matched?], page 652 for what this means.

RE_NO_SUB

>If this bit is set, then no_sub will be set to one during re_compile_pattern. This causes matching and searching routines not to record substring match information.

RE_UNMATCHED_RIGHT_PAREN_ORD

>If this bit is set and the regular expression has no matching open-group operator, then Regex considers what would otherwise be a close-group operator (based on how RE_NO_BK_PARENS is set) to match ')'.

14.2.2 Predefined Syntaxes

If you're programming with Regex, you can set a pattern buffer's (see Section 14.7.1.1 [GNU Pattern Buffers], page 653) syntax either to an arbitrary combination of syntax bits (see Section 14.2.1 [Syntax Bits], page 638) or else to the configurations defined by Regex. These configurations define the syntaxes used by certain programs—GNU Emacs, POSIX Awk, traditional Awk, Grep, Egrep—in addition to syntaxes for POSIX basic and extended regular expressions.

The predefined syntaxes—taken directly from regex.h—are:

```
#define RE_SYNTAX_EMACS 0

#define RE_SYNTAX_AWK                                                   \
  (RE_BACKSLASH_ESCAPE_IN_LISTS | RE_DOT_NOT_NULL                       \
   | RE_NO_BK_PARENS            | RE_NO_BK_REFS                         \
   | RE_NO_BK_VBAR              | RE_NO_EMPTY_RANGES                    \
   | RE_UNMATCHED_RIGHT_PAREN_ORD)

#define RE_SYNTAX_POSIX_AWK                                            \
  (RE_SYNTAX_POSIX_EXTENDED | RE_BACKSLASH_ESCAPE_IN_LISTS)

#define RE_SYNTAX_GREP                                                 \
  (RE_BK_PLUS_QM                | RE_CHAR_CLASSES                      \
   | RE_HAT_LISTS_NOT_NEWLINE | RE_INTERVALS                           \
   | RE_NEWLINE_ALT)

#define RE_SYNTAX_EGREP                                                \
  (RE_CHAR_CLASSES            | RE_CONTEXT_INDEP_ANCHORS               \
   | RE_CONTEXT_INDEP_OPS | RE_HAT_LISTS_NOT_NEWLINE                   \
   | RE_NEWLINE_ALT          | RE_NO_BK_PARENS                         \
   | RE_NO_BK_VBAR)

#define RE_SYNTAX_POSIX_EGREP                                          \
  (RE_SYNTAX_EGREP | RE_INTERVALS | RE_NO_BK_BRACES)

/* P1003.2/D11.2, section 4.20.7.1, lines 5078ff.  */
#define RE_SYNTAX_ED RE_SYNTAX_POSIX_BASIC

#define RE_SYNTAX_SED RE_SYNTAX_POSIX_BASIC

/* Syntax bits common to both basic and extended POSIX regex syntax.  */
#define _RE_SYNTAX_POSIX_COMMON                                        \
  (RE_CHAR_CLASSES | RE_DOT_NEWLINE      | RE_DOT_NOT_NULL             \
   | RE_INTERVALS  | RE_NO_EMPTY_RANGES)

#define RE_SYNTAX_POSIX_BASIC                                          \
  (_RE_SYNTAX_POSIX_COMMON | RE_BK_PLUS_QM)

/* Differs from ..._POSIX_BASIC only in that RE_BK_PLUS_QM becomes
   RE_LIMITED_OPS, i.e., \? \+ \| are not recognized.  Actually, this
   isn't minimal, since other operators, such as \`, aren't disabled.  */
#define RE_SYNTAX_POSIX_MINIMAL_BASIC                                  \
  (_RE_SYNTAX_POSIX_COMMON | RE_LIMITED_OPS)

#define RE_SYNTAX_POSIX_EXTENDED                                       \
  (_RE_SYNTAX_POSIX_COMMON | RE_CONTEXT_INDEP_ANCHORS                  \
   | RE_CONTEXT_INDEP_OPS  | RE_NO_BK_BRACES                           \
   | RE_NO_BK_PARENS       | RE_NO_BK_VBAR                             \
   | RE_UNMATCHED_RIGHT_PAREN_ORD)

/* Differs from ..._POSIX_EXTENDED in that RE_CONTEXT_INVALID_OPS
   replaces RE_CONTEXT_INDEP_OPS and RE_NO_BK_REFS is added.  */
#define RE_SYNTAX_POSIX_MINIMAL_EXTENDED                              \
  (_RE_SYNTAX_POSIX_COMMON  | RE_CONTEXT_INDEP_ANCHORS                 \
   | RE_CONTEXT_INVALID_OPS | RE_NO_BK_BRACES                          \
   | RE_NO_BK_PARENS        | RE_NO_BK_REFS                            \
   | RE_NO_BK_VBAR          | RE_UNMATCHED_RIGHT_PAREN_ORD)
```

14.2.3 Collating Elements vs. Characters

POSIX generalizes the notion of a character to that of a collating element. It defines a *collating element* to be "a sequence of one or more bytes defined in the current collating sequence as a unit of collation."

This generalizes the notion of a character in two ways. First, a single character can map into two or more collating elements. For example, the German "ß" collates as the collating element 's' followed by another collating element 's'. Second, two or more characters can map into one collating element. For example, the Spanish '11' collates after '1' and before 'm'.

Since POSIX's "collating element" preserves the essential idea of a "character," we use the latter, more familiar, term in this document.

14.2.4 The Backslash Character

The '\' character has one of four different meanings, depending on the context in which you use it and what syntax bits are set (see Section 14.2.1 [Syntax Bits], page 638). It can: 1) stand for itself, 2) quote the next character, 3) introduce an operator, or 4) do nothing.

1. It stands for itself inside a list (see Section 14.3.6 [List Operators], page 646) if the syntax bit `RE_BACKSLASH_ESCAPE_IN_LISTS` is not set. For example, '[\]' would match '\'.

2. It quotes (makes ordinary, if it's special) the next character when you use it either:

    - outside a list,[1] or

    - inside a list and the syntax bit `RE_BACKSLASH_ESCAPE_IN_LISTS` is set.

3. It introduces an operator when followed by certain ordinary characters—sometimes only when certain syntax bits are set. See the cases `RE_BK_PLUS_QM`, `RE_NO_BK_BRACES`, `RE_NO_BK_VAR`, `RE_NO_BK_PARENS`, `RE_NO_BK_REF` in Section 14.2.1 [Syntax Bits], page 638. Also:

    - '\b' represents the match-word-boundary operator (see Section 14.4.1.2 [Match-word-boundary Operator], page 651).

    - '\B' represents the match-within-word operator (see Section 14.4.1.3 [Match-within-word Operator], page 651).

    - '\<' represents the match-beginning-of-word operator (see Section 14.4.1.4 [Match-beginning-of-word Operator], page 651).

    - '\>' represents the match-end-of-word operator (see Section 14.4.1.5 [Match-end-of-word Operator], page 651).

    - '\w' represents the match-word-constituent operator (see Section 14.4.1.6 [Match-word-constituent Operator], page 651).

---

[1] Sometimes you don't have to explicitly quote special characters to make them ordinary. For instance, most characters lose any special meaning inside a list (see Section 14.3.6 [List Operators], page 646). In addition, if the syntax bits `RE_CONTEXT_INVALID_OPS` and `RE_CONTEXT_INDEP_OPS` aren't set, then (for historical reasons) the matcher considers special characters ordinary if they are in contexts where the operations they represent make no sense; for example, then the match-zero-or-more operator (represented by '*') matches itself in the regular expression '*foo' because there is no preceding expression on which it can operate. It is poor practice, however, to depend on this behavior; if you want a special character to be ordinary outside a list, it's better to always quote it, regardless.

- '\W' represents the match-non-word-constituent operator (see Section 14.4.1.7 [Match-non-word-constituent Operator], page 651).

- '\`' represents the match-beginning-of-buffer operator and '\'' represents the match-end-of-buffer operator (see Section 14.4.2 [Buffer Operators], page 651).

- If Regex was compiled with the C preprocessor symbol **emacs** defined, then '\s*class*' represents the match-syntactic-class operator and '\S*class*' represents the match-not-syntactic-class operator (see Section 14.5.1 [Syntactic Class Operators], page 652).

4. In all other cases, Regex ignores '\'. For example, '\n' matches 'n'.

14.3 Common Operators

You compose regular expressions from operators. In the following sections, we describe the regular expression operators specified by POSIX; GNU also uses these. Most operators have more than one representation as characters. See Section 14.2 [Regular Expression Syntax], page 637, for what characters represent what operators under what circumstances.

For most operators that can be represented in two ways, one representation is a single character and the other is that character preceded by '\'. For example, either '(' or '\(' represents the open-group operator. Which one does depends on the setting of a syntax bit, in this case RE_NO_BK_PARENS. Why is this so? Historical reasons dictate some of the varying representations, while POSIX dictates others.

Finally, almost all characters lose any special meaning inside a list (see Section 14.3.6 [List Operators], page 646).

14.3.1 The Match-self Operator (*ordinary character*)

This operator matches the character itself. All ordinary characters (see Section 14.2 [Regular Expression Syntax], page 637) represent this operator. For example, 'f' is always an ordinary character, so the regular expression 'f' matches only the string 'f'. In particular, it does *not* match the string 'ff'.

14.3.2 The Match-any-character Operator (.)

This operator matches any single printing or nonprinting character except it won't match a:

newline   if the syntax bit RE_DOT_NEWLINE isn't set.

null   if the syntax bit RE_DOT_NOT_NULL is set.

The '.' (period) character represents this operator. For example, 'a.b' matches any three-character string beginning with 'a' and ending with 'b'.

14.3.3 The Concatenation Operator

This operator concatenates two regular expressions a and b. No character represents this operator; you simply put b after a. The result is a regular expression that will match a string if a matches its first part and b matches the rest. For example, 'xy' (two match-self operators) matches 'xy'.

14.3.4 Repetition Operators

Repetition operators repeat the preceding regular expression a specified number of times.

14.3.4.1 The Match-zero-or-more Operator (*)

This operator repeats the smallest possible preceding regular expression as many times as necessary (including zero) to match the pattern. '*' represents this operator. For example, 'o*' matches any string made up of zero or more 'o's. Since this operator operates on the smallest preceding regular expression, 'fo*' has a repeating 'o', not a repeating 'fo'. So, 'fo*' matches 'f', 'fo', 'foo', and so on.

Since the match-zero-or-more operator is a suffix operator, it may be useless as such when no regular expression precedes it. This is the case when it:

- is first in a regular expression, or
- follows a match-beginning-of-line, open-group, or alternation operator.

Three different things can happen in these cases:

1. If the syntax bit RE_CONTEXT_INVALID_OPS is set, then the regular expression is invalid.
2. If RE_CONTEXT_INVALID_OPS isn't set, but RE_CONTEXT_INDEP_OPS is, then '*' represents the match-zero-or-more operator (which then operates on the empty string).
3. Otherwise, '*' is ordinary.

The matcher processes a match-zero-or-more operator by first matching as many repetitions of the smallest preceding regular expression as it can. Then it continues to match the rest of the pattern.

If it can't match the rest of the pattern, it backtracks (as many times as necessary), each time discarding one of the matches until it can either match the entire pattern or be certain that it cannot get a match. For example, when matching 'ca*ar' against 'caaar', the matcher first matches all three 'a's of the string with the 'a*' of the regular expression. However, it cannot then match the final 'ar' of the regular expression against the final 'r' of the string. So it backtracks, discarding the match of the last 'a' in the string. It can then match the remaining 'ar'

14.3.4.2 The Match-one-or-more Operator (+ or \+)

If the syntax bit RE_LIMITED_OPS is set, then Regex doesn't recognize this operator. Otherwise, if the syntax bit RE_BK_PLUS_QM isn't set, then '+' represents this operator; if it is, then '\+' does.

This operator is similar to the match-zero-or-more operator except that it repeats the preceding regular expression at least once; see Section 14.3.4.1 [Match-zero-or-more Operator], page 644, for what it operates on, how some syntax bits affect it, and how Regex backtracks to match it.

For example, supposing that '+' represents the match-one-or-more operator; then 'ca+r' matches, e.g., 'car' and 'caaaar', but not 'cr'.

14.3.4.3 The Match-zero-or-one Operator (? or \?)

If the syntax bit RE_LIMITED_OPS is set, then Regex doesn't recognize this operator. Otherwise, if the syntax bit RE_BK_PLUS_QM isn't set, then '?' represents this operator; if it is, then '\?' does.

This operator is similar to the match-zero-or-more operator except that it repeats the preceding regular expression once or not at all; see Section 14.3.4.1 [Match-zero-or-more Operator], page 644, to see what it operates on, how some syntax bits affect it, and how Regex backtracks to match it.

For example, supposing that '?' represents the match-zero-or-one operator; then 'ca?r' matches both 'car' and 'cr', but nothing else.

14.3.4.4 Interval Operators ({ ... } or \{ ... \})

If the syntax bit RE_INTERVALS is set, then Regex recognizes *interval expressions*. They repeat the smallest possible preceding regular expression a specified number of times.

If the syntax bit RE_NO_BK_BRACES is set, '{' represents the *open-interval operator* and '}' represents the *close-interval operator* ; otherwise, '\{' and '\}' do.

Specifically, supposing that '{' and '}' represent the open-interval and close-interval operators; then:

{count}   matches exactly *count* occurrences of the preceding regular expression.

{min,}   matches *min* or more occurrences of the preceding regular expression.

{min, max}

matches at least *min* but no more than *max* occurrences of the preceding regular expression.

The interval expression (but not necessarily the regular expression that contains it) is invalid if:

- *min* is greater than *max*, or
- any of *count*, *min*, or *max* are outside the range zero to RE_DUP_MAX (which symbol regex.h defines).

If the interval expression is invalid and the syntax bit RE_NO_BK_BRACES is set, then Regex considers all the characters in the would-be interval to be ordinary. If that bit isn't set, then the regular expression is invalid.

If the interval expression is valid but there is no preceding regular expression on which to operate, then if the syntax bit RE_CONTEXT_INVALID_OPS is set, the regular expression is invalid. If that bit isn't set, then Regex considers all the characters—other than backslashes, which it ignores—in the would-be interval to be ordinary.

14.3.5 The Alternation Operator (| or \|)

If the syntax bit RE_LIMITED_OPS is set, then Regex doesn't recognize this operator. Otherwise, if the syntax bit RE_NO_BK_VBAR is set, then '|' represents this operator; otherwise, '\|' does.

Alternatives match one of a choice of regular expressions: if you put the character(s) representing the alternation operator between any two regular expressions *a* and *b*, the result matches the union of the strings that *a* and *b* match. For example, supposing that '|' is the alternation operator, then 'foo|bar|quux' would match any of 'foo', 'bar' or 'quux'.

The alternation operator operates on the *largest* possible surrounding regular expressions. (Put another way, it has the lowest precedence of any regular expression operator.) Thus, the only way you can delimit its arguments is to use grouping. For example, if '(' and

')' are the open and close-group operators, then 'fo(o|b)ar' would match either 'fooar' or 'fobar'. ('foo|bar' would match 'foo' or 'bar'.)

The matcher usually tries all combinations of alternatives so as to match the longest possible string. For example, when matching '(fooq|foo)*(qbarquux|bar)' against 'fooqbarquux', it cannot take, say, the first ("depth-first") combination it could match, since then it would be content to match just 'fooqbar'.

Note that since the default behavior is to return the leftmost longest match, when more than one of a series of alternatives matches the actual match will be the longest matching alternative, not necessarily the first in the list.

14.3.6 List Operators ([...] and [^ ...])

Lists, also called *bracket expressions*, are a set of one or more items. An *item* is a character, a collating symbol, an equivalence class expression, a character class expression, or a range expression. The syntax bits affect which kinds of items you can put in a list. We explain the last four items in subsections below. Empty lists are invalid.

A *matching list* matches a single character represented by one of the list items. You form a matching list by enclosing one or more items within an *open-matching-list operator* (represented by '[') and a *close-list operator* (represented by ']').

For example, '[ab]' matches either 'a' or 'b'. '[ad]*' matches the empty string and any string composed of just 'a's and 'd's in any order. Regex considers invalid a regular expression with a '[' but no matching ']'.

Nonmatching lists are similar to matching lists except that they match a single character *not* represented by one of the list items. You use an *open-nonmatching-list operator* (represented by '[^'[2]) instead of an open-matching-list operator to start a nonmatching list.

For example, '[^ab]' matches any character except 'a' or 'b'.

If the syntax bit RE_HAT_LISTS_NOT_NEWLINE is set, then nonmatching lists do not match a newline.

Most characters lose any special meaning inside a list. The special characters inside a list follow.

']'   ends the list if it's not the first list item. So, if you want to make the ']' character a list item, you must put it first.

'\'   quotes the next character if the syntax bit RE_BACKSLASH_ESCAPE_IN_LISTS is set.

'[.'   represents the open-collating-symbol operator (see Section 14.3.6.1 [Collating Symbol Operators], page 647).

'.]'   represents the close-collating-symbol operator.

'[='   represents the open-equivalence-class operator (see Section 14.3.6.2 [Equivalence Class Operators], page 647).

'=]'   represents the close-equivalence-class operator.

---

[2] Regex therefore doesn't consider the '^' to be the first character in the list. If you put a '^' character first in (what you think is) a matching list, you'll turn it into a nonmatching list.

'[:'   represents the open-character-class operator (see Section 14.3.6.3 [Character Class Operators], page 647) if the syntax bit `RE_CHAR_CLASSES` is set and what follows is a valid character class expression.

':]'   represents the close-character-class operator if the syntax bit `RE_CHAR_CLASSES` is set and what precedes it is an open-character-class operator followed by a valid character class name.

'-'   represents the range operator (see Section 14.3.6.4 [Range Operator], page 648) if it's not first or last in a list or the ending point of a range.

All other characters are ordinary. For example, '[.*]' matches '.' and '*'.

14.3.6.1 Collating Symbol Operators ([. ... .])

Collating symbols can be represented inside lists. You form a *collating symbol* by putting a collating element between an *open-collating-symbol operator* and a *close-collating-symbol operator*. '[.' represents the open-collating-symbol operator and '.]' represents the close-collating-symbol operator. For example, if '11' is a collating element, then '[[.11.]]' would match '11'.

14.3.6.2 Equivalence Class Operators ([= ... =])

Regex recognizes equivalence class expressions inside lists. A *equivalence class expression* is a set of collating elements which all belong to the same equivalence class. You form an equivalence class expression by putting a collating element between an *open-equivalence-class operator* and a *close-equivalence-class operator*. '[=' represents the open-equivalence-class operator and '=]' represents the close-equivalence-class operator. For example, if 'a' and 'A' were an equivalence class, then both '[[=a=]]' and '[[=A=]]' would match both 'a' and 'A'. If the collating element in an equivalence class expression isn't part of an equivalence class, then the matcher considers the equivalence class expression to be a collating symbol.

14.3.6.3 Character Class Operators ([: ... :])

If the syntax bit `RE_CHAR_CLASSES` is set, then Regex recognizes character class expressions inside lists. A *character class expression* matches one character from a given class. You form a character class expression by putting a character class name between an *open-character-class operator* (represented by '[:') and a *close-character-class operator* (represented by ':]'). The character class names and their meanings are:

alnum   letters and digits

alpha   letters

blank   system-dependent; for GNU, a space or tab

cntrl   control characters (in the ASCII encoding, code 0177 and codes less than 040)

digit   digits

graph   same as `print` except omits space

lower   lowercase letters

print   printable characters (in the ASCII encoding, space tilde—codes 040 through 0176) punct   neither control nor alphanumeric characters

space   space, carriage return, newline, vertical tab, and form feed

upper   uppercase letters

xdigit   hexadecimal digits: 0–9, a–f, A–F

These correspond to the definitions in the C library's `<ctype.h>` facility. For example, '`[:alpha:]`' corresponds to the standard facility `isalpha`. Regex recognizes character class expressions only inside of lists; so '`[[:alpha:]]`' matches any letter, but '`[:alpha:]`' outside of a bracket expression and not followed by a repetition operator matches just itself.

14.3.6.4 The Range Operator (-)

Regex recognizes *range expressions* inside a list. They represent those characters that fall between two elements in the current collating sequence. You form a range expression by putting a *range operator* between two of any of the following: characters, collating elements, collating symbols, and equivalence class expressions. The starting point of the range and the ending point of the range don't have to be the same kind of item, e.g., the starting point could be a collating element and the ending point could be an equivalence class expression. If a range's ending point is an equivalence class, then all the collating elements in that class will be in the range.[3] '-' represents the range operator. For example, '`a-f`' within a list represents all the characters from 'a' through 'f' inclusively.

If the syntax bit `RE_NO_EMPTY_RANGES` is set, then if the range's ending point collates less than its starting point, the range (and the regular expression containing it) is invalid. For example, the regular expression '`[z-a]`' would be invalid. If this bit isn't set, then Regex considers such a range to be empty.

Since '-' represents the range operator, if you want to make a '-' character itself a list item, you must do one of the following:

- Put the '-' either first or last in the list.

- Include a range whose starting point collates strictly lower than '-' and whose ending point collates equal or higher. Unless a range is the first item in a list, a '-' can't be its starting point, but *can* be its ending point. That is because Regex considers '-' to be the range operator unless it is preceded by another '-'. For example, in the ASCII encoding, ')', '*', '+', ',', '-', '.', and '/' are contiguous characters in the collating sequence. You might think that '`[)-+--/]`' has two ranges: ')-+' and '--/'. Rather, it has the ranges ')-+' and '+--', plus the character '/', so it matches, e.g., ',', not '.'.

- Put a range whose starting point is '-' first in the list.

For example, '`[-a-z]`' matches a lowercase letter or a hyphen (in English, in ASCII).

14.3.7 Grouping Operators ((...) or \(... \))

A *group*, also known as a *subexpression*, consists of an *open-group operator*, any number of other operators, and a *close-group operator*. Regex treats this sequence as a unit, just as mathematics and programming languages treat a parenthesized expression as a unit.

Therefore, using *groups*, you can:

---

[3] You can't use a character class for the starting or ending point of a range, since a character class is not a single character.

- delimit the argument(s) to an alternation operator (see Section 14.3.5 [Alternation Operator], page 645) or a repetition operator (see Section 14.3.4 [Repetition Operators], page 644).

- keep track of the indices of the substring that matched a given group. See Section 14.7.1.8 [Using Registers], page 657, for a precise explanation. This lets you:

  - use the back-reference operator (see Section 14.3.8 [Back-reference Operator], page 649).

  - use registers (see Section 14.7.1.8 [Using Registers], page 657).

If the syntax bit RE_NO_BK_PARENS is set, then '(' represents the open-group operator and ')' represents the close-group operator; otherwise, '\(' and '\)' do.

If the syntax bit RE_UNMATCHED_RIGHT_PAREN_ORD is set and a close-group operator has no matching open-group operator, then Regex considers it to match ')'.

14.3.8 The Back-reference Operator (*digit*)

If the syntax bit RE_NO_BK_REF isn't set, then Regex recognizes back references. A back reference matches a specified preceding group. The back reference operator is represented by '*digit*' anywhere after the end of a regular expression's *digit*-th group (see Section 14.3.7 [Grouping Operators], page 648).

digit must be between '1' and '9'. The matcher assigns numbers 1 through 9 to the first nine groups it encounters. By using one of '\1' through '\9' after the corresponding group's close-group operator, you can match a substring identical to the one that the group does.

Back references match according to the following (in all examples below, '(' represents the open-group, ')' the close-group, '{' the open-interval and '}' the close-interval operator):

- If the group matches a substring, the back reference matches an identical substring. For example, '(a)\1' matches 'aa' and '(bana)na\1bo\1' matches 'bananabanabobana'. Likewise, '(.*)\1' matches any (newline-free if the syntax bit RE_DOT_NEWLINE isn't set) string that is composed of two identical halves; the '(.*)' matches the first half and the '\1' matches the second half.

- If the group matches more than once (as it might if followed by, e.g., a repetition operator), then the back reference matches the substring the group *last* matched. For example, '((a*)b)*\1\2' matches 'aabababa'; first group 1 (the outer one) matches 'aab' and group 2 (the inner one) matches 'aa'. Then group 1 matches 'ab' and group 2 matches 'a'. So, '\1' matches 'ab' and '\2' matches 'a'.

- If the group doesn't participate in a match, i.e., it is part of an alternative not taken or a repetition operator allows zero repetitions of it, then the back reference makes the whole match fail. For example, '(one()|two())-and-(three\2|four\3)' matches 'one-and-three' and 'two-and-four', but not 'one-and-four' or 'two-and-three'. For example, if the pattern matches 'one-and-', then its group 2 matches the empty string and its group 3 doesn't participate in the match. So, if it then matches 'four', then when it tries to back reference group 3—which it will attempt to do because '\3' follows the 'four'—the match will fail because group 3 didn't participate in the match.

You can use a back reference as an argument to a repetition operator. For example, '(a(b))\2*' matches 'a' followed by two or more 'b's. Similarly, '(a(b))\2{3}' matches 'abbbb'.

If there is no preceding *digit*-th subexpression, the regular expression is invalid.

14.3.9 Anchoring Operators

These operators can constrain a pattern to match only at the beginning or end of the entire string or at the beginning or end of a line.

14.3.9.1 The Match-beginning-of-line Operator (^)

This operator can match the empty string either at the beginning of the string or after a newline character. Thus, it is said to *anchor* the pattern to the beginning of a line.

In the cases following, '^' represents this operator. (Otherwise, '^' is ordinary.)

- It (the '^') is first in the pattern, as in '^foo'.
- The syntax bit RE_CONTEXT_INDEP_ANCHORS is set, and it is outside a bracket expression.
- It follows an open-group or alternation operator, as in 'a\(^b\)' and 'a\|^b'. See Section 14.3.7 [Grouping Operators], page 648, and Section 14.3.5 [Alternation Operator], page 645.

These rules imply that some valid patterns containing '^' cannot be matched; for example, 'foo^bar' if RE_CONTEXT_INDEP_ANCHORS is set.

If the not_bol field is set in the pattern buffer (see Section 14.7.1.1 [GNU Pattern Buffers], page 653), then '^' fails to match at the beginning of the string. This lets you match against pieces of a line, as you would need to if, say, searching for repeated instances of a given pattern in a line; it would work correctly for patterns both with and without match-beginning-of-line operators.

14.3.9.2 The Match-end-of-line Operator ($)

This operator can match the empty string either at the end of the string or before a newline character in the string. Thus, it is said to *anchor* the pattern to the end of a line.

It is always represented by '$'. For example, 'foo$' usually matches, e.g., 'foo' and, e.g., the first three characters of 'foo\nbar'.

Its interaction with the syntax bits and pattern buffer fields is exactly the dual of '^'s; see the previous section. (That is, "'^'" becomes "'$'", "beginning" becomes "end", "next" becomes "previous", "after" becomes "before", and "not_bol" becomes "not_eol".)

14.4 GNU Operators

Following are operators that GNU defines (and POSIX doesn't).

14.4.1 Word Operators

The operators in this section require Regex to recognize parts of words. Regex uses a syntax table to determine whether or not a character is part of a word, i.e., whether or not it is *word-constituent*.

14.4.1.1 Non-Emacs Syntax Tables

A *syntax table* is an array indexed by the characters in your character set. In the ASCII encoding, therefore, a syntax table has 256 elements. Regex always uses a char * variable `re_syntax_table` as its syntax table. In some cases, it initializes this variable and in others it expects you to initialize it.

- If Regex is compiled with the preprocessor symbols `emacs` and `SYNTAX_TABLE` both undefined, then Regex allocates `re_syntax_table` and initializes an element i either to `Sword` (which it defines) if i is a letter, number, or '`_`', or to zero if it's not.

- If Regex is compiled with `emacs` undefined but `SYNTAX_TABLE` defined, then Regex expects you to define a `char *` variable `re_syntax_table` to be a valid syntax table.

- See Section 14.5.1.1 [Emacs Syntax Tables], page 652, for what happens when Regex is compiled with the preprocessor symbol `emacs` defined.

14.4.1.2 The Match-word-boundary Operator (\b)

This operator (represented by '`\b`') matches the empty string at either the beginning or the end of a word. For example, '`\brat\b`' matches the separate word '`rat`'.

14.4.1.3 The Match-within-word Operator (\B)

This operator (represented by '`\B`') matches the empty string within a word. For example, '`c\Brat\Be`' matches '`crate`', but '`dirty \Brat`' doesn't match '`dirty rat`'.

14.4.1.4 The Match-beginning-of-word Operator (\<)

This operator (represented by '`\<`') matches the empty string at the beginning of a word.

14.4.1.5 The Match-end-of-word Operator (\>)

This operator (represented by '`\>`') matches the empty string at the end of a word.

14.4.1.6 The Match-word-constituent Operator (\w)

This operator (represented by '`\w`') matches any word-constituent character.

14.4.1.7 The Match-non-word-constituent Operator (\W)

This operator (represented by '`\W`') matches any character that is not word-constituent.

14.4.2 Buffer Operators

Following are operators which work on buffers. In Emacs, a *buffer* is, naturally, an Emacs buffer. For other programs, Regex considers the entire string to be matched as the buffer.

14.4.2.1 The Match-beginning-of-buffer Operator (\`)

This operator (represented by '`\``') matches the empty string at the beginning of the buffer.

14.4.2.2 The Match-end-of-buffer Operator (\')

This operator (represented by '`\'`') matches the empty string at the end of the buffer.

14.5 GNU Emacs Operators

Following are operators that GNU defines (and POSIX doesn't) that you can use only when Regex is compiled with the preprocessor symbol `emacs` defined.

14.5.1 Syntactic Class Operators

The operators in this section require Regex to recognize the syntactic classes of characters. Regex uses a syntax table to determine this.

14.5.1.1 Emacs Syntax Tables

A *syntax table* is an array indexed by the characters in your character set. In the ASCII encoding, therefore, a syntax table has 256 elements.

If Regex is compiled with the preprocessor symbol `emacs` defined, then Regex expects you to define and initialize the variable `re_syntax_table` to be an Emacs syntax table. Emacs' syntax tables are more complicated than Regex's own (see Section 14.4.1.1 [Non-Emacs Syntax Tables], page 650). See Section "Syntax" in *The GNU Emacs User's Manual*, for a description of Emacs' syntax tables.

14.5.1.2 The Match-syntactic-class Operator (\s*class*)

This operator matches any character whose syntactic class is represented by a specified character. '`\s`*class*' represents this operator where *class* is the character representing the syntactic class you want. For example, 'w' represents the syntactic class of word-constituent characters, so '`\sw`' matches any word-constituent character.

14.5.1.3 The Match-not-syntactic-class Operator (\S*class*)

This operator is similar to the match-syntactic-class operator except that it matches any character whose syntactic class is *not* represented by the specified character. '`\S`*class*' represents this operator. For example, 'w' represents the syntactic class of word-constituent characters, so '`\Sw`' matches any character that is not word-constituent.

14.6 What Gets Matched?

Regex usually matches strings according to the "leftmost longest" rule; that is, it chooses the longest of the leftmost matches. This does not mean that for a regular expression containing subexpressions that it simply chooses the longest match for each subexpression, left to right; the overall match must also be the longest possible one.

For example, '`(ac*)(c*d[ac]*)\1`' matches '`acdacaaa`', not '`acdac`', as it would if it were to choose the longest match for the first subexpression.

14.7 Programming with Regex

Here we describe how you use the Regex data structures and functions in C programs. Regex has three interfaces: one designed for GNU, one compatible with POSIX (as specified by POSIX, draft 1003.2/D11.2), and one compatible with Berkeley Unix. The POSIX interface is not documented here; see the documentation of GNU libc, or the POSIX man pages. The Berkeley Unix interface is documented here for convenience, since its documentation is not otherwise readily available on GNU systems.

14.7.1 GNU Regex Functions

If you're writing code that doesn't need to be compatible with either POSIX or Berkeley Unix, you can use these functions. They provide more options than the other interfaces.

14.7.1.1 GNU Pattern Buffers

To compile, match, or search for a given regular expression, you must supply a pattern buffer. A *pattern buffer* holds one compiled regular expression.[4]

You can have several different pattern buffers simultaneously, each holding a compiled pattern for a different regular expression.

regex.h defines the pattern buffer struct with the following public fields:

```
unsigned char *buffer;
unsigned long allocated;
char *fastmap;
char *translate;
size_t re_nsub;
unsigned no_sub : 1;
unsigned not_bol : 1;
unsigned not_eol : 1;
```

14.7.1.2 GNU Regular Expression Compiling

In GNU, you can both match and search for a given regular expression. To do either, you must first compile it in a pattern buffer (see Section 14.7.1.1 [GNU Pattern Buffers], page 653).

Regular expressions match according to the syntax with which they were compiled; with GNU, you indicate what syntax you want by setting the variable re_syntax_options (declared in regex.h) before calling the compiling function, re_compile_pattern (see below). See Section 14.2.1 [Syntax Bits], page 638, and Section 14.2.2 [Predefined Syntaxes], page 640.

You can change the value of re_syntax_options at any time. Usually, however, you set its value once and then never change it.

re_compile_pattern takes a pattern buffer as an argument. You must initialize the following fields:

translate initialization

translate

> Initialize this to point to a translate table if you want one, or to zero if you don't. We explain translate tables in Section 14.7.1.7 [GNU Translate Tables], page 657.

fastmap   Initialize this to nonzero if you want a fastmap, or to zero if you don't.

buffer

allocated

> If you want re_compile_pattern to allocate memory for the compiled pattern, set both of these to zero. If you have an existing block of memory (allocated with malloc) you want Regex to use, set buffer to its address and allocated to its size (in bytes).
>
> re_compile_pattern uses realloc to extend the space for the compiled pattern as necessary.

---

[4] Regular expressions are also referred to as "patterns," hence the name "pattern buffer."

To compile a pattern buffer, use:

```
char *
re_compile_pattern (const char *regex, const int regex_size,
                    struct re_pattern_buffer *pattern_buffer)
```

regex is the regular expression's address, *regex_size* is its length, and *pattern_buffer* is the pattern buffer's address.

If `re_compile_pattern` successfully compiles the regular expression, it returns zero and sets *`*pattern_buffer`* to the compiled pattern. It sets the pattern buffer's fields as follows:

buffer   to the compiled pattern.

syntax   to the current value of `re_syntax_options`.

re_nsub   to the number of subexpressions in *regex*.

If `re_compile_pattern` can't compile *regex*, it returns an error string corresponding to a POSIX error code.

14.7.1.3 GNU Matching

Matching the GNU way means trying to match as much of a string as possible starting at a position within it you specify. Once you've compiled a pattern into a pattern buffer (see Section 14.7.1.2 [GNU Regular Expression Compiling], page 653), you can ask the matcher to match that pattern against a string using:

```
int
re_match (struct re_pattern_buffer *pattern_buffer,
          const char *string, const int size,
          const int start, struct re_registers *regs)
```

pattern_buffer is the address of a pattern buffer containing a compiled pattern. *string* is the string you want to match; it can contain newline and null characters. *size* is the length of that string. *start* is the string index at which you want to begin matching; the first character of *string* is at index zero. See Section 14.7.1.8 [Using Registers], page 657, for an explanation of *regs*; you can safely pass zero.

`re_match` matches the regular expression in *pattern_buffer* against the string *string* according to the syntax of *pattern_buffer*. (See Section 14.7.1.2 [GNU Regular Expression Compiling], page 653, for how to set it.) The function returns −1 if the compiled pattern does not match any part of *string* and −2 if an internal error happens; otherwise, it returns how many (possibly zero) characters of *string* the pattern matched.

An example: suppose *pattern_buffer* points to a pattern buffer containing the compiled pattern for 'a*', and *string* points to 'aaaaab' (whereupon *size* should be 6). Then if *start* is 2, `re_match` returns 3, i.e., 'a*' would have matched the last three 'a's in *string*. If *start* is 0, `re_match` returns 5, i.e., 'a*' would have matched all the 'a's in *string*. If *start* is either 5 or 6, it returns zero.

If *start* is not between zero and *size*, then `re_match` returns −1.

14.7.1.4 GNU Searching

Searching means trying to match starting at successive positions within a string. The function `re_search` does this.

Before calling **re_search**, you must compile your regular expression. See Section 14.7.1.2 [GNU Regular Expression Compiling], page 653.

Here is the function declaration:

```
int
re_search (struct re_pattern_buffer *pattern_buffer,
           const char *string, const int size,
           const int start, const int range,
           struct re_registers *regs)
```

whose arguments are the same as those to **re_match** (see Section 14.7.1.3 [GNU Matching], page 654) except that the two arguments *start* and *range* replace **re_match**'s argument *start*.

If *range* is positive, then **re_search** attempts a match starting first at index *start*, then at *start* + 1 if that fails, and so on, up to *start* + *range*; if *range* is negative, then it attempts a match starting first at index *start*, then at *start* − 1 if that fails, and so on.

If *start* is not between zero and *size*, then **re_search** returns −1. When *range* is positive, **re_search** adjusts *range* so that *start* + *range* − 1 is between zero and *size*, if necessary; that way it won't search outside of *string*. Similarly, when *range* is negative, **re_search** adjusts *range* so that *start* + *range* + 1 is between zero and *size*, if necessary.

If the **fastmap** field of *pattern_buffer* is zero, **re_search** matches starting at consecutive positions; otherwise, it uses **fastmap** to make the search more efficient. See Section 14.7.1.6 [Searching with Fastmaps], page 656.

If no match is found, **re_search** returns −1. If a match is found, it returns the index where the match began. If an internal error happens, it returns −2.

14.7.1.5 Matching and Searching with Split Data

Using the functions **re_match_2** and **re_search_2**, you can match or search in data that is divided into two strings.

The function:

```
int
re_match_2 (struct re_pattern_buffer *buffer,
            const char *string1, const int size1,
            const char *string2, const int size2,
            const int start,
            struct re_registers *regs,
            const int stop)
```

is similar to **re_match** (see Section 14.7.1.3 [GNU Matching], page 654) except that you pass *two* data strings and sizes, and an index *stop* beyond which you don't want the matcher to try matching. As with **re_match**, if it succeeds, **re_match_2** returns how many characters of *string* it matched. Regard *string1* and *string2* as concatenated when you set the arguments *start* and *stop* and use the contents of *regs*; **re_match_2** never returns a value larger than *size1* + *size2*.

The function:

```
int
re_search_2 (struct re_pattern_buffer *buffer,
```

```
             const char *string1, const int size1,
             const char *string2, const int size2,
             const int start, const int range,
             struct re_registers *regs,
             const int stop)
```

is similarly related to `re_search`.

14.7.1.6 Searching with Fastmaps

If you're searching through a long string, you should use a fastmap. Without one, the searcher tries to match at consecutive positions in the string. Generally, most of the characters in the string could not start a match. It takes much longer to try matching at a given position in the string than it does to check in a table whether or not the character at that position could start a match. A *fastmap* is such a table.

More specifically, a fastmap is an array indexed by the characters in your character set. Under the ASCII encoding, therefore, a fastmap has 256 elements. If you want the searcher to use a fastmap with a given pattern buffer, you must allocate the array and assign the array's address to the pattern buffer's `fastmap` field. You either can compile the fastmap yourself or have `re_search` do it for you; when `fastmap` is nonzero, it automatically compiles a fastmap the first time you search using a particular compiled pattern.

By setting the buffer's `fastmap` field before calling `re_compile_pattern`, you can reuse a buffer data structure across multiple searches with different patterns, and allocate the fastmap only once. Nonetheless, the fastmap must be recompiled each time the buffer has a new pattern compiled into it.

To compile a fastmap yourself, use:

```
int
re_compile_fastmap (struct re_pattern_buffer *pattern_buffer)
```

pattern_buffer is the address of a pattern buffer. If the character *c* could start a match for the pattern, `re_compile_fastmap` makes *pattern_buffer*->fastmap[c] nonzero. It returns 0 if it can compile a fastmap and −2 if there is an internal error. For example, if '|' is the alternation operator and *pattern_buffer* holds the compiled pattern for 'a|b', then `re_compile_fastmap` sets `fastmap['a']` and `fastmap['b']` (and no others).

`re_search` uses a fastmap as it moves along in the string: it checks the string's characters until it finds one that's in the fastmap. Then it tries matching at that character. If the match fails, it repeats the process. So, by using a fastmap, `re_search` doesn't waste time trying to match at positions in the string that couldn't start a match.

If you don't want `re_search` to use a fastmap, store zero in the `fastmap` field of the pattern buffer before calling `re_search`.

Once you've initialized a pattern buffer's `fastmap` field, you need never do so again—even if you compile a new pattern in it—provided the way the field is set still reflects whether or not you want a fastmap. `re_search` will still either do nothing if `fastmap` is null or, if it isn't, compile a new fastmap for the new pattern.

14.7.1.7 GNU Translate Tables

If you set the **translate** field of a pattern buffer to a translate table, then the GNU Regex functions to which you've passed that pattern buffer use it to apply a simple transformation to all the regular expression and string characters at which they look.

A *translate table* is an array indexed by the characters in your character set. Under the ASCII encoding, therefore, a translate table has 256 elements. The array's elements are also characters in your character set. When the Regex functions see a character c, they use **translate[c]** in its place, with one exception: the character after a '\' is not translated. (This ensures that, the operators, e.g., '\B' and '\b', are always distinguishable.)

For example, a table that maps all lowercase letters to the corresponding uppercase ones would cause the matcher to ignore differences in case.[5] Such a table would map all characters except lowercase letters to themselves, and lowercase letters to the corresponding uppercase ones. Under the ASCII encoding, here's how you could initialize such a table (we'll call it **case_fold**):

```
for (i = 0; i < 256; i++)
  case_fold[i] = i;
for (i = 'a'; i <= 'z'; i++)
  case_fold[i] = i - ('a' - 'A');
```

You tell Regex to use a translate table on a given pattern buffer by assigning that table's address to the **translate** field of that buffer. If you don't want Regex to do any translation, put zero into this field. You'll get weird results if you change the table's contents anytime between compiling the pattern buffer, compiling its fastmap, and matching or searching with the pattern buffer.

14.7.1.8 Using Registers

A group in a regular expression can match a (possibly empty) substring of the string that regular expression as a whole matched. The matcher remembers the beginning and end of the substring matched by each group.

To find out what they matched, pass a nonzero *regs* argument to a GNU matching or searching function (see Section 14.7.1.3 [GNU Matching], page 654 and Section 14.7.1.4 [GNU Searching], page 654), i.e., the address of a structure of this type, as defined in **regex.h**:

```
struct re_registers
{
  unsigned num_regs;
  regoff_t *start;
  regoff_t *end;
};
```

Except for (possibly) the *num_regs*'th element (see below), the *i*th element of the **start** and **end** arrays records information about the *i*th group in the pattern. (They're declared as C pointers, but this is only because not all C compilers accept zero-length arrays; conceptually, it is simplest to think of them as arrays.)

---

[5] A table that maps all uppercase letters to the corresponding lowercase ones would work just as well for this purpose.

The `start` and `end` arrays are allocated in one of two ways. The simplest and perhaps most useful is to let the matcher (re)allocate enough space to record information for all the groups in the regular expression. If `re_set_registers` is not called before searching or matching, then the matcher allocates two arrays each of $1 + re\_nsub$ elements (re_nsub is another field in the pattern buffer; see Section 14.7.1.1 [GNU Pattern Buffers], page 653). The extra element is set to -1. Then on subsequent calls with the same pattern buffer and *regs* arguments, the matcher reallocates more space if necessary.

The function:

```
void
re_set_registers (struct re_pattern_buffer *buffer,
      struct re_registers *regs,
      size_t num_regs,
      regoff_t *starts, regoff_t *ends)
```

sets *regs* to hold *num_regs* registers, storing them in *starts* and *ends*. Subsequent matches using *buffer* and *regs* will use this memory for recording register information. *starts* and *ends* must be allocated with malloc, and must each be at least $num\_regs * \texttt{sizeof}(\texttt{regoff\_t})$ bytes long.

If *num_regs* is zero, then subsequent matches should allocate their own register data.

Unless this function is called, the first search or match using *buffer* will allocate its own register data, without freeing the old data.

The following examples illustrate the information recorded in the `re_registers` structure. (In all of them, '(' represents the open-group and ')' the close-group operator. The first character in the string *string* is at index 0.)

- If the regular expression has an *i*-th group that matches a substring of *string*, then the function sets `regs->start[i]` to the index in *string* where the substring matched by the *i*-th group begins, and `regs->end[i]` to the index just beyond that substring's end. The function sets `regs->start[0]` and `regs->end[0]` to analogous information about the entire pattern.

  For example, when you match '((a)(b))' against 'ab', you get:

  - 0 in `regs->start[0]` and 2 in `regs->end[0]`
  - 0 in `regs->start[1]` and 2 in `regs->end[1]`
  - 0 in `regs->start[2]` and 1 in `regs->end[2]`
  - 1 in `regs->start[3]` and 2 in `regs->end[3]`

- If a group matches more than once (as it might if followed by, e.g., a repetition operator), then the function reports the information about what the group *last* matched.

  For example, when you match the pattern '(a)*' against the string 'aa', you get:

  - 0 in `regs->start[0]` and 2 in `regs->end[0]`
  - 1 in `regs->start[1]` and 2 in `regs->end[1]`

- If the *i*-th group does not participate in a successful match, e.g., it is an alternative not taken or a repetition operator allows zero repetitions of it, then the function sets `regs->start[i]` and `regs->end[i]` to -1.

  For example, when you match the pattern '(a)*b' against the string 'b', you get:

  - 0 in `regs->start[0]` and 1 in `regs->end[0]`

- −1 in *regs*->start[1] and −1 in *regs*->end[1]
- If the *i*-th group matches a zero-length string, then the function sets *regs*->start[*i*] and *regs*->end[*i*] to the index just beyond that zero-length string.

  For example, when you match the pattern '(a*)b' against the string 'b', you get:

  - 0 in *regs*->start[0] and 1 in *regs*->end[0]
  - 0 in *regs*->start[1] and 0 in *regs*->end[1]

- If an *i*-th group contains a *j*-th group in turn not contained within any other group within group *i* and the function reports a match of the *i*-th group, then it records in *regs*->start[*j*] and *regs*->end[*j*] the last match (if it matched) of the *j*-th group.

  For example, when you match the pattern '((a*)b)*' against the string 'abb', group 2 last matches the empty string, so you get what it previously matched:

  - 0 in *regs*->start[0] and 3 in *regs*->end[0]
  - 2 in *regs*->start[1] and 3 in *regs*->end[1]
  - 2 in *regs*->start[2] and 2 in *regs*->end[2]

  When you match the pattern '((a)*b)*' against the string 'abb', group 2 doesn't participate in the last match, so you get:

  - 0 in *regs*->start[0] and 3 in *regs*->end[0]
  - 2 in *regs*->start[1] and 3 in *regs*->end[1]
  - 0 in *regs*->start[2] and 1 in *regs*->end[2]

- If an *i*-th group contains a *j*-th group in turn not contained within any other group within group *i* and the function sets *regs*->start[*i*] and *regs*->end[*i*] to −1, then it also sets *regs*->start[*j*] and *regs*->end[*j*] to −1.

  For example, when you match the pattern '((a)*b)*c' against the string 'c', you get:

  - 0 in *regs*->start[0] and 1 in *regs*->end[0]
  - −1 in *regs*->start[1] and −1 in *regs*->end[1]
  - −1 in *regs*->start[2] and −1 in *regs*->end[2]

14.7.1.9 Freeing GNU Pattern Buffers

To free any allocated fields of a pattern buffer, use the POSIX function `regfree`:

```
void
regfree (regex_t *preg)
```

preg is the pattern buffer whose allocated fields you want freed; this works because since the type `regex_t`—the type for POSIX pattern buffers—is equivalent to the type `re_pattern_buffer`.

`regfree` also sets *preg*'s `allocated` field to zero. After a buffer has been freed, it must have a regular expression compiled in it before passing it to a matching or searching function.

14.7.2 BSD Regex Functions

If you're writing code that has to be Berkeley Unix compatible, you'll need to use these functions whose interfaces are the same as those in Berkeley Unix.

14.7.2.1 BSD Regular Expression Compiling

With Berkeley Unix, you can only search for a given regular expression; you can't match one. To search for it, you must first compile it. Before you compile it, you must indicate the regular expression syntax you want it compiled according to by setting the variable `re_syntax_options` (declared in `regex.h` to some syntax (see Section 14.2 [Regular Expression Syntax], page 637).

To compile a regular expression use:

```
char *
re_comp (char *regex)
```

regex is the address of a null-terminated regular expression. `re_comp` uses an internal pattern buffer, so you can use only the most recently compiled pattern buffer. This means that if you want to use a given regular expression that you've already compiled—but it isn't the latest one you've compiled—you'll have to recompile it. If you call `re_comp` with the null string (*not* the empty string) as the argument, it doesn't change the contents of the pattern buffer.

If `re_comp` successfully compiles the regular expression, it returns zero. If it can't compile the regular expression, it returns an error string. `re_comp`'s error messages are identical to those of `re_compile_pattern` (see Section 14.7.1.2 [GNU Regular Expression Compiling], page 653).

14.7.2.2 BSD Searching

Searching the Berkeley Unix way means searching in a string starting at its first character and trying successive positions within it to find a match. Once you've compiled a pattern using `re_comp` (see Section 14.7.2.1 [BSD Regular Expression Compiling], page 660), you can ask Regex to search for that pattern in a string using:

```
int
re_exec (char *string)
```

string is the address of the null-terminated string in which you want to search.

`re_exec` returns either 1 for success or 0 for failure. It automatically uses a GNU fastmap (see Section 14.7.1.6 [Searching with Fastmaps], page 656).

14.8 Regular expression syntaxes

Gnulib supports many different types of regular expressions; although the underlying features are the same or identical, the syntax used varies. The descriptions given here for the different types are generated automatically.

14.8.1 'awk' regular expression syntax

The character '.' matches any single character except the null character.

'+'   indicates that the regular expression should match one or more occurrences of the previous atom or regexp.

'?'   indicates that the regular expression should match zero or one occurrence of the previous atom or regexp.

'\+'   matches a '+'

'\?'   matches a '?'.

Bracket expressions are used to match ranges of characters. Bracket expressions where the range is backward, for example '[z-a]', are invalid. Within square brackets, '\' can be used to quote the following character. Character classes are not supported, so for example you would need to use '[0-9]' instead of '[[:digit:]]'.

GNU extensions are not supported and so '\w', '\W', '\<', '\>', '\b', '\B', '\`', and '\'' match 'w', 'W', '<', '>', 'b', 'B', '`', and ''' respectively.

Grouping is performed with parentheses '()'. An unmatched ')' matches just itself. A backslash followed by a digit matches that digit.

The alternation operator is '|'.

The characters '^' and '$' always represent the beginning and end of a string respectively, except within square brackets. Within brackets, '^' can be used to invert the membership of the character class being specified.

'*', '+' and '?' are special at any point in a regular expression except:

1. At the beginning of a regular expression

2. After an open-group, signified by '('

3. After the alternation operator '|'

The longest possible match is returned; this applies to the regular expression as a whole and (subject to this constraint) to subexpressions within groups.

14.8.2 'egrep' regular expression syntax

The character '.' matches any single character except newline.

'+'   indicates that the regular expression should match one or more occurrences of the previous atom or regexp.

'?'   indicates that the regular expression should match zero or one occurrence of the previous atom or regexp.

'\+'   matches a '+'

'\?'   matches a '?'.

Bracket expressions are used to match ranges of characters. Bracket expressions where the range is backward, for example '[z-a]', are ignored. Within square brackets, '\' is taken literally. Character classes are supported; for example '[[:digit:]]' will match a single decimal digit. Non-matching lists '[^...]' do not ever match newline.

GNU extensions are supported:

1. '\w' matches a character within a word

2. '\W' matches a character which is not within a word

3. '\<' matches the beginning of a word

4. '\>' matches the end of a word

5. '\b' matches a word boundary

6. '\B' matches characters which are not a word boundary

7. '\`' matches the beginning of the whole input

8. '\'' matches the end of the whole input

Grouping is performed with parentheses '()'. A backslash followed by a digit acts as a back-reference and matches the same thing as the previous grouped expression indicated by that number. For example '\2' matches the second group expression. The order of group expressions is determined by the position of their opening parenthesis '('.

The alternation operator is '|'.

The characters '^' and '$' always represent the beginning and end of a string respectively, except within square brackets. Within brackets, '^' can be used to invert the membership of the character class being specified.

The characters '*', '+' and '?' are special anywhere in a regular expression.

The longest possible match is returned; this applies to the regular expression as a whole and (subject to this constraint) to subexpressions within groups.

14.8.3 'ed' regular expression syntax

The character '.' matches any single character except the null character.

'\+'   indicates that the regular expression should match one or more occurrences of the previous atom or regexp.

'\?'   indicates that the regular expression should match zero or one occurrence of the previous atom or regexp.

'+ and ?'   match themselves.

Bracket expressions are used to match ranges of characters. Bracket expressions where the range is backward, for example '[z-a]', are invalid. Within square brackets, '\' is taken literally. Character classes are supported; for example '[[:digit:]]' will match a single decimal digit.

GNU extensions are supported:

1. '\w' matches a character within a word
2. '\W' matches a character which is not within a word
3. '\<' matches the beginning of a word
4. '\>' matches the end of a word
5. '\b' matches a word boundary
6. '\B' matches characters which are not a word boundary
7. '\'' matches the beginning of the whole input
8. '\'' matches the end of the whole input

Grouping is performed with backslashes followed by parentheses '\(', '\)'. A backslash followed by a digit acts as a back-reference and matches the same thing as the previous grouped expression indicated by that number. For example '\2' matches the second group expression. The order of group expressions is determined by the position of their opening parenthesis '\('.

The alternation operator is '\|'.

The character '^' only represents the beginning of a string when it appears:

1. At the beginning of a regular expression

2. After an open-group, signified by '\('

3. After the alternation operator '\|'

The character '$' only represents the end of a string when it appears:

1. At the end of a regular expression

2. Before a close-group, signified by '\)'

3. Before the alternation operator '\|'

'*', '\+' and '\?' are special at any point in a regular expression except:

1. At the beginning of a regular expression

2. After an open-group, signified by '\('

3. After the alternation operator '\|'

Intervals are specified by '\{' and '\}'. Invalid intervals such as 'a\{1z' are not accepted.

The longest possible match is returned; this applies to the regular expression as a whole and (subject to this constraint) to subexpressions within groups.

14.8.4 'emacs' regular expression syntax

The character '.' matches any single character except newline.

'+'   indicates that the regular expression should match one or more occurrences of the previous atom or regexp.

'?'   indicates that the regular expression should match zero or one occurrence of the previous atom or regexp.

'\+'   matches a '+'

'\?'   matches a '?'.

Bracket expressions are used to match ranges of characters. Bracket expressions where the range is backward, for example '[z-a]', are ignored. Within square brackets, '\' is taken literally. Character classes are not supported, so for example you would need to use '[0-9]' instead of '[[:digit:]]'.

GNU extensions are supported:

1. '\w' matches a character within a word

2. '\W' matches a character which is not within a word

3. '\<' matches the beginning of a word

4. '\>' matches the end of a word

5. '\b' matches a word boundary

6. '\B' matches characters which are not a word boundary

7. '\`' matches the beginning of the whole input

8. '\'' matches the end of the whole input

Grouping is performed with backslashes followed by parentheses '\(', '\)'. A backslash followed by a digit acts as a back-reference and matches the same thing as the previous grouped expression indicated by that number. For example '\2' matches the second group expression. The order of group expressions is determined by the position of their opening parenthesis '\('.

The alternation operator is '\|'.

The character '^' only represents the beginning of a string when it appears:

1. At the beginning of a regular expression
2. After an open-group, signified by '\('
3. After the alternation operator '\|'

The character '$' only represents the end of a string when it appears:

1. At the end of a regular expression
2. Before a close-group, signified by '\)'
3. Before the alternation operator '\|'

'*', '+' and '?' are special at any point in a regular expression except:

1. At the beginning of a regular expression
2. After an open-group, signified by '\('
3. After the alternation operator '\|'

The longest possible match is returned; this applies to the regular expression as a whole and (subject to this constraint) to subexpressions within groups.

14.8.5 'gnu-awk' regular expression syntax

The character '.' matches any single character.

'+'   indicates that the regular expression should match one or more occurrences of the previous atom or regexp.

'?'   indicates that the regular expression should match zero or one occurrence of the previous atom or regexp.

'\+'   matches a '+'

'\?'   matches a '?'.

Bracket expressions are used to match ranges of characters. Bracket expressions where the range is backward, for example '[z-a]', are invalid. Within square brackets, '\' can be used to quote the following character. Character classes are supported; for example '[[:digit:]]' will match a single decimal digit.

GNU extensions are supported:

1. '\w' matches a character within a word
2. '\W' matches a character which is not within a word
3. '\<' matches the beginning of a word
4. '\>' matches the end of a word
5. '\b' matches a word boundary
6. '\B' matches characters which are not a word boundary
7. '\`' matches the beginning of the whole input
8. '\'' matches the end of the whole input

Grouping is performed with parentheses '()'. An unmatched ')' matches just itself. A backslash followed by a digit acts as a back-reference and matches the same thing as the previous grouped expression indicated by that number. For example '\2' matches the second group expression. The order of group expressions is determined by the position of their opening parenthesis '('.

The alternation operator is '|'.

The characters '^' and '$' always represent the beginning and end of a string respectively, except within square brackets. Within brackets, '^' can be used to invert the membership of the character class being specified.

'*', '+' and '?' are special at any point in a regular expression except:

1. At the beginning of a regular expression

2. After an open-group, signified by '('

3. After the alternation operator '|'

The longest possible match is returned; this applies to the regular expression as a whole and (subject to this constraint) to subexpressions within groups.

14.8.6 'grep' regular expression syntax

The character '.' matches any single character except newline.

'\+'   indicates that the regular expression should match one or more occurrences of the previous atom or regexp.

'\?'   indicates that the regular expression should match zero or one occurrence of the previous atom or regexp.

'+ and ?'   match themselves.

Bracket expressions are used to match ranges of characters. Bracket expressions where the range is backward, for example '[z-a]', are ignored. Within square brackets, '\' is taken literally. Character classes are supported; for example '[[:digit:]]' will match a single decimal digit. Non-matching lists '[^...]' do not ever match newline.

GNU extensions are supported:

1. '\w' matches a character within a word

2. '\W' matches a character which is not within a word

3. '\<' matches the beginning of a word

4. '\>' matches the end of a word

5. '\b' matches a word boundary

6. '\B' matches characters which are not a word boundary

7. '\`' matches the beginning of the whole input

8. '\'' matches the end of the whole input

Grouping is performed with backslashes followed by parentheses '\(', '\)'. A backslash followed by a digit acts as a back-reference and matches the same thing as the previous grouped expression indicated by that number. For example '\2' matches the second group expression. The order of group expressions is determined by the position of their opening parenthesis '\('.

The alternation operator is '\|'.

The character '^' only represents the beginning of a string when it appears:

1. At the beginning of a regular expression
2. After an open-group, signified by '\('
3. After a newline
4. After the alternation operator '\|'

The character '$' only represents the end of a string when it appears:

1. At the end of a regular expression
2. Before a close-group, signified by '\)'
3. Before a newline
4. Before the alternation operator '\|'

'*', '\+' and '\?' are special at any point in a regular expression except:

1. At the beginning of a regular expression
2. After an open-group, signified by '\('
3. After a newline
4. After the alternation operator '\|'

Intervals are specified by '\{' and '\}'. Invalid intervals such as 'a\{1z' are not accepted.

The longest possible match is returned; this applies to the regular expression as a whole and (subject to this constraint) to subexpressions within groups.

14.8.7 'posix-awk' regular expression syntax

The character '.' matches any single character except the null character.

'+'   indicates that the regular expression should match one or more occurrences of the previous atom or regexp.

'?'   indicates that the regular expression should match zero or one occurrence of the previous atom or regexp.

'\+'   matches a '+'

'\?'   matches a '?'.

Bracket expressions are used to match ranges of characters. Bracket expressions where the range is backward, for example '[z-a]', are invalid. Within square brackets, '\' can be used to quote the following character. Character classes are supported; for example '[[:digit:]]' will match a single decimal digit.

GNU extensions are not supported and so '\w', '\W', '\<', '\>', '\b', '\B', '\`', and '\'' match 'w', 'W', '<', '>', 'b', 'B', '`', and ''' respectively.

Grouping is performed with parentheses '()'. An unmatched ')' matches just itself. A backslash followed by a digit acts as a back-reference and matches the same thing as the previous grouped expression indicated by that number. For example '\2' matches the second group expression. The order of group expressions is determined by the position of their opening parenthesis '('.

The alternation operator is '|'.

The characters '^' and '$' always represent the beginning and end of a string respectively, except within square brackets. Within brackets, '^' can be used to invert the membership of the character class being specified.

'*', '+' and '?' are special at any point in a regular expression except the following places, where they are not allowed:

1. At the beginning of a regular expression

2. After an open-group, signified by '('

3. After the alternation operator '|'

Intervals are specified by '{' and '}'. Invalid intervals such as 'a{1z' are not accepted.

The longest possible match is returned; this applies to the regular expression as a whole and (subject to this constraint) to subexpressions within groups.

14.8.8 'posix-basic' regular expression syntax

This is a synonym for ed.

14.8.9 'posix-egrep' regular expression syntax

The character '.' matches any single character except newline.

'+'   indicates that the regular expression should match one or more occurrences of the previous atom or regexp.

'?'   indicates that the regular expression should match zero or one occurrence of the previous atom or regexp.

'\+'   matches a '+'

'\?'   matches a '?'.

Bracket expressions are used to match ranges of characters. Bracket expressions where the range is backward, for example '[z-a]', are ignored. Within square brackets, '\' is taken literally. Character classes are supported; for example '[[:digit:]]' will match a single decimal digit. Non-matching lists '[^...]' do not ever match newline.

GNU extensions are supported:

1. '\w' matches a character within a word

2. '\W' matches a character which is not within a word

3. '\<' matches the beginning of a word

4. '\>' matches the end of a word

5. '\b' matches a word boundary

6. '\B' matches characters which are not a word boundary

7. '\`' matches the beginning of the whole input

8. '\'' matches the end of the whole input

Grouping is performed with parentheses '()'. A backslash followed by a digit acts as a back-reference and matches the same thing as the previous grouped expression indicated by that number. For example '\2' matches the second group expression. The order of group expressions is determined by the position of their opening parenthesis '('.

The alternation operator is '|'.

The characters '^' and '$' always represent the beginning and end of a string respectively, except within square brackets. Within brackets, '^' can be used to invert the membership of the character class being specified.

The characters '*', '+' and '?' are special anywhere in a regular expression.

Intervals are specified by '{' and '}'. Invalid intervals are treated as literals, for example 'a{1' is treated as 'a\{1'

The longest possible match is returned; this applies to the regular expression as a whole and (subject to this constraint) to subexpressions within groups.

14.8.10 'posix-extended' regular expression syntax

The character '.' matches any single character except the null character.

'+'   indicates that the regular expression should match one or more occurrences of the previous atom or regexp.

'?'   indicates that the regular expression should match zero or one occurrence of the previous atom or regexp.

'\+'   matches a '+'

'\?'   matches a '?'.

Bracket expressions are used to match ranges of characters. Bracket expressions where the range is backward, for example '[z-a]', are invalid. Within square brackets, '\' is taken literally. Character classes are supported; for example '[[:digit:]]' will match a single decimal digit.

GNU extensions are supported:

1. '\w' matches a character within a word
2. '\W' matches a character which is not within a word
3. '\<' matches the beginning of a word
4. '\>' matches the end of a word
5. '\b' matches a word boundary
6. '\B' matches characters which are not a word boundary
7. '\`' matches the beginning of the whole input
8. '\'' matches the end of the whole input

Grouping is performed with parentheses '()'. An unmatched ')' matches just itself. A backslash followed by a digit acts as a back-reference and matches the same thing as the previous grouped expression indicated by that number. For example '\2' matches the second group expression. The order of group expressions is determined by the position of their opening parenthesis '('.

The alternation operator is '|'.

The characters '^' and '$' always represent the beginning and end of a string respectively, except within square brackets. Within brackets, '^' can be used to invert the membership of the character class being specified.

'*', '+' and '?' are special at any point in a regular expression except the following places, where they are not allowed:

1. At the beginning of a regular expression

2. After an open-group, signified by '('

3. After the alternation operator '|'

Intervals are specified by '{' and '}'. Invalid intervals such as 'a{1z' are not accepted.

The longest possible match is returned; this applies to the regular expression as a whole and (subject to this constraint) to subexpressions within groups.

14.8.11 'posix-minimal-basic' regular expression syntax

The character '.' matches any single character except the null character.

Bracket expressions are used to match ranges of characters. Bracket expressions where the range is backward, for example '[z-a]', are invalid. Within square brackets, '\' is taken literally. Character classes are supported; for example '[[:digit:]]' will match a single decimal digit.

GNU extensions are supported:

1. '\w' matches a character within a word

2. '\W' matches a character which is not within a word

3. '\<' matches the beginning of a word

4. '\>' matches the end of a word

5. '\b' matches a word boundary

6. '\B' matches characters which are not a word boundary

7. '\`' matches the beginning of the whole input

8. '\'' matches the end of the whole input

Grouping is performed with backslashes followed by parentheses '\(', '\)'. A backslash followed by a digit acts as a back-reference and matches the same thing as the previous grouped expression indicated by that number. For example '\2' matches the second group expression. The order of group expressions is determined by the position of their opening parenthesis '\('.

The character '^' only represents the beginning of a string when it appears:

1. At the beginning of a regular expression

2. After an open-group, signified by '\('

The character '$' only represents the end of a string when it appears:

1. At the end of a regular expression

2. Before a close-group, signified by '\)'

Intervals are specified by '\{' and '\}'. Invalid intervals such as 'a\{1z' are not accepted.

The longest possible match is returned; this applies to the regular expression as a whole and (subject to this constraint) to subexpressions within groups.

14.8.12 'sed' regular expression syntax

This is a synonym for ed.

Appendix A GNU Free Documentation License

Version 1.3, 3 November 2008

Copyright © 2000, 2001, 2002, 2007, 2008 Free Software Foundation, Inc.
http://fsf.org/

Everyone is permitted to copy and distribute verbatim copies
of this license document, but changing it is not allowed.

0. PREAMBLE

The purpose of this License is to make a manual, textbook, or other functional and
useful document *free* in the sense of freedom: to assure everyone the effective freedom
to copy and redistribute it, with or without modifying it, either commercially or noncommercially. Secondarily, this License preserves for the author and publisher a way
to get credit for their work, while not being considered responsible for modifications
made by others.

This License is a kind of "copyleft", which means that derivative works of the document
must themselves be free in the same sense. It complements the GNU General Public
License, which is a copyleft license designed for free software.

We have designed this License in order to use it for manuals for free software, because
free software needs free documentation: a free program should come with manuals
providing the same freedoms that the software does. But this License is not limited to
software manuals; it can be used for any textual work, regardless of subject matter or
whether it is published as a printed book. We recommend this License principally for
works whose purpose is instruction or reference.

1. APPLICABILITY AND DEFINITIONS

This License applies to any manual or other work, in any medium, that contains a
notice placed by the copyright holder saying it can be distributed under the terms
of this License. Such a notice grants a world-wide, royalty-free license, unlimited in
duration, to use that work under the conditions stated herein. The "Document",
below, refers to any such manual or work. Any member of the public is a licensee, and
is addressed as "you". You accept the license if you copy, modify or distribute the work
in a way requiring permission under copyright law.

A "Modified Version" of the Document means any work containing the Document or
a portion of it, either copied verbatim, or with modifications and/or translated into
another language.

A "Secondary Section" is a named appendix or a front-matter section of the Document
that deals exclusively with the relationship of the publishers or authors of the Document
to the Document's overall subject (or to related matters) and contains nothing that
could fall directly within that overall subject. (Thus, if the Document is in part a
textbook of mathematics, a Secondary Section may not explain any mathematics.) The
relationship could be a matter of historical connection with the subject or with related
matters, or of legal, commercial, philosophical, ethical or political position regarding
them.

The "Invariant Sections" are certain Secondary Sections whose titles are designated, as
being those of Invariant Sections, in the notice that says that the Document is released

under this License. If a section does not fit the above definition of Secondary then it is not allowed to be designated as Invariant. The Document may contain zero Invariant Sections. If the Document does not identify any Invariant Sections then there are none.

The "Cover Texts" are certain short passages of text that are listed, as Front-Cover Texts or Back-Cover Texts, in the notice that says that the Document is released under this License. A Front-Cover Text may be at most 5 words, and a Back-Cover Text may be at most 25 words.

A "Transparent" copy of the Document means a machine-readable copy, represented in a format whose specification is available to the general public, that is suitable for revising the document straightforwardly with generic text editors or (for images composed of pixels) generic paint programs or (for drawings) some widely available drawing editor, and that is suitable for input to text formatters or for automatic translation to a variety of formats suitable for input to text formatters. A copy made in an otherwise Transparent file format whose markup, or absence of markup, has been arranged to thwart or discourage subsequent modification by readers is not Transparent. An image format is not Transparent if used for any substantial amount of text. A copy that is not "Transparent" is called "Opaque".

Examples of suitable formats for Transparent copies include plain ASCII without markup, Texinfo input format, LaTeX input format, SGML or XML using a publicly available DTD, and standard-conforming simple HTML, PostScript or PDF designed for human modification. Examples of transparent image formats include PNG, XCF and JPG. Opaque formats include proprietary formats that can be read and edited only by proprietary word processors, SGML or XML for which the DTD and/or processing tools are not generally available, and the machine-generated HTML, PostScript or PDF produced by some word processors for output purposes only.

The "Title Page" means, for a printed book, the title page itself, plus such following pages as are needed to hold, legibly, the material this License requires to appear in the title page. For works in formats which do not have any title page as such, "Title Page" means the text near the most prominent appearance of the work's title, preceding the beginning of the body of the text.

The "publisher" means any person or entity that distributes copies of the Document to the public.

A section "Entitled XYZ" means a named subunit of the Document whose title either is precisely XYZ or contains XYZ in parentheses following text that translates XYZ in another language. (Here XYZ stands for a specific section name mentioned below, such as "Acknowledgements", "Dedications", "Endorsements", or "History".) To "Preserve the Title" of such a section when you modify the Document means that it remains a section "Entitled XYZ" according to this definition.

The Document may include Warranty Disclaimers next to the notice which states that this License applies to the Document. These Warranty Disclaimers are considered to be included by reference in this License, but only as regards disclaiming warranties: any other implication that these Warranty Disclaimers may have is void and has no effect on the meaning of this License.

2. VERBATIM COPYING

You may copy and distribute the Document in any medium, either commercially or noncommercially, provided that this License, the copyright notices, and the license notice saying this License applies to the Document are reproduced in all copies, and that you add no other conditions whatsoever to those of this License. You may not use technical measures to obstruct or control the reading or further copying of the copies you make or distribute. However, you may accept compensation in exchange for copies. If you distribute a large enough number of copies you must also follow the conditions in section 3.

You may also lend copies, under the same conditions stated above, and you may publicly display copies.

3. COPYING IN QUANTITY

If you publish printed copies (or copies in media that commonly have printed covers) of the Document, numbering more than 100, and the Document's license notice requires Cover Texts, you must enclose the copies in covers that carry, clearly and legibly, all these Cover Texts: Front-Cover Texts on the front cover, and Back-Cover Texts on the back cover. Both covers must also clearly and legibly identify you as the publisher of these copies. The front cover must present the full title with all words of the title equally prominent and visible. You may add other material on the covers in addition. Copying with changes limited to the covers, as long as they preserve the title of the Document and satisfy these conditions, can be treated as verbatim copying in other respects.

If the required texts for either cover are too voluminous to fit legibly, you should put the first ones listed (as many as fit reasonably) on the actual cover, and continue the rest onto adjacent pages.

If you publish or distribute Opaque copies of the Document numbering more than 100, you must either include a machine-readable Transparent copy along with each Opaque copy, or state in or with each Opaque copy a computer-network location from which the general network-using public has access to download using public-standard network protocols a complete Transparent copy of the Document, free of added material. If you use the latter option, you must take reasonably prudent steps, when you begin distribution of Opaque copies in quantity, to ensure that this Transparent copy will remain thus accessible at the stated location until at least one year after the last time you distribute an Opaque copy (directly or through your agents or retailers) of that edition to the public.

It is requested, but not required, that you contact the authors of the Document well before redistributing any large number of copies, to give them a chance to provide you with an updated version of the Document.

4. MODIFICATIONS

You may copy and distribute a Modified Version of the Document under the conditions of sections 2 and 3 above, provided that you release the Modified Version under precisely this License, with the Modified Version filling the role of the Document, thus licensing distribution and modification of the Modified Version to whoever possesses a copy of it. In addition, you must do these things in the Modified Version:

A. Use in the Title Page (and on the covers, if any) a title distinct from that of the Document, and from those of previous versions (which should, if there were any, be listed in the History section of the Document). You may use the same title as a previous version if the original publisher of that version gives permission.

B. List on the Title Page, as authors, one or more persons or entities responsible for authorship of the modifications in the Modified Version, together with at least five of the principal authors of the Document (all of its principal authors, if it has fewer than five), unless they release you from this requirement.

C. State on the Title page the name of the publisher of the Modified Version, as the publisher.

D. Preserve all the copyright notices of the Document.

E. Add an appropriate copyright notice for your modifications adjacent to the other copyright notices.

F. Include, immediately after the copyright notices, a license notice giving the public permission to use the Modified Version under the terms of this License, in the form shown in the Addendum below.

G. Preserve in that license notice the full lists of Invariant Sections and required Cover Texts given in the Document's license notice.

H. Include an unaltered copy of this License.

I. Preserve the section Entitled "History", Preserve its Title, and add to it an item stating at least the title, year, new authors, and publisher of the Modified Version as given on the Title Page. If there is no section Entitled "History" in the Document, create one stating the title, year, authors, and publisher of the Document as given on its Title Page, then add an item describing the Modified Version as stated in the previous sentence.

J. Preserve the network location, if any, given in the Document for public access to a Transparent copy of the Document, and likewise the network locations given in the Document for previous versions it was based on. These may be placed in the "History" section. You may omit a network location for a work that was published at least four years before the Document itself, or if the original publisher of the version it refers to gives permission.

K. For any section Entitled "Acknowledgements" or "Dedications", Preserve the Title of the section, and preserve in the section all the substance and tone of each of the contributor acknowledgements and/or dedications given therein.

L. Preserve all the Invariant Sections of the Document, unaltered in their text and in their titles. Section numbers or the equivalent are not considered part of the section titles.

M. Delete any section Entitled "Endorsements". Such a section may not be included in the Modified Version.

N. Do not retitle any existing section to be Entitled "Endorsements" or to conflict in title with any Invariant Section.

O. Preserve any Warranty Disclaimers.

If the Modified Version includes new front-matter sections or appendices that qualify as Secondary Sections and contain no material copied from the Document, you may at your option designate some or all of these sections as invariant. To do this, add their titles to the list of Invariant Sections in the Modified Version's license notice. These titles must be distinct from any other section titles.

You may add a section Entitled "Endorsements", provided it contains nothing but endorsements of your Modified Version by various parties—for example, statements of peer review or that the text has been approved by an organization as the authoritative definition of a standard.

You may add a passage of up to five words as a Front-Cover Text, and a passage of up to 25 words as a Back-Cover Text, to the end of the list of Cover Texts in the Modified Version. Only one passage of Front-Cover Text and one of Back-Cover Text may be added by (or through arrangements made by) any one entity. If the Document already includes a cover text for the same cover, previously added by you or by arrangement made by the same entity you are acting on behalf of, you may not add another; but you may replace the old one, on explicit permission from the previous publisher that added the old one.

The author(s) and publisher(s) of the Document do not by this License give permission to use their names for publicity for or to assert or imply endorsement of any Modified Version.

5. COMBINING DOCUMENTS

You may combine the Document with other documents released under this License, under the terms defined in section 4 above for modified versions, provided that you include in the combination all of the Invariant Sections of all of the original documents, unmodified, and list them all as Invariant Sections of your combined work in its license notice, and that you preserve all their Warranty Disclaimers.

The combined work need only contain one copy of this License, and multiple identical Invariant Sections may be replaced with a single copy. If there are multiple Invariant Sections with the same name but different contents, make the title of each such section unique by adding at the end of it, in parentheses, the name of the original author or publisher of that section if known, or else a unique number. Make the same adjustment to the section titles in the list of Invariant Sections in the license notice of the combined work.

In the combination, you must combine any sections Entitled "History" in the various original documents, forming one section Entitled "History"; likewise combine any sections Entitled "Acknowledgements", and any sections Entitled "Dedications". You must delete all sections Entitled "Endorsements."

6. COLLECTIONS OF DOCUMENTS

You may make a collection consisting of the Document and other documents released under this License, and replace the individual copies of this License in the various documents with a single copy that is included in the collection, provided that you follow the rules of this License for verbatim copying of each of the documents in all other respects.

You may extract a single document from such a collection, and distribute it individually under this License, provided you insert a copy of this License into the extracted document, and follow this License in all other respects regarding verbatim copying of that document.

7. AGGREGATION WITH INDEPENDENT WORKS

A compilation of the Document or its derivatives with other separate and independent documents or works, in or on a volume of a storage or distribution medium, is called an "aggregate" if the copyright resulting from the compilation is not used to limit the legal rights of the compilation's users beyond what the individual works permit. When the Document is included in an aggregate, this License does not apply to the other works in the aggregate which are not themselves derivative works of the Document.

If the Cover Text requirement of section 3 is applicable to these copies of the Document, then if the Document is less than one half of the entire aggregate, the Document's Cover Texts may be placed on covers that bracket the Document within the aggregate, or the electronic equivalent of covers if the Document is in electronic form. Otherwise they must appear on printed covers that bracket the whole aggregate.

8. TRANSLATION

Translation is considered a kind of modification, so you may distribute translations of the Document under the terms of section 4. Replacing Invariant Sections with translations requires special permission from their copyright holders, but you may include translations of some or all Invariant Sections in addition to the original versions of these Invariant Sections. You may include a translation of this License, and all the license notices in the Document, and any Warranty Disclaimers, provided that you also include the original English version of this License and the original versions of those notices and disclaimers. In case of a disagreement between the translation and the original version of this License or a notice or disclaimer, the original version will prevail.

If a section in the Document is Entitled "Acknowledgements", "Dedications", or "History", the requirement (section 4) to Preserve its Title (section 1) will typically require changing the actual title.

9. TERMINATION

You may not copy, modify, sublicense, or distribute the Document except as expressly provided under this License. Any attempt otherwise to copy, modify, sublicense, or distribute it is void, and will automatically terminate your rights under this License.

However, if you cease all violation of this License, then your license from a particular copyright holder is reinstated (a) provisionally, unless and until the copyright holder explicitly and finally terminates your license, and (b) permanently, if the copyright holder fails to notify you of the violation by some reasonable means prior to 60 days after the cessation.

Moreover, your license from a particular copyright holder is reinstated permanently if the copyright holder notifies you of the violation by some reasonable means, this is the first time you have received notice of violation of this License (for any work) from that copyright holder, and you cure the violation prior to 30 days after your receipt of the notice.

Termination of your rights under this section does not terminate the licenses of parties who have received copies or rights from you under this License. If your rights have been terminated and not permanently reinstated, receipt of a copy of some or all of the same material does not give you any rights to use it.

10. FUTURE REVISIONS OF THIS LICENSE

The Free Software Foundation may publish new, revised versions of the GNU Free Documentation License from time to time. Such new versions will be similar in spirit to the present version, but may differ in detail to address new problems or concerns. See http://www.gnu.org/copyleft/.

Each version of the License is given a distinguishing version number. If the Document specifies that a particular numbered version of this License "or any later version" applies to it, you have the option of following the terms and conditions either of that specified version or of any later version that has been published (not as a draft) by the Free Software Foundation. If the Document does not specify a version number of this License, you may choose any version ever published (not as a draft) by the Free Software Foundation. If the Document specifies that a proxy can decide which future versions of this License can be used, that proxy's public statement of acceptance of a version permanently authorizes you to choose that version for the Document.

11. RELICENSING

"Massive Multiauthor Collaboration Site" (or "MMC Site") means any World Wide Web server that publishes copyrightable works and also provides prominent facilities for anybody to edit those works. A public wiki that anybody can edit is an example of such a server. A "Massive Multiauthor Collaboration" (or "MMC") contained in the site means any set of copyrightable works thus published on the MMC site.

"CC-BY-SA" means the Creative Commons Attribution-Share Alike 3.0 license published by Creative Commons Corporation, a not-for-profit corporation with a principal place of business in San Francisco, California, as well as future copyleft versions of that license published by that same organization.

"Incorporate" means to publish or republish a Document, in whole or in part, as part of another Document.

An MMC is "eligible for relicensing" if it is licensed under this License, and if all works that were first published under this License somewhere other than this MMC, and subsequently incorporated in whole or in part into the MMC, (1) had no cover texts or invariant sections, and (2) were thus incorporated prior to November 1, 2008.

The operator of an MMC Site may republish an MMC contained in the site under CC-BY-SA on the same site at any time before August 1, 2009, provided the MMC is eligible for relicensing.

ADDENDUM: How to use this License for your documents

To use this License in a document you have written, include a copy of the License in the document and put the following copyright and license notices just after the title page:

```
Copyright (C)  year  your name.
Permission is granted to copy, distribute and/or modify this document
under the terms of the GNU Free Documentation License, Version 1.3
or any later version published by the Free Software Foundation;
with no Invariant Sections, no Front-Cover Texts, and no Back-Cover
Texts.  A copy of the license is included in the section entitled ''GNU
Free Documentation License''.
```

If you have Invariant Sections, Front-Cover Texts and Back-Cover Texts, replace the "with...Texts." line with this:

```
with the Invariant Sections being list their titles, with
the Front-Cover Texts being list, and with the Back-Cover Texts
being list.
```

If you have Invariant Sections without Cover Texts, or some other combination of the three, merge those two alternatives to suit the situation.

If your document contains nontrivial examples of program code, we recommend releasing these examples in parallel under your choice of free software license, such as the GNU General Public License, to permit their use in free software.

Index

N

P

O

Q

T

X

Y